I0449186

Workers of the World, Unite!

Unity & Struggle

Journal of the
International Conference of
Marxist-Leninist Parties
and Organizations

ICMLPO

No. 44 – May of 2022

Unity & Struggle

Journal of the International Conference
of Marxist-Leninist Parties and Organizations

Published in English, Spanish, Turkish,
Arabic, Portuguese, German and Danish
as the responsibility of the Coordination Committee
of the International Conference

Any opinions expressed in this journal belong
to the contributors.

Postal Address: Verlag AZ, Postfach 401051,
D-70410, Stuttgart, Germany
info@arbeit-zukunft.de

North American edition available from:

American Party of Labor
www.americanpartyoflabor.com

Red Star Publishers
www.RedStarPublishers.org

Reconstruction communiste Canada
pueblo1917@gmail.com

También disponible en español

Contents

From the Congress to the BJP

It is a great tragedy of Indian history that India was partitioned in 1947 as a solution of the communal question, but communalism[1] survived in India and became worse during the rule of the Congress[2]. The situation gradually deteriorated and communalism took new form as Hindutva[3]. Thus India has now come under the rule of the Hindutvavadi BJP[4] and communalism has assumed the form of a monster. To understand the cause of this development it is necessary to look at the history of British colonial rule in India.

-2-

James Mill was a man of great erudition and the first British historian of India. In his book, 'The History of British India', he divided Indian history into Hindu, Muslim, and British periods. The first two periods were divided on the basis of religion. But the third period was called British, instead of Christian. It was a deliberate mischief and done with a view to introduce religious communalism among Indians.

The division on the basis of religion was also done wrongly. The entire pre-Sultanate period of Indian history was distorted and characterized as Hindu. It was a deliberate falsehood. For in that period

---

[1] In this case, the term *communalism* is used to connote the manipulation of the religious symbols and feelings of the population by social elites for their own political and material interests. – *(Spanish) Translator's note.*

[2] This refers to the **Indian National Congress party**, also known as the **Congress Party** or simply **Congress**. – *Translator's note.*

[3] Hindutva in a religious sense is defined as the Hindu spirit; it is currently used as a political term to refer to Hindu nationalism, which identifies India with Hinduism and Hinduism with India. – *Translator's note.*

[4] Bharatiya Janta Party (Indian People's Party) of Prime Minister Narendra Modi. – *Translator's note*

India was ruled also by great Buddhist kings and emperors like Ashoke, Kanishka, Harshabardhan, and the Pals, who ruled Eastern India for four hundred years. There were also other minor Buddhist kings. All kings and emperors of the Sultan and Mughal periods were portrayed as oppressors of the Hindus and enemies of Hinduism. His special target was the Mughals. James Mills died in 1836 but his historical writings influenced later historians. Indian historians like R. C. Dutt, R. C. Majumdar, Jadunath Sarkar and others wrote history following the line indicated by James Mill and communalised it. These communal historians largely shaped the politics of late nineteenth and the first half of the twentieth century India.

-3-

The British government particularly targeted the Mughals and tried to show that the British rule was beneficial to the Hindus. In 1857 both Hindus and Muslims fought unitedly against the British and declared the last Mughal emperor Bahadur Shah as their emperor. Bahadur Shah had no active role in the uprising, but he and the Muslims became the principal targets of the British. Prime Minister Lord Palmerston ordered the demolition of Mughal buildings in Delhi. William Dalrymple, describing the situation at that time, wrote in his book, 'The City of Djinns', "The recapture of Delhi by the British on 14 September 1857 led to the wholesale destruction of great areas of the city. The Red Fort was plundered and much of it razed to the ground; what remained of one of the most beautiful palaces became a grey British barracks. It was only by a hair's-breadth that the great Mughal Jama Masjid was saved from similar destruction....Three thousand Delhi-wallahs were tried and executed—either hanged, shot or blown from the mouths of cannons.... The last Emperor was sent off to exile in Rangoon in a bullock cart; the princes, his children, were all shot. The inhabitants of the city were turned out of the gates to starve in the countryside outside; and even after the city's Hindus were allowed to return, Muslims remained banned for two whole years. The finest mosques were sold off to Hindu bankers for use as bakeries and stables."

In fact, all the Mughal buildings in Shahjahanabad of old Delhi were destroyed. The great palaces and mansions of Mughal ameers and generals, the huge Chandni Chowk bazar, the imposing guest house built by Shahjahan's daughter Jahanara and other important structures were razed to the ground. This act was not less barbaric than the destruction of the Buddha statues in Bamiyan of Afghanistan. Historians did not criticize it, they remained silent. The whole episode was allowed to be forgotten.

-4-

During the pre-British period the Muslims were employed in the army and the administration of the Mughals. There were few landlords among the Muslims. Some Hindus were also employed in the army and administration, but land and zamindares were owned mostly by them. With the Mughal empire gone, the Muslims lost their jobs in the army and administration and they had no alternative employment. They were hostile to British rule and did not take part in the activities of the British-owned business and financial houses. On the other hand, the Hindus welcomed and took the opportunities opened before them. They were employed in the British business houses and also worked as Mutsuddis, Banians, moneylenders and in other capacities.

The colonial administration introduced a new system of education and built schools and colleges where English was taught. The Hindus took full advantage of this and advanced in learning. It helped them to get employment in government departments and also in private business organizations. The Muslims generally deprived themselves of this opportunity and very few of them took to English education. As a consequence of all this, the Muslims lagged behind the Hindus in the sphere of education and economic life. They remained poor and uneducated. A gap was thus created between the economically solvent and educationally advanced Hindus and the poor and backward Muslims. The gap widened in the nineteenth century and became the most important and determining factor in the political developments of British India.

Also in the sphere of land ownership and zamindaris[5] Muslims faced a difficult situation. According to the provisions of the Permanent Settlement of 1793, the zamindars had to pay nine-tenth of the collected revenues to the government within a stipulated time. Most zamindaris began to fail to deposit the fixed rent and the zamindaris were sold in auction. The auctioned zamindaris were bought by the Calcutta-based Mutsuddis, Banias, merchants and usurers, who possessed liquid money. The Muslims had no money and except a few,

---

[5] Owners of agricultural farms. – *Translator's note*

all zamindaris went to a new class of Hindus. This disparity enhanced the gap between the Hindus and Muslims in the nineteenth century and reached a critical stage by the turn of the century.

-5-

Reducing this gap between the Hindus and Muslims became the greatest concern of Muslims in the whole of India. But in Bengal it took the form of a movement. Some influential leaders and a section of the middle-class Muslims in East Bengal demanded a separate province by partitioning Bengal. This actually coincided with the British government decision to partition Bengal apparently for administrative reasons. It was true that reorganization of the Bengal Presidency[6] was necessary for its huge size, but creating hostility among the Hindus and Muslims was also in their agenda. For this purpose they actually inspired and encouraged the partitionwalas of East Bengal like Nawab Salimullah. The disparities in economic, social and political spheres between the Hindus and Muslims were supposed to gradually reduce under a separate provincial administration dominated by Muslims.

-6-

Bengal was partitioned in 1905, thirty-five years before the Lahore Resolution. The Hindus of Bengal, the zamindars and landowners, business communities, men employed in government and commercial organizations, writers and cultural workers and political leaders, all belonging to the upper castes, unitedly opposed the arrangement and demanded the annulment of partition. The resistance movement became very powerful and at the same time it heightened communal tension between the Hindus and Muslims. In the face of this resistance and after successfully achieving their political objectives, the British government annulled the partition of Bengal in 1911.

What is interesting to note in this context is that in spite of the question of Hindu-Muslim disparity becoming a live political issue, the Congress remained stubbornly opposed to any concession to the

---

[6] The Bengal Presidency, later reorganized as the Province of Bengal, was once the largest subdivision of British India after the dissolution of the Bengal Subah, with its headquarters in Calcutta. – *Translator's note*

Muslims for reducing the gap between the two communities. This was despite Gandhi's support for the Khilafat movement.

The Khilafat movement against the British government was a pseudo-religious movement and it had no real anti-imperialist character. It had nothing to do with the plight of the Indian Muslims and it didn't hurt the interest of Hindus. Gandhi supported the movement. Bal Gangadhar Tilak also lent his support. Gandhi gave a call to 230 million Indian Hindus to cooperate with the Khilafat movement. At the same time, he also started his non-cooperation movement. But this kind of movement cannot really create and promote good relation between communities. The Hindu-Muslim relation deteriorated following the end of the Khilafat movement.

Jinnah was a secular politician. He opposed the Khilafat movement and tried to prevent Muslim League joining it. But Muslim League decided to join the movement. Jinnah left the Muslim League and went to England, where he joined the legal profession.

-7-

In Bengal disparity became a very important political issue and Chittaranjan Das of the Bengal Congress, in collaboration with Fazlul Huq and other Muslim leaders, prepared a formula for reducing Hindu-Muslim disparity. In 1923, they signed an agreement called the 'Bengal Pact' in which, among other things, there was provision for equal (50:50) share of jobs for the two communities. At the same time Chittaranjan declared that in the event of formation of a Congress government in Bengal it would reserve sixty per cent jobs for the Muslims till such time as the Hindus and Muslims reach the same level in this area. With the same end in view he suggested reservation of eighty per cent seats for Muslims in the Calcutta Corporation. There was a big row against Chittaranjan by some Hindu members of the Congress and Gandhi rejected it. Chittaranjan died soon afterwards.

-8-

On November 8, 1927, the British government announced a seven-member Parliamentary Commission under the leadership of Sir John Simon. No Indian was included in the Commission. Both the Congress and the Muslim League boycotted the Commission. After the declaration of the formation of the Simon Commission, the Congress Working Committee sponsored an All-Party Conference on

February 12, 1928. In that Conference a committee was formed under the presidency of Motilal Nehru, taking leaders from different parties with a view to deciding the main aspects of the future constitution of India. On December 20, 1928, in the joint convention of the Congress and the Muslim League and in the All-Party Conference held in Calcutta the report of the Nehru Committee was submitted.

The report recommended dominion status for India, selection of the members in the centre and provincial councils by joint electorate, reservation of seats for the minorities in the centre and provincial councils, no reservation of seats for the Muslims of the Punjab and Bengal, reservation of seats on the basis of population for a particular period of time, etc.

After holding discussions on this report, Jinnah proposed amendments which included reservation of one-third seats in the Central Council for the Muslims, reservation of seats for the Muslims of the Punjab and Bengal on the basis of population till an election system on the basis of adult franchise is introduced, transferring residuary powers to the provinces, etc. Tej Bahadur Sapru appealed for accepting Jinnah's proposals with a view to maintaining communal balance. But it was opposed by Hindu Mahasabha representative Jayakar and Motilal Nehru. Gandhi did not take part in this controversy and remained silent all along. When Jinnah's amendments were given to the vote, they were rejected. Jinnah was very much shaken by this defeat. To him this was 'parting of the ways between the Hindus and Muslims.' Henceforward he gave up all efforts for Hindu-

Muslim unity and understanding and sought to preserve and secure Muslim interest within the framework of communal politics. That was the normal and easiest way for securing and preserving the rights of religious minorities within the structure of bourgeois politics.

This All-Party Conference was a vastly important landmark in the history of India's politics. It saw the parting of the ways between the Hindus and Muslims as Jinnah's secularism broke down. Jinnah's breakdown symbolized the breakdown of secularism in the constitutional politics of India.

After being convinced that the Muslims had nothing to get from the Congress, Jinnah took the communal path. To him the Muslims were the only minority in India who mattered and they had to be organized in order to confront the Congress. He had his bourgeois class orientation, had no broad political vision and lacked farsightedness. Otherwise he would have realized that a much more effective way of confronting Hindu communalism of the Congress was to establish good and fraternal relations with other political forces and national minorities like the Scheduled Caste Hindus, Sikhs, nationalities of North-East India, etc. That kind of national unity would have been able to curb the power of big Hindu capital and pave the way for a democratic solution of the minority question in India.

-9-

The British government convened a Round Table Conference for holding discussions between the British government and leaders of various political parties of India. The first session was held in London in 1930 and two others followed. B. R. Ambedkar, leader of the oppressed and marginalized Scheduled Caste Hindus, argued for a separate electorate for the untouchables. But claiming himself as the leader and real representative of the untouchables, Gandhi rejected Ambedkar's demand for a separate electorate because that would largely affect the majority status of the Hindus. Being afraid of such developments, he later appeared as the saviour of Scheduled Caste Hindus and re-named them as 'Harijans' or the People of God. He also brought out a newspaper called *Harijan*[7]. This undoubtedly was

---

[7] Harijan is a term popularized by Mohandas Gandhi to refer to Dalits, traditionally called untouchables, a sector that is born and leads a life of marginalization, exclusion and violation of human rights. – Translator's note.

a deceitful posture. Because Gandhi was wholly dedicated to the interest of the upper caste Hindus.

After the Round Table Conference, Ramsay MacDonald, the British Prime Minister, announced that the untouchables would be awarded separate electorate for a period of twenty years. At the time Gandhi was detained in Yerawada Central Jail in Poona. From there he announced that unless the provision for separate electorate for untouchables was revoked, he would fast until death.

A month later he actually began his fast. It was immediately followed by mounting frenzy. Ambedkar was held responsible for the fast and was accused for trying to kill Gandhi. He was in a difficult situation. That was not the time for logic and reason. Ambedkar did not want to be held responsible for Gandhi's death. He withdrew his demand for a separate electorate for the untouchables and agreed to have reservation. After four days of the fast on 24 September 1932 Ambedkar visited Gandhi in the prison and signed a pact, the Poona Pact, as it came to be known. Among the other signatories were the Marwari industrialist and Gandhi's patron G. D. Birla and V. D. Savarkar, the President of Hindu Mahasabha. Thus Gandhi finally 'settled' the Scheduled Caste issue. He was able to keep the Scheduled Castes within the fold of Hinduism and use them politically, and at the same time preserve the prison house of the caste system in the interest of the upper caste. The Scheduled Castes renamed as Dalit, are still languishing in the same prison house, which Gandhi protected and preserved in the 1930s.

Later, when the situation calmed down Ambedkar wrote, "There was nothing noble in the fast. It was a foul and filthy act.... It was a vile and wicked act. How can the untouchables regard such a man as honest and sincere?" (Quoted by Arundhati Roy. The Doctor and the Saint. From Babashaeb Ambedkar: Writings and Speeches. BAWS).

Ambedkar was so deeply aggrieved and embittered by the actions of Gandhi that afterwards in 1937, in the preface to the second edition of his famous book 'Annihilation of Caste', he wrote, "I shall be satisfied if I make the Hindus realize that they are the sick men of India, and their sickness is causing danger to the health and happiness of other Indians."

-10-

The British colonial government was fully cognizant of the political situation in India. They were playing their own game of stoking political animosity between the Hindu Muslim communal forces. Despite of all the claptrap of the national freedom movement, the Congress and the Muslim League had little steam of their own. In the language of Maulana Mohammad Ali they were pursuing a 'begging and praying' politics.

Gandhi was renowned as the greatest national leader of India. But his nationalism was a politics of compromise. He wanted to extract concessions from the British colonial government, but never opposed it beyond a limit. Whenever the possibility of such limit-crossing arose, Gandhi intervened and stopped the movement. He launched non-cooperation movement, but always showed a curious unwillingness to let it develop into violent confrontation with the government. In order to justify this, he propounded his theory of Ahimsa or non-violence. But Ahimsa of that vintage was a misnomer. What is interesting to note is that his non-violence was meant only for Indians. He always opposed any form of violence by Indians. His opposition to the violence at Chowri Chowra was famous. But he was never found to oppose and denounce violence by the British colonial government. He refused to condemn the massacre of thousands of innocent Indians by the British Indian army in Jallianwala Bagh in 1919. He refused to condemn the hanging of Bhagat Singh in 1931. When soldiers of the Garhwal Regiment refused to open fire on innocent people in Kissakhani Bazaar of Peshawar in 1931, being inspired by his ideal of Ahimsa he openly disapproved it, saying that a soldier must obey the orders of superiors, otherwise there would be no discipline in the army! When they would be in power they would need a disciplined army!! By supporting the soldiers of the Garhwal Regiment he did not want to encourage indiscipline!!!

Gandhi actually never practised what he preached. This was true not only in the above-mentioned cases, but also in what he did in his dealings with the Muslims and the lower caste Hindus. His secularism and his love for the 'Harijans' was nothing but a sham. His opposition to British colonialism had the same character. He loved freedom but did not demand India's independence till the late twenties. In fact, the Indian bourgeois leaders like Gandhi, Jinnah, Nehru, Patel, etc. were all spineless. They could not think of India's independence without the cooperation of the British government! And indeed, finally they got it with the unmistakable 'cooperation' of the British government.

-11-

The relation of the Congress leaders with G. D. Birla was very close. Dr. Sarvapalli Radhakrishnan's son, Sarvapalli Gopal has said in his biography of Jawaharlal Nehru that Gandhi, Patel, Rajendra Prasad and others used to take money from Birla regularly. Nehru declined to take it directly from Birla. So he gave it to Gandhi and Nehru took it from him! Though Birla was Gandhi's patron and looked after him, yet he always tried to give the impression that he lived a poor man's life. He travelled in the third class, but his third class was not the third class of ordinary passengers. Once Sarojini Naidu wittily said, "we have to spend a great lot of money to keep Bapu in poverty."

After Gandhi's death, Birla published some documents in two volumes called, 'Bapu'. It was Gandhi's practice to send a copy of everything to Birla—letters written to various political leaders and representatives of the British government, political documents, even private letters. These letters, including letters written to Birla are all included in these two volumes. A close look at these clearly reveals who was whose Bapu.

-12-

The character of the Indian National Congress was undergoing a transformation in the thirties. It was a broad platform of various interests. Progressive elements like the Communist Party, M. N. Roy[8] and liberals were associated with it. As the influence and control of Hindu landowners, upper class Hindu businessmen and industrialist Marwaris like G. D. Birla and the house of Tata grew in the Congress, progressive elements began to leave it in the late thirties. A large number of people known as nationalist Muslims, who were loyal members of the Congress, deserted it and most of them joined the Muslim League. Even it was not possible for Subhas Bose to stay in

---

[8] M. N. Roy was a founder of the Communist Party of India. He participated in the Third International and from which he was expelled in 1929; in 1940 he created the Radical Democratic Party. After a few years, Roy concluded that party politics was incompatible with his ideal of organized democracy. This resulted in the dissolution of the Radical Democratic Party in December 1948 and the launching of a movement called the Radical Humanist Movement.

the Congress. He had to leave it. The communal and reactionary character of the Congress became quite evident.

The Pakistan Resolution of the Muslim League in 1940, also known as the Lahore Resolution, was based on the two-nation theory. The Congress and other organizations denounced it as communal. The two-nation theory was communal, but not new.

-13-

In the 1860s, Nabagopal Mitra established the 'Hindu Mela' and the 'Jatiya Sava' or the National Association, an organization for propagating nationalism. By nationalism they meant Hindu nationalism. In the Hindu Mela in 1867, they declared that Hindus were a distinct nation. But why did the need arise to declare themselves as a separate nation? Against whom was this declaration directed? There was little doubt that it was the Muslims who were considered opponents in the field of opportunities which were opened before them at the time.

The Hindu Mela was an important event. Rajnarayan Basu, a prominent leader of the Brahmo Samaj, claimed in his autobiography that he inspired Nabagopal Mitra to convene the Hindu Mela. Though a Brahmo, he also designated the Hindus as a distinct nation. But he was not the only Brahmo to subscribe to this idea. There were others. What is apparently astonishing is that the Brahmos who renounced Hinduism and formed a different religious group did not desist at times from identifying themselves with the Hindus. In 1871, Rajnarayan Basu gave his famous lecture on the superiority of Hindu religion in a meeting organized by Jatiya Sava of Nabagopal Mitra and presided over by the most important Brahmo leader Debendranath Tagore, father of Rabindranath. The umbilical cord of the Brahmo Dharma was not severed from Hinduism.

Shankaracharya set his religious movement to counter and oppose the tide of Buddhism in the eighth century. Shree Chaitanya preached his version of Hinduism in response to the advances of Islam in the sixteenth century. The Brahmo Dharma appeared in Bengal in the nineteenth century at a time when educated middle class young people inclined towards Christianity. Because of this the Brahmo Dharma also had a distinct class character. There were no peasant, worker or poor people in the Brahmo Samaj. It was a religion of the upper and the middle classes.

The Brahmo Dharma had no definite ideological foundation. It was, in fact, a weak reaction against a weak trend of Christianity. It had no scripture of its own. They adhered to the Vedanta and the Upanishads. They came out of Hinduism, but most of them regarded themselves as Hindus in a broad sense of the term and had a sense of belonging to the 'Hindu nation'. This was because the Brahmo Dharma was, in reality, a sect of Hinduism. They had considerable influence on the educated middle-class Hindus and for that, along with the Hindus, their adherence to the idea of a distinct Hindu national identity was an important factor in the nineteenth century.

Bankimchandra Chatterjee famously propagated the idea of a Hindu Raj in India and was the greatest representative of social and political reaction in the nineteenth century and was the chief theoretician of Hindu communalism. Two-nation theory was implicit in his teachings. Rabindranath greatly influenced the Bengalis and shaped their language and culture. But Bankimchandra's religious influence was a driving force in the second half of the nineteenth century and afterwards. The terrorist organizations sought inspiration from his writings and did not recruit Muslims.

No one in the Congress and other parties criticized religious revivalism and communalism of Bankimchandra. On the contrary, the Congress adopted his revivalist 'Bande Mataram' song as a national song of India. Even Rabindranath was enamoured of Bande Mataram'. It is surprising that even the Naxalites did not criticize Bankimchandra. They felled statues of Ishwar Chandra Vidyasagar and Rabindranath, but the statues of Bankimchandra remained untouched. This is an aspect of the political situation which cannot be underestimated or ignored.

During the awakening of Hindu nationalism, the Hindu Mela was an aggressive stance of the Hindus. The seed of communalism as a political line was sown on the eve of the rise of Hindu nationalism. The two-nation theory of Nabagopal Mitra and Rajnarayan Basu of the Brahmo Samaj was offensive in character. The two-nation theory of Jinnah, as embodied in the Pakistan Resolution, was formulated to face the advancement of the Hindu bourgeoisie and protect and promote the interest of the backward Muslims. It was defensive in character.

The post 1940 period saw the dominance of communalism in the politics of India. At that time four main contradictions obtained in the Indian situation—the contradiction of the people of India with the colonial British government, the contradiction between the various regions, the communal contradiction and the class contradiction. In the middle of the forties, communal contradiction and peoples' contradiction with the government subordinated the other two contradictions and became the most dominant factors. These contradictions were resolved by independence and partition of the country.

-14-

In March 1946 the British government, with the ostensible objective of granting independence to India, sent a Cabinet Mission to Delhi for talks with the Indian leaders. After about three months of procrastinated negotiations between the Cabinet Mission and the leaders of Congress and League, an agreement was reached. Independent India was to have a federal government with three units— one in West India, the second in East India, and the third in the Central and Southern regions. Jinnah agreed to this and gave up his demand for Pakistan. All seemed well. But suddenly Jawaharlal Nehru, the newly elected president of the Congress, declared in a press conference that they were not bound by the agreement and were free to take their own decisions. The proposed Constituent Assembly would decide what form of government independent India would have.

With this declaration Jawaharlal Nehru actually torpedoed the agreement. Though apparently this was done abruptly, yet it is wrong to think that Nehru acted unilaterally without the connivance and consent of Patel and Gandhi. Patel was actually a Hindu of the RSS variety (the government led by Narendra Modi has built a tall statue of Patel in Ahmedabad) and a very powerful leader of the Congress. He hated the Muslims and did not want to have anything to do with them. Working with them in a federal government was the last thing he wanted. Neither he nor Gandhi opposed Nehru's declaration. No explanation was asked from him by any Congress committee. Abul Kalam Azad was annoyed, but he did not make any public statement. He was a leader of little consequence in the Congress. Later he wrote about this in his book 'India Wins Freedom'. There was also some soft criticism in certain small circle of the Congress.

The inevitable followed. Jinnah considered Nehru's declaration as an act of betrayal, accused the Cabinet Mission, Viceroy and the Congress of a breach of trust, and returned to his demand for Pakistan. The die was cast. Jawaharlal Nehru and the Congress created a situation in which Pakistan became unavoidable.

After Nehru's press conference, Jinnah convened the Muslim League council in Bombay on July 30. A decision was taken to observe August 16 as 'Direct Action Day'. In a press release on August 14, Jinnah declared that the main aim and objective of the 'Direct Action Day' on August 16 was to create consciousness among the Indian Muslims to meet with the situation they were going to face.

The Bengal Muslim League called a public meeting on August 16 at the Calcutta Maidan. A huge short meeting was held, but riots broke out in the city. It continued fiercely for a few days in which thousands of innocent Hindus and Muslims were killed. It raised Hindu-Muslim animosity and hatred to a level never seen before.

The Congress and the Muslim League organizations had no direct involvement in the riots. The situation which developed after the failure of the Cabinet Mission Plan created conditions for this kind of hostilities and the British government took full advantage of this. They engineered the riots through elaborately organized network of agents in the Hindu Mahasabha, Congress and the Muslim League. The Hindus and the Muslims blamed each other for the riots, but everybody forgot the British, who were always criticized for the divide and rule policy. Hence forward riots continued and spread to different parts of India and became a factor in the subsequent political developments. It made the situation helpful for the British government to grant India independence on their terms and partition the country according to their plan.

P. C. Joshi, Secretary of the Communist Party of India (CPI), wrote a pamphlet on the Punjab riots. In that he described, on the basis of concrete evidence, how the British-Indian government engineered the riots.

-15-

Suniti Kumar Ghosh, a very eminent Marxist thinker and historian, wrote in his enormously important book, 'India and the Raj': "Viceroy Wavell noted, perhaps not unjustly, that Patel was strongly influenced by the capitalists and lived in the pocket of one of them, G. D. Birla. Not only Gandhi and Patel but other close associates of theirs had also pleasant relationship with the big bourgeois, though the bounties they enjoyed were certainly not equally generous. Rajendra Prasad acknowledged how he was benefitted by such relationship. S. Gopal writes that the Birla family provided fairly substantive monthly allowances to many leading Congressmen. It would be no wonder if those who paid the piper called the tune. 'By his close association with many millionaires and sheths such as Jamnalal Bajaj, Ambala Sarabhai, Ghanashamdas Birla and others', writes Rani Dhavan Shankardas, 'the Mahatma gained a financial strength without which Congress politics could scarcely be carried out and which was no less vital than the strength which sheths gained from him."

A detailed study and investigation of this relationship of the Congress and Congress leaders like Gandhi, Patel, Nehru, Rajendra Prasad, etc. with the Indian big bourgeoisie is likely to be very revealing. It will throw clear lights on the Congress as servitors of the big bourgeoisie. It will show that as the successor of the Congress, the BJP is now on the same boat. The Congress had its Birla, Tata, Jamnalal Bajaj, Ambalal Sarabhai, etc. The BJP has Ambani brothers, Adani, Tata, etc. The same tradition runs from the Congress to the BJP without any semblance of difference.

-16-

After the failure of the Cabinet Mission Plan, the British government prepared an elaborate plan for the partition of India and sent Lord Mountbatten in March 1947 to execute it. With great efficiency and amazing speed Mountbatten addressed his task. The way he moved indicated that he was thoroughly briefed on the character and habits of important Indian political leaders. He played his cards with consummate skill.

The partition of India was no longer a disputable issue when Mountbatten arrived in India. It was assumed by all parties as a settled matter. But a new political dispute arose. The Congress demanded that in the context of India's partition, Bengal and Punjab would also have to be partitioned according to Hindu and Muslim majority areas. The identity of the Congress as a communal organization of the Hindus could no longer be hidden behind the mask of Indian nationalism. West Bengal was the main seat of Marwari comprador capital. Birla and other Marwari capitalists could not let it go to Pakistan. It was for this that Nehru and Patel demanded the partition of Bengal. Even before the arrival of Mountbatten, Nehru wrote a letter to Lord Wavell on 9 March 1947, in which he "suggested the partition of Bengal and Punjab even if India was not partitioned. Birla's Hindustan Times had raised the same demand which was echoed by Shyamaprasad Mukherjee of the Hindu Mahasabha". (Suniti Kumar Ghosh: India and the Raj. Shahtya Samsad. 2007. p, 596).

There was resistance in Bengal against partition. Leaders of the Congress like Sarat Chandra Bose and Kiran Shankar Roy and the Muslim League leaders sat together and decided to oppose it. They prepared a plan for a united sovereign Bengal. But the central Congress leadership intervened. The provincial Congress Committee began to hold its meetings in which they invited Shyamaprasad Mukherjee, President of Hindu Mahasabha, but excluded Sarat Bose and Kiran Shankar, though they were the two most important Congress leaders in Bengal. Being directed by the centre, the Provincial Committee opposed the move for a united Bengal and demanded partition. However, on behalf of the Congress and the Muslim League a draft plan for a sovereign united independent Bengal was prepared and it was signed by Sarat Bose and Abul Hashim. Jinnah gave it a lukewarm support, but the Congress rejected it.

Gandhi wrote to Sarat Bose: "I have gone through your draft. I have now discussed the scheme roughly with Pandit Nehru and Sardar. Both of them are dead against the proposal and they are of opinion that it is merely a trick of dividing Hindus and Scheduled Caste leaders. With them it is not a suspicion but almost a conviction." (Sarat Chandra Bose Papers). In reply to another letter of Sarat Bose, Gandhi wrote to him, "I have your note. There is nothing in the draft stipulating that nothing will be done by mere majority. Every act of the government must carry with it the cooperation of at least two-thirds of Hindu members in the Executive and Legislative." (Sarat Chandra Bose Papers).

Here, very clearly, Gandhi was expressing his opinion as a Hindu for safeguarding the interest of Hindus from majority Muslims. The Congress demanded its Pakistan in Bengal in unmistakable communal terms. In that situation Sarat Bose said to Gandhi in a letter, "It grieves me to find that the Congress which was once a great national organization is fast becoming an organization of Hindus only." (Sarat Chandra Bose Papers).

In March and April Mountbatten met Indian leaders more than once by rotation and continued consultations with his own advisors. He had long and several discussions with Gandhi, Nehru and Patel among the Congress leaders and the Muslim League President, Jinnah. He also met other leaders like Maulana Azad, Liaquat Ali Khan, Baldev Singh, etc.

From the very beginning Mountbatten developed a special kind of pleasant relationship with Nehru, who became almost a family member of the Mountbattens. Mountbatten capitalized on this relationship for his diplomatic purposes. Nehru virtually became a collaborator of Mountbatten. This was not a sudden development. The Nehrus, father and the son; Gandhi, Patel, Rajendra Prasad, Rajagopal Achariya, etc. were all well-linked with the British-Indian administration. Their secret and collaborationist activities very largely determined the course of British India's political developments. Examples of their loyalty to and cooperation with the British government were numerous. But there are few takers of this among the historians and middle-class intellectuals. So leaders like Gandhi, Nehru, Patel, etc. continue to survive as idols of the Indian national movement.

In June Mountbatten presented his award. According to this award proposals were made to divide India into two parts, India and Pakistan; to divide Bengal and Punjab, to hold plebiscites for taking the opinions of Sylhet and North-West Frontier Province and to form two separate Constituent Assemblies for India and Pakistan. In the evening of June 3, 1947, Mountbatten, Nehru, Jinnah and Baldev Singh made radio broadcasts approving the proposal.

The way India was partitioned favoured the Congress. In the language of Jinnah the Muslim League got a truncated and moth-eaten Pakistan. The last Viceroy of Imperial Britain, Lord Mountbatten became a darling of the Congress. They made him the first Head of State of independent India. It was a big political scandal. Nehru as Prime Minister formed his cabinet. It was not a coalition ministry. But in it he included Shyamaprasad Mukherjee, President of the Hindu Mahasabha.

-17-

The partition of India, and consequently Bengal and the Panjab, in 1947 instead of solving the religious minority problem, which was its ostensible objective, consolidated firmly the rule of religious majorities in what previously constituted British India. There was nothing surprising in this, because the 1940 Lahore Resolution of the Muslim League proposed to create separate states in the Muslim majority areas of East and West India. Thus, in real terms, there was no question of solving the religious minority problems in India either for the Muslims or for the Hindus or other peoples in the declared objectives of either the Indian National Congress or the Muslim League. What became quite clear during the Indian independence movement in the 1940s was that both the Congress and the Muslim League were trying to consolidate the interest of the Indian feudal-bourgeois classes belonging to the Hindu and the Muslim majority respectively. The former under the garb of a united India in the name of Indian nationalism, and the latter in the form of separate states for the Muslim minorities of India, who actually constituted majorities in the Eastern and Western parts of Northern India.

What was quite amazing during the struggle for independence in the 1940s was that the Muslims of the clearly Hindu majority areas in India, like the United Provinces, Bihar, Assam and the Southern provinces, joined the ranks of the Muslim League in large numbers in demanding Pakistan which according to the Lahore Resolution itself, did not include their areas. This was a tragic historical example of how emotionally-charged, powerful political propaganda can sweep away minimal common sense, judgment and even considerations of thoughtful self-interests, and create political blindness in the masses, and also in the literate and highly educated sections of the people.

The pretentions of the Congress to Indian nationalism, supposed to safeguard the interest of all sections of the people, irrespective of their religion, caste and language, broke down when the very important question of preserving the unity of the Punjab and Bengal was raised at the time of independence. The Congress made a radical and formal departure from its long-standing position of secular nationalism when it demanded the partition of Bengal in the same language and for the same considerations which formed the raison d'etre of the Pakistan demand of the Muslim League.

The rule of big Hindu and Marwari capital was inaugurated in independent India. Congress leaders like Gandhi, Nehru and Patel worked for it. They stood for a united India because in united India Hindus would be the majority and the rule of the majority would protect and promote the interest of Hindu landlords, industrial and business classes belonging to the upper caste at the expense of the other minorities and the lower caste Hindus. Independent India was smaller in size than united India, but it provided the above-mentioned interests with all the opportunities which they wanted to have in a united India.

-18-

The cow was and still is an important political issue in India's politics. In July and August 1947, on the eve of independence, Rajendra Prasad became very active for prohibiting cow slaughter. He put pressure on Nehru to declare a ban on cow slaughter and wrote letters to him. Nehru was communal but not of the Rajendra Prasad hue. Moreover, at that time it was not possible for him as Prime Minister to prohibit cow eating and ban cow slaughter. So he ignored Rajendra Prasad's letters, but since 1947 cow slaughter was significantly reduced in most Indian states. It was discouraged. During Indira Gandhi's Prime Ministership her son Sanjay Gandhi demolished all kebab shops around the Delhi Jama Masjid and enforced a ban on cow slaughter in the city.

The BJP prime minister Narendra Modi has practically enforced a ban on cow slaughter throughout India except in West Bengal and Kerala and along with his cohorts of the BJP and the Sangh Parivar are persecuting the Muslims, Christians and the Dalits, often with fake charges of cow slaughter and beef eating. Many of them have been killed.

On January 30, 1948, Gandhi was assassinated by an RSS[9] man. The government banned the RSS. But a little later, Sardar Patel, the Interior Minister, lifted the ban on RSS.

-19-

The limited opportunities which were available to the Muslims in the pre-independence period, began to be reduced in independent India. In the field of education and jobs they began to lag behind. The possibility of reducing the gap between the Hindus and the Muslims disappeared. Communal riots continued to happen in different areas in India, particularly, in North India. The central and state governments failed to stop occurrences of riots and it created a sense of insecurity in the minds of Muslims. Still the Muslims generally voted for the Congress who remained in power at a stretch for thirty years till 1977. In 1977 a non-Congress government came to power. Then in 1982 the Congress won the election and Indira Gandhi returned as Prime Minister. Following her death in 1984, her son Rajiv Gandhi

---

[9] The Rastriya Swayamsevak Sangh, abbreviated RSS, is an Indian far-right paramilitary and Hindu nationalist organization. – *Translator's note.*

succeeded her as Prime Minister. After Rajiv Gandhi a Congress government was formed by Narasimha Rao.

-20-

Since the 1980s communal forces began to gain strength and get organized. The BJP[10] emerged as the most powerful communal organization. Other RSS gharana parties like Viswa Hindu Parishad, Bajrang Dal, Shiv Sena, etc. also began to get organized. Communalism, instead of weakening, began to gather unprecedented strength.

Issues like Babri Masjid, a sixteenth century mosque at Ayodhya, were brought to the forefront. The RSS Sangha Parivar parties, including the BJP demanded the demolition of the mosque and building a Hindu temple at the site. They alleged, without any historical evidence whatsoever, that the Babri Masjid was built by the Moghul emperor Babar destroying a temple which stood at Ramchandra's birthplace.

The Sangh Parivar parties, led by the BJP, raised the movement for destruction of the mosque at a high level, but the Congress government of Narsimha Rao was indifferent. Finally, on December 6, 1992, thousands of RSS karsevaks attacked the Babri mosque and demolished it.

The government of Narsimha Rao did not take any step to stop the karsevaks. They could have easily stopped them by surrounding the mosque by the army. But nothing at all was done. What was extremely surprising was that instead of sitting in his office at that critical time and handling the situation Prime Minister Narsimha Rao spent the day at his home in the puja ghar (prayer room). Who can doubt the complicity of the Congress government of Narsimha Rao with the RSS in demolishing the Babri mosque in such circumstances?

Jawaharlal Nehru's inclusion of Shyamaprasad Mukherjee, President of Hindu Mahasaba and a rabid communalist, in his first cabinet, Sardar Patel lifting the ban on the RSS, Narsimha Rao's role during the demolition of the Babri mosque and the actual demolition of the mosque by the karsevaks are tied unmistakably by the same thread, the thread of communalism.

-21-

---

[10] Indian People's Party.

With the demolition of the Babri mosque communalism, instead of weakening, began to grow in strength. The BJP emerged as the second national party after the Congress, and was nearing the corridors of power. Atal Bihari Vajpayee, leader of the BJP, became Prime Minister of India for 13 days in 1996. He again became Prime Minister in a coalition ministry for 13 months in 1998-99, followed by a full term as Prime Minister from 1999 to 2004.

In 2001 the BJP came to power in Gujarat and Narendra Modi, a former RSS pracharak[11] and BJP member, became the Chief Minister. Soon after assuming power Narendra Modi engineered a communal conflagration in Gujarat in 2002 in which thousands of innocent Muslims were killed and driven out from their homes. He remained Gujarat's Chief Minister till 2014, when he became Prime Minister of India. The BJP also formed governments in a number of other states and consolidated its power as the biggest political party in India.

-22-

In 2004 Congress returned to power at the centre. In March 2005 Prime Minister Manmohan Singh constituted a commission called the Sachar Committee, with Justice Rajendra Sachar as the Chairman, for studying the social, economic and educational condition of the Muslims of India. The Committee in its report described the miserable condition of Muslims and while doing so said that their condition was worse than that of the Dalits. They made certain recommendations, but the government did not take any step for changing the condition of the Muslims.

Before this in 1979, the Janata Party government of Morarji Desai constituted a commission, called the Mandal Commission, with B. P. Mandal as chairman, for enquiring into the condition of lower caste Hindus. It submitted its report, but the successive Congress governments of Indira and Rajiv Gandhi suppressed it. Later it was published by Prime Minister V. P. Singh in August 1990. The report described the miserable condition of the intermediate castes and made some recommendations. V. P. Singh declared that they would implement them, and actually began to take steps. The Commission

---

[11] Pracharak is a spokesperson, propagator of ideas, and recruiter for the organization. – Translator's note.

recommended reservation of jobs, promotional measures in the field of education etc.

That created a crisis in the government. It was a coalition government in which BJP was a component. They strongly opposed the decisions. There began a widespread agitation of upper caste Hindu students and others against it, as they felt that their privileges would be curtailed. The agitation was stoked by the BJP and their fellow parties and reached a high pitch. BJP left the coalition and the government of V. P. Singh fell.

The Mandal Commission report revealed what the successive Congress governments did or did not do for the oppressed castes. The Sachar Committee Report revealed what the successive Congress governments did or did not do for the Muslims. The conditions of the Dalits and Muslims continued to be miserable.

Muslims constitute fifteen per cent of the population in India, but their employment is not more than two per cent. In West Bengal the population of Muslims is more than thirty per cent, but their employment is less than two per cent. Educationally they lag far behind the Hindus. A leftist government led by the CPI(M)[12] was in power in West Bengal for thirty-four years. But the condition of Muslims remained unchanged!

-23-

In 2014 BJP won in the general election and Narendra Modi became Prime Minister. With that India came under the rule of fascists by shedding all pretentions to democracy. They openly declared that the Muslims were invaders and outsiders and were not to be considered as Indians. They would make India a Hindu state, a Ram Rajya, and govern the country according to the laws of Hindutva.

The BJP has presented a new version of Hinduism called Hindutva, a kind of religious fundamentalism. But in reality there cannot be any fundamentalism in Hinduism. Fundamentalism requires a religious book, a scripture, unqualified allegiance to which is absolutely binding. Or in other words, without textual reference there cannot be any religious fundamentalism. The Tripitak, the Talmud, the Bible, the Koran, the Granth Sahib are such text of the Buddhists, the Jews, the Christians, the Muslims and the Sikhs respectively. But Hinduism has no such scripture. One can remain a Hindu even

---

[12] Communist Party of India (Marxist). – Translator's note.

without any faith in the Vedas, the Upanishads, Ramayana, Maha-bharata and the Gita. Even an atheist like Charvak is considered a Hindu.

The core of Hinduism is the caste system. Communalism is not integrally related to religion, but the caste system is. For this, after some years communalism will disappear in the wake of economic and social developments. The caste system will gradually weaken but remain, for how long is anybody's guess.

By presenting Hinduism as a kind of religious fundamentalism, the RSS and the parties of the gharana, including the BJP practically dish out a false Hinduism. The Hindutvavadis indulge in all sorts of silly verbalism while trying to glorify Hindutva. But they have not been able to lay down in concrete terms any religious ideological basis of it. In reality it is nothing but a virulent religious fascism at the service of the upper caste Hindus and the big bourgeois of India. In India today, Narendra Modi of the BJP, Prime Minister of India, is presiding over a fascist system of government in the name of religion.

From the Congress to the BJP is not a long jump. It is a transition.

August 10, 2021

Notes for an Analysis of Crypto Assets and the Blockchain from the Viewpoint of Marxist Political Economy

"The bourgeoisie cannot exist without constantly revolutionising the instruments of production, and thereby the relations of production, and with them the whole relations of society.... Constant revolutionising of production, uninterrupted disturbance of all social conditions, everlasting uncertainty and agitation distinguish the bourgeois epoch from all earlier ones."
– Marx and Engels, *Manifesto of the Communist Party*

The crypto-asset industry[1], which has an economic, political, geopolitical and social impact internationally, promises the utopia of financial transactions without centralized control, the supposed democratization and transparency of transactions with decentralized replicas of records, secured by a cryptographic algorithm hosted on blockchain. The crypto-asset industry does not sell a token or computer code; it sells the hope of investing money with an exponentially high rate of return; it sells the dream of economic freedom.

Up to March 2022, at least 18,000 different crypto assets were registered on the internet; it is estimated that more than 300 million people worldwide 'own' some kind of crypto assets. In Ukraine more than 12.7% of the population 'owns' crypto assets, in other countries there are similar figures: Russia (11.9%), Venezuela (10.3%), Singapore (9.4%), Kenya (8.5%), USA (8.3%), India (7.3%) and South Africa (7.1%). The legal status of crypto assets varies among countries. In 2021 El Salvador became the first country to recognize bitcoin as legal tender. Regulations in the US, Canada, the European Union, Iceland, Australia and the UK tend to recognize the right to own and exchange crypto assets without their being legal tender. On the other

---

[1] Crypto assets are widely and generally used to refer to cryptocurrencies, and other cryptographic derivative products.

hand, China[2], Bolivia and at least 50 other countries have established restrictions or prohibitions around the 'mining', holding and/or exchange of crypto assets.

To study the phenomenon of crypto assets from Marxist political economy, it is worth starting from some questions: What is a crypto asset? Is it a monetary commodity or a currency? Is it fictitious capital? Does it have or represent any value? Does it represent a democratization of the financial system? In academic circles there are some preliminary approaches to the theoretical debate (Fridmanski, Alizart, Abdulhakeem and Qinmei), and some organizations of the ICMLPO, such as Revolusjon (Norway), have published articles and notes that open the way for the necessary debate and precise characterization of the phenomenon in all its forms. In *The Method of Political Economy*, Marx argued that the world is knowable, that despite its complexity society is governed by universal laws of development; starting from concrete reality in a dialectical process of theorization that must be validated based on objective reality as a criterion of truth.

Monetary Commodities and Capital

"It is not money that renders commodities commensurable. Just the contrary. It is because all commodities, as values, are realised human labour, and therefore commensurable, that their values can be measured by one and the same special commodity, and the latter be converted into the common measure of their values, i.e., into money. Money as a measure of value, is the phenomenal form that must of necessity be assumed by that measure of value which is immanent in commodities, labour-time."

– Marx, *Capital* – Volume I Chapter III, pg. 97

"It is only in the markets of the world that money acquires to the full extent the character of the commodity whose bodily form is also the immediate social incarnation of human labour in the abstract."

---

2 The ban on 'mining' crypto assets in China at the end of 2021 was a consequence of the energy impact that mass mining had in that country; before the ban it was estimated that almost 75% of energy consumption of the bitcoin network was concentrated in Chinese regions due to the low price of electricity.

– Marx, *Capital* – Volume I Chapter III, pg. 141

The monetary commodity fulfills the function of being a universal measure of value; it is a material expression of the value of other commodities that allows an equitable exchange of two different commodities. The value of each commodity is essentially the labor power socially necessary for its production or transformation. Therefore, the monetary commodity is a representation of the value of labor power, whose validity as a means of intermediation enjoys a generalized acceptance within the market.

By transforming itself from a means of intermediation and payment into a means of accumulation, money is transformed into capital, applying the general formula of capitalism (M – C ... P ... C' – M'). The value of the commodity is the result of the labor socially necessary for its production, therefore the productive process –labor power – that transforms raw materials into a commodity creates an added value that is not remunerated to the worker in its entirety. That added value, or surplus value, is the cornerstone of capitalism – the accumulation of capital as a result of the labor of others.

Money Fetishism and Fictitious Capital

"As interest-bearing capital, and particularly in its direct form of interest-bearing money capital... capital assumes its pure fetish form, M — M' being the subject, the saleable thing.... a form, in which all its specific attributes are obliterated and its real elements invisible."

– Marx, *Capital* – Volume III, pg. 390

The social character of labor under capitalism conceals the direct relationship between labour power and the transformation of raw material into commodities. The commodity assumes in itself a 'mystical' character, the market assigns it a subjective value (exchange value), the object is conceived as if it had a value by itself and as if it had the ability to relate to other objects independently. That is, the commodity becomes a fetish, it is personified.

Commodity fetishism under capitalism reaches its 'purest' form in interest-bearing money capital or usurious capital, whose cycle of reproduction 'skips' the intermediate steps of the productive process and is reduced to the two extremes of the process – "money exchanged for more money, a form that is incompatible with the nature of money, and therefore remains inexplicable from the standpoint of the circulation of commodities." (Marx, Capital – Volume I, pg. 162). This fetishized capital appears to have its own ability to generate more capital, through interest; by depositing a quantity of money in the bank it not only remains protected, but 'works by itself' and generates returns.

The metamorphosis of the monetary commodity into paper money transformed the role of banks, through promissory notes, credit notes, checks, etc.; each bank guaranteed the bearer the existence of a specified quantity of money. In Imperialism, the Highest Stage of Capitalism, Lenin explained the process of merging productive and unproductive capital into finance capital, under which banks assume a fundamental role, since they "transform inactive money capital into active, that is, into capital yielding a profit; they collect all kinds of money revenues and place them at the disposal of the capitalist class" (pg. 31).

Just as the depositor had the paper money representation of the value guarded by the bank, so the borrower had the paper money representation of the value of the credit. Fictitious or speculative capital is a representation by promissory notes and credit notes of a non-existent capital, but of a determined and accepted value. The promissory note, bond or check issued by a bank that objectively does not have a backing creates a bubble of speculation. Marx in Volume I Chapter III of Capital details the episodes of crisis in the mid-19th century in England because of the rampant speculation of private banks. The liquidity crisis of private banking led to the transformation of the Bank of England into the first modern central bank.

The Collapse of the Bretton-Woods System

"Following the devaluation of the dollar, there were falls also in the currencies of other countries, such as the French franc, the Italian lira, the German mark, etc. In fact. as a result of the crisis, the 'Bretton-Woods system', with its exchange rate for the dollar, has collapsed.... The United States of America has no obligation in regard to the parity of the dollar."

– Hoxha, *The Superpowers*, pg. 160

At the end of World War II the major imperialist powers at the Bretton Woods Conference agreed on a new international monetary framework, created the International Monetary Fund (IMF), laid the background for the World Bank (WB), and established the international standard known as Special Drawing Rights (SDR). The SDR as a unit of account is backed by an international reserve and until 1971 its exchange value depended on the US dollar pegged to the gold standard, with a value set at US $35 per ounce of gold.

In 1971 the Nixon administration unilaterally imposed the dollar standard in international trade without requiring it to be solvent in gold reserves. It opened the possibility of unlimited financial speculation, since the Federal Reserve can order the unlimited printing of more paper money without any backing. Financial speculation has been quantified since the breakdown of the gold standard by observing the variation in the gold-dollar ratio, which went from $35 per ounce to reach more than $1,970 per ounce in 2020. The economic recession of 2001 was a pretext for an unprecedented devaluation of the dollar against gold, which accelerated further in the 2008 crisis and the 2020 crisis.

In the absence of a stable parity between the dollar and gold, the IMF modified the structure of the SDR that is currently calculated based on a proportional basket of currencies composed of the US dollar, the euro, the pound sterling, the Japanese yen and the Chinese yuan/renminbi that was incorporated in 2015. In 2021, in order to confront the impact of the health pandemic, 456 trillion SDRs (approx. $650 trillion US) were 'created' to 'inject liquidity' into the world economy, proportionally allocating to each country according to its contributions to the IMF's reserves.

'Monetary sovereignty' and trusted entities

"In one way or the other they all interfere brutally in the internal affairs of others by means of weapons, politics, diplomacy and the 'influx of dollars' and all kinds of credits."

– Hoxha, *The Superpowers*, pg. 224

The establishment of central banks as regulators of monetary policy and with the exclusive power to issue coins and banknotes of the national currency is one of the characteristics of modern capitalist nation-states. Like all branches of the state, the central bank is neither autonomous nor independent; it is an instrument at the service of the ruling class. In the case of the US Federal Reserve, the main private banks in the country intervene openly in decision-making, while in other countries the sections of the bourgeoisie contest the nuances of monetary policy among themselves through lobbying and the electoral apparatuses. The supposed 'monetary sovereignty' of nation-states is nothing more than the right of the ruling classes to establish its policies at will.

Regional integrations such as the European Union have their own institutions to impose their hegemonic control; in the European Central Bank (ECB) only 4 of the 28 member states concentrate more than 58% of the shareholding power. The monetary-financial apparatus works with a 'revolving door' logic, that is, an executive who yesterday was a director of a private bank, today is a senior executive of the IMF and tomorrow could be president of the central bank. Christine Lagarde, the current president of the ECB, before taking office was managing director of the IMF and minister of economy and finance of the French government. Chile's current finance minister, Mario Marcel, before taking office was president of the Central Bank of Chile and held management positions at the Inter-American Development Bank (IDB) and the World Bank. The current Chancellor of the Exchequer of the United Kingdom, Rishi Sunak, has a track record within the Goldman Sachs investment group and private investment funds. Ghana's Minister of Finance and Planning, Ken Ofori-Atta, is a director of Enterprise Group Ltd, Trust Bank and the International Bank of Liberia, and chairs the Africa board at the World Bank.

In countries with dependent and backward economies, the local oligarchy is nothing more than the transmission belt of the mandates of their imperialist bosses. Through the memoranda of 'understanding' that determine international credits (that is, the foreign debt) from the IMF or some 'friendly' country, the imperialist powers hold dependent economies hostage. The central banks are nothing more than branches of the IMF and/or other creditors, because if they do not obey the mandates of Washington, Frankfurt or Beijing, the countries run the risk of sanctions, economic blockades, freezing of international reserves or restrictions on the purchase of foreign currency.

After the collapse of the Bretton-Woods system in 1973 the main private banks of Europe and North America met in Belgium to establish international standards for interbank transfers, establishing the system known as SWIFT, which currently processes an average of 45 million bank transfers per day.

With its headquarters in Belgium, as a private company SWIFT is subject to European legislation and has been used to apply sanctions against Iran (2012-2016) and against Russia in 2022, in both cases restricting the access of banks of the respective countries to international financial transactions. Also in 2012, U.S. federal agencies intervened and confiscated the shipment of $26,000 between two European business owners because it dealt with the import of Cuban tobacco. The supposed freedom of enterprise of capitalism is subjected to the political-economic interests of the dominant imperialist bloc.

The need to facilitate international trade has promoted technological leaps, the telegraphic transfer messages of the 1970s have been transformed into electronic transfers over the Internet, with clearing and settlement systems. This technological leap was accompanied by a transformation of paper currency into electronic currency, as a functional representation of the current currency, from the expansion of the use of credit and debit cards, and later payments through mobile wallets, QR codes and mobile applications. The guarantee or trust that exists within the SWIFT system is based on the financial institutions that in turn have the backing of the central bank of their respective country.

What is the value of a currency?

"The fluctuations in the value of the paper currencies of various capitalist countries are important not only for the bourse d'èchange (Stock exchange), but they are linked closely with credits, the sale of commodities, and many other factors, and are accompanied with grave consequences, both internally and abroad..."

– Hoxha, *The Superpowers*, pg. 161

National or regional currencies in the free market generally have an exchange value subject to supply and demand. The exchange rate and consequently the purchasing power of a currency depends on a number of factors, including: the trade balance (imports vs. exports), external debt, international reserves (Forex) as well as gold reserves and / or foreign currencies and the Sovereign Wealth Fund. The gold support of the US economy corresponds to 8,133 tons of the precious metal, which represents 65.5% of its international reserves, in the case of Germany its reserve of 3,359 tons corresponds to 65.4% of its reserves, while the 2,298 tons of gold reserves of Russia represent 20.94% of its reserves and 1,948 tons of China are only 3.24% of its international reserves. 58.8% of international foreign exchange reserves are in US dollars, 20.64% in euros, 5.57% corresponds to the Japanese yen, 4.78% to the pound sterling, 2.79% to the Chinese yuan/renminbi, and the remaining 7% is divided among other currencies (Canadian dollars, Australian dollars, Swiss francs).

The national or regional currencies are abstract representations of the total reserves of the State (whether these are in gold, currencies, bonds, etc.); these reserves in turn are an abstract representation step by step until reaching "that measure of value which is immanent in commodities, labour-time." (Marx, *Capital* – Volume I, pg. 97).

The aftermath of the 2008 crisis

"Parties or movements of illusory and often reactionary protest against the oligarchies and the EU have been strengthened, offering alternatives within the system, without presupposing the revolutionary defeating of capitalism. Their 'hobbyhorses' are: the recovery of national sovereignty, criticism of EU interference and austerity policies, problems of immigration, multiculturalism, the responsibility of the banks in the crisis, the theory of the 'plot', the idea of 'betrayal' of the people, etc."

– ICMLPO – European Meeting 2018,
The fight against populism in Europe

The financial crisis of 2008 reshaped the map of the financial giants internationally. The bursting of the 'mortgage bubble' in the United States, that is, the sharpening of the unsustainable gap between the (speculative) financial economy and the real economy in the mortgage market due to the systematic issuance of derivative financial products without objective support, put an end to some of the most important financial conglomerates in the world. The Lehman

Brothers group filed for bankruptcy, Bear Sterns was acquired by JP Morgan and Merrill Lynch by Bank of America; the US government allocated more than $700 billion to bail out private banks, benefiting Wells Fargo, State Street, Bank of America, JP Morgan Chase, Citigroup, Morgan Stanley, Goldman Sachs, Capital One, American Express, Discover, along with hundreds of other financial institutions. Germany, Belgium, Cyprus, Spain, Greece, Iceland, Ireland, the Netherlands, Portugal, the United Kingdom and Switzerland also 'injected liquidity' into the banking system with generous 'rescue' packages.

That the governments of bourgeois states decide to hand over public funds to private banks, under the pretext of safeguarding the 'stability of the financial system' only reaffirms what Marx and Engels said in the Manifesto of the Communist Party: " The executive of the modern State is but a committee for managing the common affairs of the whole bourgeoisie." As expected, the internal contradictions of the financial oligarchy are expressed in the relationship of the financial groups rescued, merged or bankrupted as a result of the crisis.

The massive expansion of the financial bailout and the benefiting banks, while the working peoples experienced in their own skin the effects of the capitalist crisis – eviction and unemployment – created the ideal context for the formation of 'anti-establishment' ideas, questioning the 'political caste' and the bankers, against state intervention in the economy, which have been indicted by populist groups of various kinds. The economic and political crisis of the current capitalist system, deepened by the COVID-19 health pandemic, has unleashed a wave of anti-popular measures, massive layoffs and wage cuts, along with the suspension of democratic freedoms and greater measures of state repression. Populism, with its variations in each country, has as its common thread the exaltation of individual effort and investment as the only guarantee of material success, completely ignoring the unequal conditions in any class society. The Meeting of Marxist-Leninist Parties and Organizations of Europe in 2018 showed that the populist movements "propose reactionary and fictitious responses to these problems, without questioning the pillars of the system of exploitation."

Is the solution in an algorithm?

At the beginning of 2009 Satoshi Nakamoto (pseudonym) launched bitcoin (the first cryptocurrency), and currently in whose first blog he reproduced the text: 'The Times January 3, 2009 Chancellor on Brink of Second Bailout for Banks'. Bitcoin was designed as a peer-to-peer electronic transaction system; given the distrust in the financial system Nakamoto argued that a computer protocol based on cryptographic algorithms with a record replicated in a decentralized way is the solution to the ills of the financial system.

Faced with the financial system of centralized control that depends on the 'trust' placed in the institutions that make up the banking system, the blockchain (chain of blocks) proposes a trustless decentralized registry, under a consensus of proof of work, saving every transaction using a series of cryptographic algorithms that form part of a publicly replicated chain. This is democratizing utopia that each person can have an encrypted copy of each transaction made in the chain for themselves as well as for third parties.

The cryptographic algorithms of the blockchain are based on the logic of incorporating in each new record parts of the chain that precede it in order to validate and verify, so that each transaction made becomes part of the new transactions, and altering a transaction would also imply the need to alter all subsequent transactions in all replicas of the blockchain. This algorithmic model implies that each record requires greater computational strength and therefore a greater quantity of energy resources, added to the wear and tear of the equipment, the law of the decreasing trend of the rate of profit is affirmed, each new block 'mined' requires greater investment.

The 'mining' of crypto assets such as bitcoin, in its first years of existence could be carried out with a personal computer, today it has become a billionaire industry, with gigantic 'farms' of servers that monopolize the mining of the main crypto assets. In April of 2021, more than 98.3% of new bitcoins globally were 'mined' among the 14 largest conglomerates (pools) in the market; among these the 8 largest conglomerates 'mined' more than 82.4%. The myth of decentralization or the democratization of control collapses in the face of the evident tendency of concentration of 'mining' equipment in the hands of a handful of big business owners.

According to The Economist (2022), the annual energy consumption of bitcoin networks in 2021 was 204 TWh (terawatt-hours, that is trillion Wh), an amount equivalent to the annual consumption of countries such as South Africa or Australia. The cost of a single bitcoin transaction is 1173 kWh (kilowatt hours, that is thousand Wh) which is equivalent to the average consumption of a home in the UK for three months. Although transactions in other crypto assets such as Ethereum (87 kWh), Litecoin (18 kWh) and Cardano (0.5 kWh) consume exponentially less energy per transaction, electronic transactions with credit or debit cards still have a substantially lower consumption since with 1 kWh approximately 650 transactions can be processed.

Not having the technical or energy capacity to mine from home, the average 'entrepreneur' or investor in crypto assets is dedicated to the exchange of various crypto assets over the internet. This exchange is carried out in a way very similar to what takes place in a stock exchange, although without the intermediation of banks or centralized entities. The vacillating market price of crypto assets in general terms takes as a model some of the most far-reaching crypto assets (bitcoin, ethereum, litecoin, etc.) or stablecoins3 such as USDT (equivalent to one US dollar), so its exchange value is ultimately subject to a legal tender. The Russian roulette of speculative 'investment' can create large profits or losses; this practice is reinforced by the 'populist' discourse that exalts individual effort as a supposed creator of wealth.

What are crypto assets?

"A commodity is, in the first place, an object outside us, a thing that by its properties satisfies human wants of some sort or another. The nature of such wants, whether, for instance, they spring from the stomach or from fancy, makes no difference."
– Marx, *Capital* – Volume I, pg. 43

The anti-establishment, anti-banking, etc. conspiracy theory rhetoric of populism in the aftermath of the 2008 crisis, poses among the fundamental problems to be solved: the insecurity and instability of the banking system and the corruption and inefficiency of state intervention or of the 'political caste' in the economy. From this

---

3 Stablecoins are crypto assets with a fixed and stable exchange rate related to a national currency or some natural resource, but in general they have no real backing.

exposition of the problem it creates needs such as: economic security for personal savings, privacy and freedom to transact without state control, investments or ventures with high returns, the social status of being an entrepreneur or investor in the emerging virtual market and even the sense of belonging, among others.

The 'possession' of crypto assets can satisfy several of the needs raised, and by satisfying a human need it therefore has a use value; thus it meets the first element of a commodity. The objective measure of use value is a representation of the labor socially necessary for its production; in the case of crypto assets a complete analysis of the productive process must consider the intellectual and manual work of computer codes, the intellectual and manual work of operation and maintenance of 'mining' farms, the productive process of specialized equipment (GPU [graphics processing unit], servers, etc.) that enable 'mining' and recording of transactions, intellectual and manual work in marketing.

The second aspect of a commodity is its exchange value, a quantification relation that allows for the exchange of one commodity for another. No matter how volatile, unstable and speculative the exchange value of crypto assets is, they meet this factor. The fetishistic character of the commodity in the case of crypto assets acquires dimensions similar to the fetishism of money, since it makes invisible any relationship with the labor power under the assumption that only computers and algorithms intervene in the transactions. The crypto-asset's fetish endows it with a supposedly inherent potential to create profit, in addition to the ability to satisfy subjective and psychological needs.

For Marxist political economy a monetary commodity is a commodity that serves as a measure of value so that it is a means of exchange, it is a means of payment and finally it is a means of hoarding (accumulation), which has widespread social acceptance.

In 2010 one of the first commercial transactions with bitcoin intermediation was recorded, the purchase of two pizzas for 10,000 ฿ (bitcoins); in October 2021 this quantity of bitcoins was equivalent to more than $669 million US. Currently, the purchasing power of crypto assets in general terms is subject to the exchange rate with the US dollar, which tends to have a volatile and speculative behavior. An example of this volatility was between May 13 and 14 of last year, when the exchange value of bitcoin suddenly fell from $58 thousand

US to $49 thousand US due to the negative comment of the tycoon Elon Musk regarding its energy consumption.

While thousands of merchants internationally accept payment for their products and services in various crypto assets, the use of crypto assets as a medium of exchange is subject to the exchange rate of currencies or legal tender at the time of making the transaction. Thus, in a matter of seconds the cost of a given product in crypto assets can vary drastically. While under capitalism market conditions (relations of supply and demand) can cause sudden changes in the exchange value of a commodity, the relative stability of a commodity as a unit of measure of value is a key factor for its social acceptance as a monetary commodity.

A monetary commodity is a means of payment, it must have generalized social acceptance4 for the amortization of public or private debts, the payment of rents, public services and taxes. In September 2021, after 20 years of dollarization, the government of Nayib Bukele in El Salvador established the bitcoin as legal tender, against the 'recommendations' of the IMF, so that any public or private transaction can be paid in dollars or bitcoin. The bitcoin market in El Salvador appeals to tourist enthusiasts and large investment companies. There is a possibility that in the future one or more of the most far-reaching crypto assets may consolidate their social acceptance as a means of payment, which at this time is still quite marginal.

Crypto-asset transactions have decentralized ledgers that can verify their validity from any machine connected to the network, but these transactions, however valid they may be internally, do not necessarily represent an external value, they do not have any real support. Just as the indulgences sold by the church in the Middle Ages effectively had the signature of the pope and therefore had full validity within the church, the bearer of the indulgence had the pass to a fictitious reality, without the right to question. It may be undeniable that you have X amount of crypto assets in your virtual wallet, but the volatility of the exchange rate of the crypto asset can turn the

---

4Social acceptance does not necessarily imply the status of legal tender. In Bolivia for example national legislation only recognizes the national currency (Boliviano) as legal tender; however there is a wide social acceptance of the US dollar as a means of payment for real estate, vehicles, rentals, electronic products, industrial equipment, bank loans, etc.

savings of an 'entrepreneur' into pennies. While fictitious capital is an objectively measurable value of speculative capital with no real backing, crypto assets are not objectively a unit of measure of value.

The function of the monetary commodity as a means of accumulation implies that it must maintain a relatively stable value over time. Gold reserves are a very good example of this function; although the collapse of the Bretton-Woods system broke the parity of the US dollar with the gold standard, the precious metal is still an important part of the real support of the main currencies of the capitalist world. The short existence of crypto assets, the high speculation and volatility of their exchange value, the lack of real support, and the 'decentralization' in management that facilitates the evasion of responsibilities to corporations that make up the bulk of the networks are some of the elements that hinder the use of crypto assets as a means of accumulation.

Therefore, we can characterize crypto assets as commodities that satisfy social needs (fundamentally subjective) – that is, they have use value, in their creation the socialized labor power intervenes directly and indirectly; it has an exchange value, which due to its intrinsically fetishistic character tends to be very variable, subject to market 'conditions' (supply and demand). The instability of the exchange value and therefore its ineffectiveness as a unit of measure of value, its limited social acceptance as a means of payment, the absence of real support and its unviability as a means of accumulation are factors that rule out the characterization of crypto assets as a monetary commodity at this time.

Central Bank Digital Currencies: Antithesis of Crypto Assets?

Given the volatility of the exchange value of crypto assets and the absence of centralized control mechanisms, at least 104 countries5 have initiated research processes and pilot tests of Central Bank Digital Currency (CBDC) programs. While electronic currency is an expression of paper money in transactions without physical bills or coins (for example credit cards, mobile wallets or QR code payments), CBDCs are digital currencies whose transactions are recorded with variations of blockchain technology with cryptographic

---

5 Bolivia is one of the few countries that by banning all use of crypto assets in the country has not proposed any sovereign development in this regard.

algorithms to ensure their veracity. But unlike crypto assets CBDCs, instead of 'decentralizing' the record of transactions through replicas, centralizes the registration and control in the institutions of the financial CBDC. The centralization of the registry and its non-replication obviously affects the reduction of energy costs compared to traditional crypto assets. Based on the same technological framework as the blockchain, CBDCs are the antithesis of the postulates of decentralization or 'democratization' of crypto assets. At the same time, by having the record of all financial transactions carried out, the State could achieve new levels of control. In its exploratory phase there are various approaches for the implementation of CBDCs, but as a general rule CBDCs aim to be legal tender in their respective countries, with the support mechanisms that paper money currencies have.

At the same time, SWIFT has announced that it will implement a new international transfer protocol based on blockchain records, which will represent a significant technological leap for the financial sector, reaffirming the role of CBDCs as a representation of national currencies. Since 2014, in defense of their own economic interests, Russia and China have created international transfer, clearing and settlement systems that process exchanges in rubles and yuan/renminbi as alternatives to SWIFT.

Blockchain technology, in addition to its applications in the financial sector, also has an important edge with smart contracts in order to process and validate data of all kinds. The blockchain seems to offer a viable model for the verification of personal documents and other data in countries with fragile institutions and with high degrees of corruption and bureaucracy, in which any public document requires endless rubrics, seals and stamps to 'validate' its authenticity. In this sense, various initiatives have emerged from local and national governments, universities and other entities that seek to alleviate the bureaucratic burden with computer processes. But it is clear that the optimization of the institutions of the bourgeois state does not change its class character.

Based on Marxism-Leninism, it is clear that the building of a new society without exploitation or oppression and with full social justice will not be the work of an algorithm or a technological leap but the result of the organized struggle of the working class. The bourgeoisie, in order to save its class dictatorship, resorts to all possible means; it is capable of sacrificing its own institutions in order to maintain its status as a ruling class. In this sense, the phenomenon of crypto assets is an economic manifestation of the rise of populism, a bourgeois instrument to channel social discontent. Blockchain technology, with an optimization of its energy consumption at the service of the working classes has endless potential practical applications.

April 2022

Capitalism and War

The invasion of Ukraine by 100,000 Russian soldiers was immediately condemned by the International Conference of Marxist-Leninist Parties and Organizations (ICMLPO), which demanded an end to the aggression and respect for the sovereignty and self-determination of the Ukrainian people. But despite the appeals, the UN General Assembly resolutions and the thousands of demonstrations, the Russian bombings continue to kill civilians and destroy cities.

Known as a grain-exporting country with immense fertile land, Ukraine sees its population going hungry. Some four million people have fled the war, 10% of the population. Those who have remained in Ukraine, a total of 36 million, live without food, medicine or heat. Thousands of people have died and seven million have been left homeless because missiles and bombs have destroyed their homes. Mariupol, a city of 400,000 inhabitants and of great importance to the Ukrainian economy because of its port on the Sea of Azov connected to the Black Sea, has been almost completely destroyed and 180,000 people are besieged without food or water. A children's hospital and a theater in the city that housed civilians were hit by missiles, killing 300 people in a matter of seconds. Russia is repeating in Ukraine what the US and NATO did in Syria, Afghanistan, Iraq and Libya.

There have also been deaths on the Russian side. According to Ukraine, 7,000 Russian troops have been killed. Russia recognizes 1,500 soldiers killed and 4,000 wounded. The Russian people, despite the order to arrest those participating in the demonstrations, continue to hold hundreds of demonstrations against the war and for peace.

The heads of the capitalist governments, who used to smile at dinners on luxury yachts, now exchange accusations and threats. The pretexts of the imperialist countries to invade countries are varied, but the objectives are the same: to dominate the peoples, to seize the wealth of the invaded country and to enrich the world big bourgeoisie at the expense of the slaughter of human beings.

The representatives and leaders of the governments of the United States, Germany, Italy, the United Kingdom and France deliver incendiary speeches against Russia, they show their compassion for the victims of the war and say they are saddened by the pain of Ukrainians. However, they send mercenaries and weapons to Ukraine, increase their troops in Europe, move their warships and warplanes to the border of Russia, declare economic war and threaten to start World War III and swear that they want peace. Believe it or not.

Russia is as capitalist as the United States

To hide the fact that behind Putin's actions is the Russian bourgeoisie, that is, the capitalist class that has investments in the London and New York stock exchanges and owns billions in US and European Union debt securities, the political analysts of the big media propagate that "Russia is led by an autocrat and that Russian billionaires are not bourgeois, but oligarchs." They want to hide the relationship of capitalism to war and to the bourgeoisie with this barbarism.

They forget that since the triumph of the Russian Socialist Revolution of 1917, the world bourgeoisie has done everything possible to overthrow socialism and restore capitalism in that country, even invading it with 27 foreign armies. They were defeated by the Red Army, the same one that saved humanity from Nazi fascism. After a few decades, the bourgeoisie returned to power in Russia and re-

established private ownership of the means of production and the exploitation of man by man.

Now bourgeois analysts display a surprising amnesia and claim that "Russia is not entirely capitalist and the Russian ruling class is not a bourgeoisie." Lies don't travel far. Putin, like Macron, Biden and Scholz, is a bourgeois politician at the service of the Russian capitalist class, the class that exploits the Russian workers and owns industries, banks, gas and dominates all Russian parties except the revolutionary parties that are underground.

Whose weapons are killing the Ukrainian people?

This lie also crumbles when one asks who benefits from this war and who enriches themselves from another carnage in the world.

In fact, amid the bodies shattered by bombs, there is a small group of people who are increasing their fortunes: the owners of the war industries of the major capitalist countries. This group, also called the military-industrial complex, is the most powerful lobby in the U.S. Congress, in the Russian, German, and French parliaments, and also in China. The owners of the war industries own banks, investment funds, aircraft companies such as Boeing, automobile industries, pharmaceutical laboratories and even co-produce films to influence world public opinion to consider war inevitable.

One might think that the Russians are killing Ukrainians only with Russian weapons; after all Russia ranks 5th among the countries with the largest war industry. But that is not exactly the case. From 2015 to 2021, ten European countries sold the Russian government missiles, bombs, torpedoes, military ships and assault tanks. The total value of these sales to Putin earned the coffers of European private companies 346 million euros. France sold 44% of these weapons and Germany 35%. The rest was exported by Italy, Austria, Bulgaria, the Czech Republic, Croatia, Finland, Spain and Slovakia. Oh, didn't they know that Russia, which annexed Crimea in 2014, was going to invade Ukraine? They are hypocrites. Does any country buy bombs and missiles to put in the dining room or store in warehouses? Now they lament the deaths and destruction of Ukraine, which would be far fewer if these European capitalist vultures had not sold weapons to the Russian capitalist government.

In addition, since November 2021, Putin met with Germany, France and the United States and warned that Russia would not accept Ukraine's entry into NATO, since it was surrounded on all sides by the troops of the US-European military alliance.

In reality, the heads of government who today are showing an apparent horror at the war are the same ones who promoted similar barbarities in Afghanistan, Syria and Iraq and supported, on March 26, Saudi Arabia's bombing of Yemen, which killed dozens of people.

In addition, these heads of government in their secret meetings are celebrating the possibilities that the war is opening up for their new military orders. Then they justify the arms race with the famous phrase: "if you want peace, prepare for war."

There is more: the stocks of the arms industry have reached all-time highs even with the end of the war in Afghanistan; rising fuel prices will allow private oil companies to make greater profits and large raw material companies will benefit from rising food prices.

Indeed, the closer the world gets to a third world war, the more the production of bombs, missiles, visible and invisible military aircraft and the manufacture of nuclear weapons will increase, and an avalanche of dollars will go into the pockets of the billionaires who own shares in these companies. Of course, material and human resources will be ruined and the economic, social, political and health crisis will be profoundly aggravated. But capitalism has not developed to guarantee better living conditions for the peoples or to build a world of peace, but to oppress and exploit human beings.

As the report by the Stockholm International Peace Research Institute (SIPRI), published on December 6, shows, the total value of arms sales exceeded 3 trillion reais ($531 billion US) last year. The US, the country that most promotes wars and invasions in the world, is the largest arms seller, controlling 39% of the market, and owns the five largest arms companies in the world. China accounts for 13 percent of global arms exports, totaling $66.8 billion, and has five companies among the world's 100 largest. India and China are the two countries that buy the most weapons from Russian companies, which earned $15 billion and, as we have seen, France, Germany and Italy have sold arms to Russia. There is no homeland here, there are dollars and gold, and profits increase as wars grow.

Capitalism wants more war

Many people are asking when the war will end. But if it is true that Putin wants to take over Ukraine, it is also true that the United

States, inspired by Hitler, has never hidden its dream of dominating Russia. Let us also remember that the war against Syria is 11 years old and is not yet over, despite the fact that 500,000 people have died and 11.5 million Syrians are refugees, many of whom live in concentration camps and are prevented from entering Europe.

On the other hand, the capitalist powers are preparing for new wars and not for ending them. NATO, the military arm of the United States and the main European countries, with the entry of Poland, Slovakia, Romania, the Czech Republic, Estonia, Slovenia, Latvia and Lithuania, has greatly increased its firepower. Meanwhile, on February 4, China and Russia announced an "agreement without limits", that is, a military and economic agreement.

In addition, the United States increased the presence of its troops in Europe to a total of 100,000 troops at numerous military bases, armed even with nuclear missiles, and in January it sent two gigantic aircraft carriers to the South China Sea with the aim of "containing the influence of evil." The European Union has decided to rewrite its core document, called the EU's Strategic Compass for Security and Defence, adding that among the possible scenarios is a new world war.

The war budget of the U.S., pompously called the Defense Budget, approved by Congress, is $768 billion, plus $27.8 billion for the production of new nuclear weapons. Russia has an estimated military expenditure of $178 billion. Germany decided to triple its military budget by 2022, which was $59 billion and rose to $159 billion. On March 7, China increased its military budget by 7.1%, reaching a total of $229.47 billion, a third of what the United States will spend. The United Kingdom allocates $71.6 billion to defense.

This is true. In December, the UN announced that $6 billion would be enough to end hunger for 42 million people, the equivalent of 1% of the U.S. military budget planned for 2022. In February this year, the FAO, the Food and Agriculture Organization of the United Nations, estimated that 800 million people go hungry in the world.

Conclusion: if the capitalist governments did not allocate such large resources to the military-industrial complex, industry would not produce that many destructive bombs and missiles, and wars would not take place so often. But the bourgeois governments are at the service of the capitalist class, which is guided by profit and business; human beings are only a means for this minority of vampires to get rich.

How to achieve a world at peace?

To expect the rapacious imperialist powers to stop the arms race and the capitalists to renounce their gigantic war profits is a vain illusion. To believe that there will be no new world war because the world would be destroyed is to close one's eyes to the successive wars that have occurred and to history itself; see Hiroshima and Nagasaki.

The world capitalist class commits hundreds of atrocities every day against human beings and nature. The total number of refugees exceeds 300 million people; 2.2 billion live without access to water and 4.2 billion lack basic sanitation. Global warming causes disasters and tragedies everywhere and, according to the UN, one million plant and animal species are in danger of extinction.

So the destruction of humanity is already underway, and it is not by any meteorite. It is not a question of whether or not there will be a new world war, but what we must do to stop it.

The truth must be told. There is only one way to avoid destruction: workers all over the world must unite, strengthen the revolutionary parties in every country and join the fight against the rotten governments of the bourgeoisie, in order to destroy those responsible for wars and hunger and, once and for all, do away with the domination of this minority of billionaires over humanity.

In other words, it is necessary to replace the governments of the bourgeoisie with independent governments of the workers and peasants that will defend the interests of the vast majority of society and use the enormous and formidable resources that humanity possesses to end poverty and unemployment, protect nature, produce vaccines and end epidemics, to promote culture, harmony and peace among the peoples. Let us unite and fight for universal brotherhood, take the world from the hands of these hypocritical bourgeois exploiters.

Only in this way will World War III be avoided and lasting peace achieved.

In 1915, V.I. Lenin, the great leader of the October Revolution, stated with foresight: "Capitalism has become reactionary... mankind is faced with the alternative of adopting socialism or of experiencing years and even decades of armed struggle between the "Great" Powers for the artificial preservation of capitalism... and national oppression of every kind." ("The Principles of Socialism and the War of 1914-1915," Collected Works, Volume 21.)

March 30, 2022

The War in Ukraine: A War of Imperialist Aggression and Redivision of Territories for World Hegemony

The war triggered by Russia's massive military intervention in Ukraine is a manifestation of inter-imperialist rivalries in the context of the crisis of the international imperialist system. It is the result of the struggle for the redivision of territories in the Baltic and Eastern European region between Russia on the one hand and the US and its NATO allies in the European Union on the other.

Russia's imperialist war of aggression in Ukraine is the culmination of a process that began in 2014 with Russia's military occupation of Crimea under the pretext of defending the discriminated Russian-speaking population. Similar ambitions also exist in the Donbass. Russia is fighting over these territories and all of Ukraine with the United States and the NATO member countries, which since the implosion of the USSR and the independence of the Baltic countries of Eastern Europe have been expanding their political, economic and military influence for geostrategic interests. The tensions have not stopped rising between the rival imperialist powers with the massive presence of Russian military troops on the border of Ukraine since February and US imperialism has not stopped issuing warnings as if it wanted to invade this country to legitimize its rivalry with Russia and mobilize its European allies, members of NATO, behind it.

The current war is aggravating the inter-imperialist contradictions and providing the opportunity to the imperialist powers to strengthen the militarization of the societies, to considerably increase their arms budgets to the detriment of the social sectors (education, health) and public services as well as the weapons trade for the profit of the arms merchants, the military-industrial complex. The European imperialist powers are massing troops and armaments in the European countries bordering Ukraine; the US through NATO is strengthening its military presence in Poland and using that country as a rear base to exert its political and military influence in Ukraine.

The consequences of this reactionary war are dramatic first for the Ukrainian people and then for the peoples of the world.

This war is aggravating the deep crisis of the world imperialist system, which was just recovering from the Covid-19 pandemic which, in addition to the health crisis, plunged the economies of the developed capitalist countries and the dominated countries into a recession with the consequences of unemployment, high costs of living, impoverishment for the working class, peoples and youth. At the same time, the monopolies and financial oligarchies have become richer thanks to the measures taken by the bourgeoisies for their benefit in the context of the restrictions imposed on the peoples. "The fortune of the world's billionaires has increased more in the 19 months of the pandemic than in the last decade. Since the pandemic, the world counts a new billionaire every 26 hours, while 160 million people have fallen into poverty.... The top 5 fortunes in France have doubled their wealth since the beginning of the pandemic. They alone own as much as the poorest 40% of the population in France." (OXFAM 2021 Inequality Report: Key Figures)

This war, considered the most serious in Europe since the Second World War and that of the Balkans in the 1990s following the aerial bombardments and ground fighting, resulted in a heavy toll in human lives and material damage in a few weeks. It is the most serious humanitarian crisis in Europe with more than 3.7 million refugees fleeing to countries bordering Ukraine (Poland, Romania, Moldova) and the countries of the European Union. The UN estimates that there are 6.5 million internally displaced people in Ukraine.

The member countries of the European Union, in particular the imperialist powers (Germany, France, Italy) and the United Kingdom, are exploiting this dramatic refugee situation with demagogy in order to give themselves a humanitarian face and as defenders of the peace and sovereignty of Ukraine. This is while in recent years, the European Union, faced with the arrival of asylum seekers fleeing the wars in Syria, Afghanistan, Sudan, Ethiopia, etc., has taken repressive measures against these populations in distress. Migrants have been detained in centers with appalling prison conditions and deported after being refused refugee status. The issue of Ukrainian refugees is being used by these imperialist powers in the framework of rivalries with Russia. This does not hide the discrimination, the stigmatization of migrants, the rise of xenophobia and racism propagated by the extreme right-wing parties and even within the highest authorities of the bourgeois states, especially during the periods of electoral campaigns. The current campaign for the presidential elections in

France is a vivid illustration of this with the media platforms offered to the racist Eric Zemmour and to Marine Le Pen of the racist and fascist Rassemblement National (National Rally) party.

Economic and social consequences of the war in Ukraine.

The war in Ukraine has its consequences on the economic level where the Western imperialist powers (US and its European allies), in spite of their internal contradictions linked to specific interests, are waging economic war with Russia through economic sanctions.

The immediate consequences are the soaring prices of foodstuffs (wheat, corn) and agricultural inputs (potash, nitrogen fertilizers), of which Russia and Ukraine are the main exporters at the world level. The same is true for fossil fuels (oil, gas and coal), of which Russia is a major exporter, especially to Europe.

Food insecurity, which has been growing in recent years and was heightened during the Covid-19 health crisis, will deepen with the risk of large-scale famine in many countries, especially in Africa.

The context of the war will dry up the sources of supply represented by Russia and Ukraine, which together account for 1/3 of the world wheat trade. Many African countries, including Burkina Faso, Egypt, Morocco, Algeria, Tunisia, the Democratic Republic of Congo, Somalia, Sudan, etc. depend on these countries for 50% of their wheat imports. On March 7, the price of a ton of wheat rose to 400 euros, while its usual value is between 180 and 230 euros per ton. The price of daily bread for the masses of people is in danger of becoming unaffordable.

In addition to food, the prices of transportation, fuel and all the basic necessities of life will rise and make life ever more expensive for the popular masses in urban and rural areas.

The imperialist powers, despite the soothing speeches and endless diplomatic ballets for peace, are war-mongers who do not care about the dramatic consequences for the peoples. For the profits of the arms monopolies, they provoke conflicts in order to conquer territories.

Geostrategic implications of the war in Ukraine

Russia's war of imperialist aggression in Ukraine amply confirms its dimension as a war of redivision of territories between imperialist powers. It is deepening the inter-imperialist rivalries that use war as a means of controlling strategic territories and plundering mineral and agricultural resources. As Lenin clearly stated: "Imperialism is the source of war". We can see this today in Syria, in Yemen, in the Sahel in West Africa, which has been transformed into a powder keg where French imperialism, in difficulty, maintains a massive military presence in the face of its US, Russian, Turkish, Indian and Brazilian rivals. Armed terrorist groups are used to legitimize military interventions while also playing their own game through drug, commodity and human trafficking.

What is happening before our eyes in Ukraine: Russia, faced with difficulties due to Ukrainian resistance and the rejection of this reactionary war by the Russian people, and its international isolation, is going to cling to the territories it already controls militarily: Crimea and the Donbass.

This is a compromise that its rivals can temporarily tolerate, because they do not lose out.

Indeed, the United States and its European allies in NATO are strengthening their military and economic presence in the countries bordering Ukraine and will exert significant influence in this area of major strategic importance.

China is trying to take advantage of the fierce struggle between these two coalitions, without ignoring the rivalries between China and the US superpower.

The working class and the peoples of Europe and the world will pay a heavy price for the disastrous economic and social consequences.

The peoples of Africa should be convinced more than ever of the imperialist nature of Russia, which like other imperialist powers engages in military interventions against the national sovereignty and territorial integrity of another country. Currently in some African countries, neo-colonies of French imperialism, mainly the working class, the people and the youth are demonstrating massively in the streets to demand the departure of French troops and military bases. Some fringes of the radical reformist petty bourgeoisie have illusions about Russia, which is wrongly considered a potential ally in the fight against terrorism and for the national and social liberation of the African peoples.

More than ever, the democratic and revolutionary movements with the enlightenment of the Marxist-Leninist parties must base their actions on the fundamental principles of the anti-imperialist struggle. Namely: we cannot rely on one superpower to fight the other. One cannot rely on one superpower or imperialist power to fight the dominant imperialism in one's country. One cannot rely on the dominant imperialism in one's country to fight a superpower or an imperialist power.

Faced with the war of aggression of Russia in Ukraine, the position of principle is to:

denounce this reactionary war which is basically a war of redivision of territories between imperialist powers.

support the resistance of the people in Ukraine for the defense of national sovereignty.

denounce the maneuvers of the Western imperialist powers (the United States and its European allies in NATO)

support the struggles of the proletariat and peoples against militarization and war budgets and for their democratic and social rights.

Central Committee of the Revolutionary Communist Party of Volta

October 2021

Lessons of an Ongoing Electoral Process

Introduction

Having examined the latest national events, it should be noted that the Colombian political scene has become increasingly dynamic and complex since the end of the elections of March 13. In those elections, Colombians had the opportunity to choose, on the one hand, the members of the Congress of the Republic, both its House of Representatives and its Senate, and on the other, the presidential candidates of those coalitions and parties that decided to choose their candidates through an interparty consultation.

Although the results of the elections held this March 13 are still partial (according to official data it is necessary to scrutinize 1% of the tables and rule on the dozens of lawsuits filed with the Electoral Organization on the partial results so far made public) the controversy over these elections and the political significance of their results are growing at the national and international level. The following lines include the main assessments of this election made by our party, of which we inform you today, with the firm conviction that your contributions, ideas and comments will enrich the perspective of change that the revolutionaries of Colombia and the world are committed to.

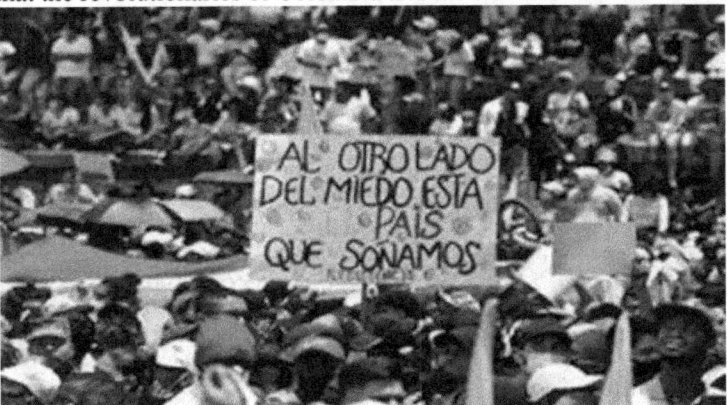

In the various demonstrations the rejection of the assassins of social leaders, of the massacres and disappearances, as well as all forms of criminalization of social protest was widespread.

Legislative elections

To begin with, we consider it pertinent to point out that **the headache of the Colombian oligarchy,** which for decades has governed this country, has become intense, permanent and so acute that some of its sectors are beginning to suffer from insomnia and despair. The weak results obtained by the different political factions that represent the Colombian oligarchy (recognized because they are parties that currently participate in the government coalition) show a marked loss of their representation in Congress, which detracts from their strength, legitimacy, the power to convene people and maneuverability.

Looking at the results in the Senate, of the 108 senators that make up the current senate of the republic, 83 seats belong to the traditional parties of the government coalition; with the electoral results of this March 13, the representation of these parties in the upper house was reduced to 52 senators.

In the House of Representatives the situation is not different; of the 172 representatives that make up this legislative body, the oligarchic parties of the government coalition currently have 146 representatives. Now, if we take into account that for this new Congress of 2022-2026 the number of seats in the House of Representatives will increase to 188 given the creation of the Special Peace Constituency that will add 16 new seats to this House, it must be pointed out that with the results made public so far the oligarchic parties will also lose representation. The results show that the representation of the oligarchic factions (adding all the territorial, international, indigenous, Afro and special peace constituencies) is reduced to 110 representatives.

In short, of the 296 Congress members elected, 162 (55%) belong to the oligarchic parties of the current government coalition , the rest, that is, 134 (45%) belong to organizations of the popular and democratic camp. As can be seen , **the representation achieved by the oligarchic factions in the new Congress, which will take office on August 7, is a Pyrrhic majority, which will make it quite difficult to approve and legitimize the policies of those who defend the current establishment.**

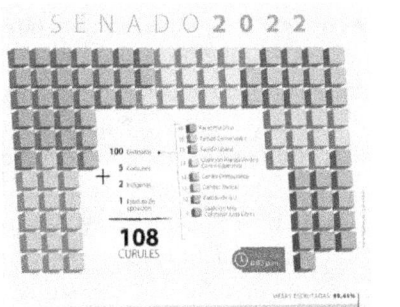

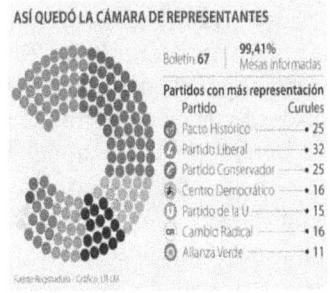

Official results published by the National Registry

In the same vein, we consider it important to emphasize a notorious fact of this electoral process, rarely seen in Colombian politics: the sinking of the ruling party. The Democratic Center, the party that was the winner in the last elections and which leads the current government coalition, clearly reduced its representation in Congress, from 51 members (19 senators and 32 representatives) in 2018 to 28 (13 senators and 15 representatives) in 2022. There is no doubt that these results clearly show the resounding defeat of former President Álvaro Uribe Vélez, President Iván Duque and all the machinery of corruption put in place for these elections. In the same way, the decline of a political force like that of Uribismo, which despite having enjoyed the power of the State and the government in Colombia for two decades, has still not found a way to save it from discredit and the growing popular rejection from which this organization, its spokespersons and leaders suffer. However, the treacherous and violent campaign carried out by all the Uribistas against the victorious forces in these elections are a warning that this fascist force will hardly being among the losers.

As for the results obtained by the democratic, progressive and left-wing forces, they all unequivocally point to the progress achieved and the possibility of victory that currently aids their forces, leaders and representatives. Indeed, we are facing a historic fact never seen in the political life of the country, since it is the first time in a legislative election that the forces of the popular and democratic camp have achieved a representation of 45% of Congress. Certainly, the effects are multiple and they are already beginning to be felt across all aspects of national political life. We are sure that this potential undoubtedly will play a very important role in the presidential campaign and winning of a democratic government.

In this framework of ideas, it is important to emphasize the progress achieved, **as one more result of the mobilization and struggle waged by the Colombian people in recent years.** This has not only served to unmask and reverse several of the reforms and policies of the current government, but also to open the road and point out the need for a radical and profound change in the economic, social and political life of the nation. Peace, bread, work, health and a democratic government committed to well-being, social justice, rights and freedoms include the banners of greater agitation in the strikes, marches and mobilizations that have been spreading throughout the national territory. The strike of November 21, 2019, the social outbreak that began on April 28, 2021, and all the days of struggle carried out in this period, have done nothing but fortify the forces against this government, which persists in repressing with blood and fire the dissatisfied population, showing the war-like treatment of the people by the State in our country.

The national strike of April 28 showed the social unrest, dissatisfaction and rejection of the government of Iván Duque

In fact, what was seen in the elections of March 13 expresses, on the one hand, the discontent, dissatisfaction and social rejection that today is manifested in the different regions of the country against the government of Iván Duque. He is the supporter like no other of corruption, the increase in the power of the mafias, the criminalization of protest, the curtailment of freedoms and rights, inequality, hunger and poverty of the majority of the population. On the other hand, this emphasizes the quantitative and qualitative advances of the popular struggle in Colombia, since it not only shows a growth of discontent and mass actions. We also find a greater participation of young people and women, as well as a better understanding of the need to go beyond the winning of a government that takes up as a challenge the materialization of the democratic reforms that the Colombian people are most demanding.

As part of this general effort of the forces and organizations of the popular camp, **we emphasize as exemplary the role that the forces of opposition to the government of Iván Duque have been playing and that have earned them widespread recognition and popular support.** The denunciations of the corruption prevailing in this government; the neglect suffered by the population during the pandemic; the assassinations, massacres, disappearances and other violations of human rights; the rejection of the government's warlike policy, the blatant repression and violation of the peace agreements; the disastrous economic and social policy applied by this government, the tax increases, servility and government protection of the monopolies, especially finance capital; the increasing inequality, hunger and poverty; the rejection of this behavior of the government in increasingly kneeling to US imperialism; are, among others, issues that in the particular case of the opposition to the government caucus in Congress has permanently addressed demands, solutions and fair measures, in accordance with the urgency and gravity of the national problems.

Gustavo Petro in Pereira-Risaralda

In obtaining the results, **we also emphasize the skills of the forces that make up the Historic Pact and the indisputable leadership of the current presidential candidate Gustavo Petro.** All the forces of the Historic Pact committed their financing, guarantees, campaign infrastructure and activities. These were mainly reflected in and contributed to the events that took place in the different regions of the country. Even the national and international press emphasized the massive participation, the solidity of the proposals presented and the countless cultural activities that accompanied these events. We interpret as a correct approach to challenge the D'Hondt method [of proportional representation] and the electoral legislation, which is decided regarding the closed list [in which the party has chosen its list of candidates, and the voter can only choose the party and not a specific candidate], the *jurles* [poll workers who check the voter's identity and count the votes] and electoral witnesses [of the political parties who observe the election – *all translator's notes*], the watching and counting of the votes. One area where we obviously need to improve is the choice of candidates at both the regional and national level.

What about fraud?

As for the allegations of fraud that have been made throughout the pre-counting and counting of the votes so far, we cannot overlook the fact that **these elections have been marked by uncertainty and the vehement intention of the government to twist the electoral results in its favor.** Uncertainty, since the rules of the game for these elections were substantially modified by the government of Iván Duque. They used every trick were not enough to choose the National Registrar of their taste and preference; with the support of the government's parliamentary caucus it also modified the law of guarantees by suspending the prohibition of public procurement at election time. It changed the Electoral Code (fortunately it was not applied due to the delay of the Constitutional Court in deciding on the constitutionality of this new law); the purchase of the new software for the counting of the votes by the National Registry did not lack its scathing preference either.

Once the elections were held, irregularities came to light showing that it was not a transparent process. It was proven that the largest omission in the counting of the votes was due to the rigged design of the E-14 forms; for the specific case of the Historic Pact this form did not have a normal sheet to write the votes by the jurors, as the other parties did; its location in the form was at the end of one of the sheets and before the logo of one of the traditional parties. That design led to an error, because when scanning the form, the votes in favor of the Historic Pact did not appear and therefore in more than 29,000 tables the votes did not appear. If these omissions had been exposed in a timely manner, the Historic Pact would have received 500,000 more votes that would have allowed it to increase its representation to 20 senators and 30 representatives.

Another denunciation that has been made has to do with the double counting of votes at about 23,000 tables. Many bad-faith jurors, in conducting the count, counted the vote for a candidate from an open list, as one vote for the candidate and one vote for the party. It was possible to prove that this double counting of the votes favored the traditional parties that had an open list and not the Historic Pact that participated with closed lists.

It was also proven that the votes for the consultation of the Historic Pact, the senate and the house do not agree; while for the consultation 5,818,735 votes were obtained, the Senate obtained 2,669,299 votes and the house obtained only 2,549,276 votes. On a qualitative examination, it is true that these votes were different, it is also true that the differences between them were abysmal. It was proven that many of the votes for the Historic Pact were not even counted.

Among the irregularities there were also spaces in the forms, numbers superimposed on the originals and other modifications, which in the specific case of Uribismo, were used to say that these are not valid results and therefore the votes must be recounted, which is not contemplated in Colombian electoral law.

As events evolve, votes for the Historic Pact continue to appear, both in the consultation to choose the presidential candidate, where Petro's votes continue to increase, and for the Senate and the House of Representatives, with the consequent effect that the number of seats for the Historic Pact will increase as does the anger, the lies and all the hindrance of the government, the Democratic Center and the forces related to the status quo seeking to ignore, with legalisms, demands and even claiming the existence of fraud in favor of the Historic Pact, the results and the victory of the popular forces.

In this context it is quite striking and paradoxical that the fraud outlined by the government and the irregularities denounced in the contest, the democratic forces have to go out to protect the votes, defend the elections, their results, because **the birds are shooting at the shotguns** [that is, the roles are reversed – *translator's note*].

Cross-party consultations

At the same time as the legislative elections were being held, the consultations of the parties that decided to choose their presidential candidate through this mechanism were also taking place. The parties of the Colombian right formed their coalition called "Equipo por Colombia" ("Team for Colombia") and chose the former mayor of Medellín Federico Gutiérrez as their candidate. The coalition "Centro Esperanza" ("Center of Hope"), in essence of a petty bourgeois type, chose the former governor of Antioquia Sergio Fajardo. The Historic Pact, a coalition formed by the Colombian democratic, progressive and left-wing forces. chose as their presidential candidate the former mayor of Bogotá and current senator Dr. Gustavo Petro.

As a living expression of the popular upsurge, the growth and advance of the forces that promote democratic change in Colombia, the consultation with the most votes was the Coalition of the Historic Pact. **Its result was historic; the 5,818,375 votes obtained in this consultation, plus the results obtained in the legislative elections,**

place the Historic Pact as the leading political force in the country.

Coalición Pacto Histórico:

Total votación: 5 818 375
Votos no marcados: 122 479
Votos nulos: 111 138

As to the vote for the right, the numbers show its retreat; in the primaries held in 2018 this same force achieved 5,960,612 votes; its winning candidate, Iván Duque, achieved 4,038,101 votes on that occasion. In the primaries held on March 13, this same coalition, strengthened with the participation of other right-wing forces, obtained 4,145,691 votes. The chosen candidate Federico Gutiérrez, supported by all the government machinery, got 2,161,686 votes. **Given the situation, the result is still catastrophic for the right-wing forces of the government**; its defeat is undeniable, neither its tricks, nor its buying of votes, nor the electoral machinery, in short, all the mechanisms so far used has not helped Uribismo or the government to maintain and ensure a victory.

Total votación: 4 145 691
Votos no marcados: 76 737
Votos nulos: 79 312

There was another force did not obtain the expected results, in our opinion due to the weakness of its proposals, its flirtation with the government, as well as its indecisiveness both in the rejection of neoliberal policies and in the defense of democratic reforms. In addition, the lack of unity of these forces is evident, with the aggravating factor that, in many parts of the country, these are forces inclined to Uribismo and compromised by serious problems of corruption. In the case of candidate Fajardo, there were strong accusations of the irregular management in the Public Companies of Medellín (EPM) and the building of the Hidroituango dam.

The results obtained by the "Centro Esperanza" coalition were 2,287,603 votes and its winning candidate Sergio Fajardo obtained only 723,475 votes. Actually, the leaders and forces that make up this coalition will have to make great efforts in order to put forward a strong name and candidate for the next presidential election.

Coalición Centro Esperanza:

Total votación: 2 287 603
Votos no marcados: 62 978
Votos nulos: 65 160

Sergio Fajardo	Juan Manuel Galán	Carlos Amaya	Alejandro Gaviria	Jorge Enrique Robledo
ASI	NUEVO LIBERALISMO	SOMOS VERDE	COLOMBIA tiene futuro	DIGNIDAD
723.475	487.019	451.223	336.504	161.244

With all the forces thrown into the ring in a contest for the presidency of the republic, the official candidates are: Gustavo Petro, for the "Historic Pact"; Federico Gutiérrez, for the "Team for Colombia" coalition; Sergio Fajardo, for the "Centro Esperanza" team; Ingrid Betancourt, for the "Green Oxygen" party; Rodolfo Hernández, for the "League of Anti-Corruption Members of the Government"; Enrique Gómez, for the "National Salvation" party; Luis Pérez, for the "Colombia piensa en grande" ("Columbia thinks big") movement, and John Milton Rodríguez, of the "Colombia Justa-Libres". ("Colombia Just and Free") Movement.

Understanding that there is much to discuss on this issue, we think it is pertinent to bear in mind the following elements of importance:

• In a context of the worsening of the economic, social and political crisis in the country, the forces of the establishment are continuing their retreat and their behavior as forces opposed to change and social progress. In order to overcome this and remain in the government, the continuity of fascistization, neoliberalism and dependence **would deepen the Colombian crisis and conflict.**

- To defeat the rising popular forces today there would also be a push for changes in obtaining and redistributing wealth, as well as in the rate of profit and its distribution. This would raise the level of exploitation of the broad popular masses. **The imposition of a de facto policy in Colombia, as has happened in many other countries, will mean that the rich get richer and the poor get poorer.**

- The growth and development of the popular forces obviously forsees an important change in the balance of forces that favors the popular camp and its project. **The achievement of a democratic government in the Colombian context would strengthen the forces of change by expanding the possibilities of moving towards a democratic opening** that would expand the freedoms, rights and well-being of the population.

- As the force that represents change in Colombia, the Historic Pact is assisted by the great challenge of moving towards the creation of **a broad political and mass front**, which would act as a pole of attraction, promote the broadest popular participation and enable the achievement of a democratic government.

- **The teachings of the past remain valid.** Unity as a force and premise for change; the purposeful spirit, tactical astuteness and flexibility in order to advance; no sectarianism, no mistakes of opportunism, will continue to be values and lessons to emphasize at a time when the possibilities of becoming the government are expanding.

- **In a transformative perspective the democratic struggle constitutes for the proletariat and its party a valuable exercise** that must be strengthened and made the most of in order to accumulate and strengthen forces, that is, to grow, organize the masses, renew and develop the cadres, with a perspective that assures and broadens confidence in the socialist ideology and future.

Central Executive Committee
Communist Party of Colombia Marxist-Leninist

Bogotá, March 30, 2022

Denmark	Dorte Grenaa Workers' Communist Party, APK

Healthcare Professionals –
A Global Commodity

The pandemic has revealed to such an extent, that the capitalist system cannot ensure the health of the people and the working class, but that health under capitalism is a commodity that is bought and sold and a goal for profit.

In many countries, healthcare workers have been on strike, carried out actions and protested against the increasingly high-pressure conditions around working hours, working conditions, wages, cuts in staff and equipment – both in the private and public health services. In Denmark there was a national strike of the nurses last year, 2021. First, there was a legal strike organized by the trade union leadership in connection with collective labour – bargaining – that ended with the Social Democratic government intervening in favour of the state as employer and subsequently there were several so-called illegal strikes and stoppages in rotation from hospital to hospital around the country, organized by the health workers themselves.

For many years, the state and government have cut budgets and staff, privatized, denied women – who make up the majority – equal pay, and worsened working conditions to the point where a great many leave the health occupations and fewer new ones are trained and educated.

It is not only in Denmark that there is a catastrophic shortage of employees and professionally competent staff in the public healthcare, education, and social sectors. It is the same situation in the rest of Europe – on other continents, indeed on a global scale.

Market conditions mean that both private companies in the health industry and the public health sector, which are now running on market principles, are doing everything possible to keep their costs as low as possible. Keep wages down, push efficiency and lower quality, fewer employees for more tasks and whatever else can lower the cost of labour.

One of the solutions for the richer imperialist countries is to import cheaper labour from poorer countries, either as a permanent solution or to cover temporary fluctuations in how large the state wants the number of health professionals to be.

More recruitment of cheaper foreign health workers as a labour force is one of the focal points of Danish government policy.

From a capitalist and employer point of view, it is pure logic. Health workers have become a global commodity that can be bought cheaper in poorer countries. It is pure capitalist win-win: the salary level can be kept low, and at the same time money can be made from a situation with shortage of staff. Capitalist exploitation of labour is increasing, and imperialist exploitation of the depended countries is increasing by making them pay for the education of health workers prior to migration.

The global imperialist health industry has put trade with health workers into system. Large international recruitment companies have been established for health professionals – doctors, nurses, caregivers, midwives. These companies ensure that all the stages of this trade in health workers' labour, imports and exports, agreements and contracts with the States concerned are concluded. So just as rich countries like Denmark trade in poor Filipino women who, under the guise of au-pair girls, are underpaid domestic workers and nannies for the wealthy or work as underpaid maids in hotels, so are health professionals traded.

Since the 1990s, private capitalists have been able to suck a huge amount of capital and profit out of privatisation and the dismantling of public health and welfare systems. Not least in Eastern Europe and the Nordic countries, where these were quite developed, with major

consequences for the working class and the people. This has created the conditions of a global healthcare industry under market conditions. In Europe, the construction and expansion of the European Union of the big monopolies, EU, has been boosted by the establishment of "the free movement of labour" throughout the EU's internal market. In Capitalist economics the money flows into the sectors where profits are highest and not where it is most needed in society, or what would benefit public health or create long-term social solutions, which would be the case in a socialist society.

Transnational recruitment companies

There are several multinational care chains, hospital, and other health chains, which also operate in Denmark as an obvious health industry worldwide. There are groups such as Aetna International, which offers governments help in the health service to achieve their financial goals, get more for health dollars, increase operational efficiency, and increase employee efficiency. This specific company, as an example, is operating in Europe, Asia Pacific (Singapore, Hongkong, China, Thailand, Indonesia, Vietnam, and the Philippines), Qatar and Dubai in the Middle East and in the United States.

And then there are the recruitment companies – the link between migrant health workers in their home country and the employers in the country that imports them.

Health professionals must be skilled and licensed, which is why their recruitment is more complex and systematised than in the case of unskilled labour. Recruiters function as initial clearing houses for hospitals by verifying that candidates meet the minimum employment requirements. Each hospital system has specific recruitment procedures that recruitment companies know how to navigate. They also negotiate placement fees and supplement their income by selling other services that can make the trade more flexible. The companies often cooperate with state and public authorities, and in countries such as the Nordic ones with the nurses' trade unions.

Under imperialism, the migration patterns of a global labour force are not only spontaneous networks of global labour cycles, but also negotiated chains of transnational labour.

From Eastern to Western Europe and on to the Middle East

Nurses are one of the largest groups of trained, educated migrant workers worldwide.

When the revisionist regimes in Eastern Europe collapsed in the late 1980s, one of the consequences was that the former public systems such as the health system were privatized on a wide scale and bought up by Western companies that just withdrew the money from the country. Another consequence was mass unemployment and falling living conditions, despite all the lies and promises of capitalism. This made a chain of cheaper nurses from the former East Germany into the West German hospitals and yet another chain of West German nurses into Denmark in the 1990s. At the same time, the was a large flow of Swedish nurses to Denmark, due to a massive neoliberal privatisation and reorganisation of the Swedish public health system at that time, which caused high unemployment and deteriorating conditions among Swedish nurses.

As most Eastern European countries joined the EU, imports of health workers into western EU countries were made significantly easier. However, they were still discriminated against in relation to full pay and fixed contracts under the guise of lack of competences, trial periods, training, etc.

Although Romania is one of the five countries from which Denmark imports the most health workers today, the flow from eastern countries is now going less into Western Europe and instead into the Middle East, especially into Saudi Arabia, which is one of the world's largest importers of health workers. This has led to a shift in the "value of many Eastern European nurses on the market". Whereas before in Europe they were marketed as the bottom of the chain, as only hardworking and docile, the Czech nurses for example are now being sold as competent, flexible, and adaptable labour to the Middle East.

Danish neo-liberal and Social Democrat politicians are also trying, through new technology, to replace health professionals. Not just with technical equipment but digitization to a point which they call "virtual hospital and treatment courses" where you are treated in your own home via computer.

Denmark – part of the global import chain

The number of applications for authorisation from nurses trained abroad has increased significantly in recent years in Denmark but has been going on since the mid-1990s. Today, these are mainly nurses with training and education from outside the EU/EEA – especially from the Philippines and Iran.

In the 2000s, under the neo-liberal Fogh government, the policy was that Denmark should exploit the "surplus" of nursing workers in the Baltic states. The government's plan was for the foreign nurses to initially work as social and health assistants, while improving their professional level and learning Danish. Thus a great many nurses from non-EU countries end up doing this both in Denmark and the rest of the EU for years. In addition, the Danish state with usual capitalist logic closed the qualification education in Danish language and hospital and work culture that Copenhagen University College's Nursing School and the Ministry of Integration previously stood for.

In the 2010s, the Social Democrats pursued the same policy. The Chair of the Danish Regions Health Committee, Ulla Asthman stated at that time: *"It is quite deliberate and simply necessary for us to bring the foreign nurses in here in order for us to cope with the recruitment problems of the future."*

The Danish regions and hospitals spend many millions of kroner each year paying global recruitment agencies to import cheaper labour. And so, they spend tax money destined for the Public Health sector and educational sector on the parasitic private intermediaries that the global recruitment and "care and health business chains" have developed into. It was not without reason that Karl Marx called capitalism a rotten and parasitic system that constantly expands with expensive intermediaries.

The consequences of imperialism

The consequences of privatization, marketisation and migrant chains are extensive, not least in the poorest and dependent countries in the world, where the catastrophic shortage of health workers is increasing. Migrant flows as a business are particularly critical in the field of health, not least for those countries that are losing their resources, but also for the people of the countries that receive them. In contrast to be unskilled worker on a construction site or in other so-called service industries, the work culture, the communication in the work of the health sector is of direct importance to the patient and colleagues, whether skilled or unskilled.

The rich imperialist countries are not only draining the dependent countries of health workers, but they are also making poorer countries pay for their education. The fact that the majority of migrant health workers are women also raises the issue that they can no longer take responsibility for caring for children, the elderly and the sick in the family they left behind in their home country, for which they were previously responsible. And all the unpaid women's work they previously did is not replaced by expanded public welfare and care systems, which has both huge human and social consequences for the people and for society.

At the same time, public care systems in the Nordic countries, with the privatization of neoliberalism, are so eroded that an increasingly number of female labourers are being imported from the poorest countries to fill in the worst gaps for the middle and upper classes. This in turn deepens the social problems of poorer countries. The fact that it is the poorest and the working class who are most affected by deteriorating social and health conditions in both dependent and imperialist countries is clear.

While rich imperialist countries steal and exploit the human and economic resources of the poor and dependent countries for their own benefit, they are competing among themselves for the cheapest, most flexible, and hardest-working labour. This is rotten from start to finish.

When it comes to the health professionals and workers themselves, both migrant workers and the employees of the recipient country are squeezed into a downward spiral, where they are set up to compete against each other over lower wages and worse working conditions.

From the migrant countries, several health worker trade unions have tried to call out the recipient countries about the consequences of this development and called on the trade unions, such as the Danish Nursing Council, DSR, for help to stop the export-import model. However, until now they have had no luck. The policy of the leadership of the DSR is that recruiting foreign nurses is a positive step to address the shortage of nurses; they advocate a "diverse" health service and are working closely with the state and employers on this line.

This calls for and demonstrates to such an extent the need for international solidarity between health workers, in the individual workplace, between national health professionals and professional organizations and trade unions across national borders. This is a common cross-trade struggle in the national health system, but also a common international fight across borders among the workers and employees.

Everywhere, this development demonstrates the need to develop the struggle of public servants and the working class for higher wages and better working conditions into a political struggle directly against those responsible and their neoliberal privatisation policies. And into a struggle for a revolutionary overthrow of the capitalist social system, which produces the deteriorating living conditions of the working class and the people.

Common struggle

For the Communist Party of Labour, APK, it is an important issue both nationally and internationally. The policy of migrant health-worker recruitment as a solution must be rejected and met with demands to ensure higher and equal pay, work, and employment conditions. The consequences of the current policy must specifically be raised in the current discussion on the future and reforms of the Danish public health and care system, which is very much about combating privatization and demanding a strong public health care sector not operating on marked terms.

However, for many health professionals and employees who do not directly belong to the working class or do not see themselves as part of it, there is little doubt that their working conditions, with the marketisation of the public sector, are increasingly similar to those of the working class. The efforts and work to build a common united class struggle and movement with the rest of the working class must be strengthened.

In our platform for "The work and tasks of the Party in the workplaces and in trade unions", APK states, among other things, that: *"The solidarity of the working class must always be specifically involved, developed, and strengthened in order to use the common strength of the class. By extending the economic struggle to a political struggle with common demands on those responsible, unity and solidarity can be developed and unfolded. Local and individual negotiations and 'free-choice' arrangements make the worker feel alone and isolated, whereas the collective strength of the working class and public servants is the way forward ...*

"The international solidarity of the working class will always be at the heart of the struggle of the working class and the work of its Communist Party. Specifically among the growing number of employees who, though scattered in many countries, work in the same multinational company. And as concrete and active solidarity with the workers' struggles and the many battles that workers all over the world are facing against the consequences of neoliberal reforms,

against capitalist and imperialist exploitation and oppression, wars and the destruction of resources and survival opportunities, and for a socialist future."

November 20, 2021

Dominican Republic	Communist Party of Labor (PCT)

On the Question of Democracy in the Dominican Republic

Some proposals for reforms to the State put forward by the government have generated a national debate on the question of democracy, which appears unclear, without a class perspective, and without the context of the relation of political and social forces that is necessary to deal with it properly.
The Communist Party of Labor (PCT) is taking part in this debate

I. Introduction

Democracy is a question referring to the State, to power, which is central to any political party or movement. Therefore, it will always be important to deal with it in the political debate and struggle, because it is about the concrete political struggle, in the concrete situation.

In our country a debate is being raised about some proposals for political reforms made by the government; and we communists and revolutionaries must take part in it.

For this it is important to have a clear theory and a historical and political context on the question of the State and democracy, to be concrete in our proposals and demands, without losing the strategic perspective.

Some Dominican revolutionaries claim they fight for democracy in general. Often in their speeches they confuse demands that are nothing more than reforms of the moment within the framework of the relation of political forces with others of a strategic nature, which can only be achieved when the popular revolution has triumphed and uses its strength to create a new political and legal system.

They do not distinguish between a period of accumulation of revolutionary forces, setting specific demands and tasks, and a period in which the question of a rupture, or the revolutionary leap towards the seizure of power, is raised.

In our country are we in a period of a revolutionary rupture with the established order; or is this a period of accumulation of forces to lead to a rupture? This is a relevant question that must be answered when we address the issue of the struggle for democracy in the particular political situation.

II. Marxism-Leninism and democracy

From a general theoretical and historical point of view, for Marxism-Leninism, democracy means socialism, since it means the control of society by the majority, by the working class over the bourgeoisie. It is a situation in the class struggle in which the formerly oppressed class has seized political power by overthrowing the former oppressor class and has established its political regime, of democracy for the majority and dictatorship for the minority. The political and social system of the working class in power would be absolutely opposite to that of the bourgeois.

It is difficult to find in the classics of Marxism-Leninism a specific theme that addresses the issue of democracy in particular. This ideal of the democratic regime, it is worth repeating, under socialism is found in fragments, among other works such as The Communist Manifesto, The German Ideology, Critique of the Gotha Program, all by Karl Marx and Frederick Engels; The Civil War in France, The 18th Brumaire of Luis Bonaparte, both by Karl Marx; The Origin of the Family, Private Property and the State, by Fredrich Engels; The State and the Revolution, April Thesis and Report on Bourgeois Democracy and the Dictatorship of the Proletariat and About the State, by V.I. Lenin. There are others, also by other authors, such as Joseph Stalin and Antonio Gramsci.

The general, theoretical approach of the Marxist-Leninists is that, contrary to the ideas of the predominance of the free market, of bourgeois liberal democracy; socialist democracy proposes central planning of the main areas of the economy. To the separation of the three branches of the State and the situation in which representatives of the people are elected every four years under representative democracy; socialist democracy places the unity of government and legislation in one single body, formed by leaders selected directly by the people, recallable at any time. The Paris Commune (1871) was an embryonic model of this power.

For Marxism-Leninism, the theoretical starting point for approaching the question of democracy links the material conditions of society to the legal-political institutions that correspond to these conditions. It is the relationship between the infrastructure and superstructure that has been popularized in manuals and texts for educational purposes.

Dealing with this relationship, in the course of history that led to the establishment of capitalist relations of production, and its consequent expression in political power, in the Communist Manifesto, Karl Marx and Friedrich Engels pointed out: "Each step in the development of the bourgeoisie was accompanied by a corresponding political advance of that class."

It takes possession of total power, it establishes its State, and consequently its democracy, when large-scale industry and the market become universal; that is, when capitalist relations of production are imposed in a dominant way. The bourgeoisie defeats the other classes, subordinates them on the economic and political plane, and then establishes the capitalist state. Marx and Engels refer to this in the Communist Manifesto by saying: "The executive of the modern State is but a committee for managing the common affairs of the whole bourgeoisie."

It also tore down the previously dominant values. To establish its full role, the bourgeoisie also had to establish its own values. Even personal dignity, say Marx and Engels, had to be subjected to a single value, that of exchange value, of commodities. All the previously known freedoms were subjected to a single freedom, that of trade. Everything was subjected to their interests.

Lenin confirmed these general ideas about the class character of democracy in his thesis and report presented in 1919 to the first congress of the Third International. This was when the revolution of

October 1917 had already triumphed, and in many countries a revolutionary movement was developing with the prospect of winning power. The Bolsheviks proposed to establish the power of the working class; while the opportunist groups that distanced themselves from revolutionary socialism took up reformism as a strategy, and questioned the ideas and efforts of the victorious communists to impose a proletarian system, with democracy for the working class and its allies, and coercion for the overthrown bourgeoisie and its allies.

These opportunists demanded a "pure democracy," "democracy in general," outside of the class struggle. Their approaches did not ask the questions: Which democracy? Democracy for whom?

The one of the bourgeoisie is an economic, political, and ideological power. It is the one of the ruling class because it dominates these three dimensions. Its bourgeois state is a broad network of political institutions (executive power, national congress, city councils, parties, central board of elections, and electoral courts); legal institutions (high courts, tribunals, prisons); military institutions (bodies of the armed forces and the national police) and ideological institutions (churches, universities, schools, press, television, radio) whose purpose is to guarantee the stability and development of the interests of the bourgeoisie.

In general Marxist theory, there is no place for the liberal postulate according to which the State represents the total community and is an expression of the public, of the general interest.

So we must be clear that when we communists and revolutionaries defend what is public: spaces, schools, universities, and public hospitals, we are demanding concessions from the bourgeoisie; we are moving in the sphere of reforms. These demands on the bourgeois government, and the gains when they are achieved, are steps forward in the process of the general struggle for revolutionary emancipation. They are not an end in themselves.

Because, in general, the State institutes public services in its strategic project as a necessity of its global domination. It builds roads, neighborhoods, housing developments, avenues, and streets, mainly for the flow of commodities, and to reassesses territories, in order to do business with them. It also makes a model of society as it wants to model it.

For example, the city and its transformations are directly related to changes in the mode of production and the consequent changes in the sphere of ideas. Thus, it can be said that there is a city that results immediately from the first industrial revolution (1760-1840); that brings people from rural regions closer to the centers where industries are functioning, since capital needs to have available labor nearby. It concentrates them in neighborhoods in which schools, entertainment centers and grocery stores also appear. And it can be said that this is a city that, as a result of so-called neoliberal globalization, destroys historical centers of people; it integrates roadways and bridges at different levels; it establishes shopping malls that, in addition to being places for the realization of value in the distribution and sale of commodities, are meant to be public spaces for the socialization of people who no longer have traditional parks. In addition to being expelled to the "bedroom communities" far from the center of the cities, it destroys parts of the land available for agricultural production and there builds housing developments for the social strata of different economic incomes.

Thus, the city is also a space for class struggle. Which type of city corresponds to the interest of the bourgeoisie, and which to the working classes, is an issue related to the struggle for political power.

Everything up to this point refers to a theoretical approach, a general framework, which seeks to emphasize the general ideal of society that the communists intend to build. A formulation that enters into the sphere of essential principles; if you will, of the maximum program of the communists.

III. It is important to study and always review the issue of the State, of the Republic, which is to a large degree the issue of democracy

To analyze the Republic in a concrete way, that is, to make a concrete analysis of the State at each historical moment, is a condition to guide political thought and action correctly. Because the State can assume different forms according to the circumstances, from which there arises the need to define policies specific to the occasion, but we communists and revolutionaries must never lose sight of its class essence.

We should carefully study the work of Karl Marx The 18th Brumaire of Louis Bonaparte, which is an analysis of the political process in France between 1848 and 1852, in which Louis Napoleon Bonaparte took power, with the aim of blocking the revolutionary process of that period. He took up the executive function and placed it above all other institutions: the political, legal and military, even those of the bourgeois class itself; but he coordinated them all and put them into action with the aim of guaranteeing the essence of the State as an instrument of domination of that class.

The importance of this work lies in the fact that Karl Marx emphasizes the fact that, regardless of whether a person assumes absolute control of all the aspects of the State, which is different from the ideal of the liberal State that conceives of the independence of the three powers, it maintains its essence as an instrument of class domination.

Obviously, in this model of State domination, contradictions are created that can go beyond the contradiction between the bourgeoisie and the working class, because some bourgeois section does not feel represented. It would be up to the revolutionaries to analyze the concrete situation and, in order to advance towards the achievement of their strategic objectives, they should define the policy that would allow them to take advantage of any splits within the ruling class.

Under these circumstances, the question is not to evaluate the fact that in general the State is bourgeois and as such it is a machine of oppression of the working class and working masses, and that it is necessary to tear it down. This formulation is correct from a theoretical and even historical point of view, as there are already experiences in which this domination has been overcome and it has been possible to generalize a theoretical affirmation of the possibility of the overthrow of the bourgeoisie. The question is, *what are the practical, that is, political, possibilities, of doing it at a given moment in light of the situation of a rise or ebb of the revolutionary movement.*

III. 1. Nuances in the management of the Dominican State since 1966

It is worth noting that, in the Dominican Republic, after the War of April 1965, a regime similar to the Bonapartist one was imposed, headed by Joaquín Balaguer (1966-78). It promoted a counter-revolutionary and developmentalist process, aimed at reshaping the political and social hegemony of the ruling classes, which had been broken after the fall of the Trujillo dictatorship in 1961. This created a political crisis, with its class conflicts between sectors of the bourgeoisie on the one hand, and on the other, the beginning of the mobilization of the workers and other popular sectors demanding public rights and freedoms and a democratic redistribution of wealth.

This regime needed to eliminate the possibility of a new popular revolt, to create the minimum political and social stability needed for the penetration of U.S. capital and capitalist accumulation in general.

Hence the repression against the revolutionary, democratic and trade union movement in general and its developmentalist policy. In the period 1966-1978 this opened the floodgates to industrial development and to the policy of import substitution which at the same time promoted the free zones (the maquilas), and the growing dominance of finance capital.

Seen from the perspective of the popular interests and the revolutionary movement, the winning of public liberties and democratic rights should have been the main issue, as in fact it was for most of the parties and groups of the left. Any fight for political and social reform at that time was a contradiction. The struggle for reforms has a component of political education for the workers and the popular masses in general; and the mobilization in the streets and squares is the main stage to fight for this. But, in the twelve-year regime of Joaquín Balaguer, there were no minimum conditions for propaganda, vital for political education; nor for free meeting and association, vital for public demonstration. Thus the struggle for reforms lacked the minimum conditions to be waged.

Those who, under these conditions, placed at the center of their tactics the fight for reforms, whatever they were, and for electoral participation, made a political mistake.

In the country there was a political turning point in 1978. The twelve-year government ended with the electoral victory of the Dominican Revolutionary Party, PRD, of that time. A space for political tolerance was opened up that has lasted until today. Anti-communist laws were repealed, prisoners were released, and political exiles were allowed to return. The winning of certain public liberties and democratic rights was achieved.

The political circumstances won through years of popular struggle made it possible to demand advanced political reforms. It was not a moment of rupture, of a revolutionary leap, but of an accumulation of forces.

A program of political reforms and of the integration into the government of popular sectors was expected from the PRD, given its situation as a party that claimed to be social democratic. In the leadership and middle levels of that party, there were many people in favor of institutional political changes. Economic and political modernization within the framework of a liberal bourgeois system was the main political expectation of the country after the departure of the conservative government of Balaguer.

But this did not happen.

The left and the popular sectors in general took advantage of the political opening to call for immediate demands, salary increases and other demands of the popular neighborhoods; *but we never demanded a political reform that would in any way open splits in the State through which political proposals could enter.*

Under subsequent governments, although the space for political tolerance opened in 1978 was maintained, the State has continued to be essentially centralized, with a presidential structure, at the service of an economic property concentrated in a few families. This has been one of its main aspects since the time of the Trujillo dictatorship (1930-1961).

Between 2004 and 2020, under the governments of the Dominican Liberation Party, PLD; institutions were perverted to guarantee their continuity in power. More than a republic, they headed a system in which from the presidency they could superimpose or subject the other powers of the State to their interests, without repealing the constitution. They fused together the party, the State, and many social organizations.

Based on the use and abuse of state power, they created new rich people, their own economic group; they entered into competition with the traditional economic groups, and in this way they contributed to establishing a nuance in the management of the State starting with the taking office of the Modern Revolutionary Party, PRM (2020-2024).

With regard to the latter, it should be noted that bourgeois groups that previously limited themselves to financing the electoral campaigns of the parties, and felt represented by them at the head of the State, now demanded to become representatives themselves, occupying important positions in the cabinet, and encouraging their people so that at some point they could become candidates for the presidency of the republic.

After the rupture of the hegemony with the fall of Trujillo and the subsequent War of April 1965, Balaguer imposed a Bonapartist regime, governing for the interests of the bourgeoisie, but without integrating it into the government. Now after the results of 16 years of the PLD government, President Luis Abinader of the PRM is integrating it to occupy important positions. The vice president, Raquel Peña, represents the interests of the bourgeoisie of the Cibao [the central and northern, most populous region of the country – *translator's note*]; the minister of the presidency, Lisandro Macarrulla, equivalent to the head of ministers, represents the Vicini group, and David Collado, the minister of tourism, also represents the same group. And besides these, other officials are in the leadership of important areas of the State.

The policy of public-private alliance is a backbone of the government's economic policy and seeks to give a greater role to the accumulation of private sector capital, based on the platform and public resources. This fact *determines the essential direction of the government, before which the alternative definitions correspond*. This is the format of the continuity of a centralized power, which corresponds to economic property concentrated in a few hands; this is the fundamental issue in the current political struggle.

This, essentially, is the problem to be overcome, proposed by the program of the glorious patriots of June 14-20, 1959, who passed through Constanza, Maimón and Estero Hondo, to overthrow the Trujillo dictatorship by means of arms, and to replace it with an advanced democratic regime.

Here we are now, 60 years after the fall of Trujillo dictatorship.

IV. What is therefore to be done?

The answer lies in determining whether we are at a period of rupture in the Dominican political process, or whether we are at a period of accumulation of revolutionary forces. The answer to this question determines the tactic.

If we are at a period of rupture, then the slogan must be *Down with bourgeois democracy!* No fight for reforms, with the consequent proposal of the system that will replace it. At a moment of upsurge in the revolutionary movement, no reforms are demanded. On the contrary, we must take up replacing the old order with a new one.

This was what V.I. Lenin recommended in his thesis and report to the first congress of the Third International, held in March 1919. The socialist revolution of October 1917 in Russia had already triumphed; but, in addition, in some countries of Europe, there was an upsurge in the revolutionary movement, and the question of power and its character was of an immediate, practical nature. Socialist democracy was the order of the day.

But are we in the Dominican Republic at a period when the breakdown of the established order and its replacement by a revolutionary democratic order is an immediate or short-term goal?

It would be confusing wishes with reality to state that the seizure of power is an immediate task of the Dominican revolutionary process. When making a necessary analysis of the situation, which includes the balance of the relation of forces and their potential in the short and medium term, we must be perfectly honest in defining the political situation, which is one of the accumulation of forces. It is not one of rupture. Therefore, we must propose policies and tasks that correspond to the view of the political moment.

The political program of the glorious revolutionaries who came from abroad in a guerrilla expedition on June 14-20, 1959, with the aim of overthrowing the Trujillo dictatorship, suggests an advanced democratic change of the regime. A constituent assembly to break the concentration of political power, and to do the same with the centralization of economic property and of land in particular; freedom of trade union organization, etc. are approaches that are relevant and can be factors of broad unity and popular mobilization. This is the main political issue at the moment.

March 2022

Ecuador	Pablo Miranda Marxist-Leninist Communist Party of Ecuador – PCMLE

The Class Nature of the Communist Party[1]

In the late 1950s and early 1960s, modern revisionism, headed by Khrushchev, seized power in the Soviet Union and in the leadership of the Communist Party of the USSR. From then on, in a sustained process, the reversion to capitalism took place, culminating in its complete restoration, after the collapse of "real socialism" and the dissolution of the USSR in 1991.

For the process of capitalist restoration to be carried through to the end, the Khrushchevite revisionists accomplished the task of changing the class nature of the communist party. In the supposed updating and development of Marxism-Leninism, they elaborated the thesis of the party of the whole people. According to them, the advances of socialism allowed the elimination of classes and class contradictions, that "democracy and freedom would reign." Thus, the party of the working class would disappear and give place to the party of the whole people (including the classes and class sectors then existing in the USSR, added to the remnants of the old ruling classes and the new rich who emerged from the maelstrom of corruption and opportunism). In reality, the once battle-tested Bolshevik party did not become a party of the whole people but rather a political organization at the service of the bureaucracy and the new rich and an instrument for the restoration of capitalism, for the oppression of the working class and other laboring classes.

In the 1970s and '80, the revisionists in the leadership of the communist parties of Western Europe, particularly the leaders of the French Communist Party, advanced more rapidly and renounced Leninism and democratic centralism. The leaders of the Italian Communist Party went so far as to change the name of the party; some transformed the militant communist parties that led the resistance struggle against Nazism into harmless parties that collaborated with the bourgeoisie of their countries; above all, they fulfilled the

---

[1] This was published for the first time in 2014. We are reproducing it today because of the importance of this issue.

infamous role of ideologically and politically disarming the working class. The Spanish revisionists followed a similar path, they became monarchists under the pretext of the transition from Francoism. All of them proclaimed the renunciation of the interests of the working class, they became props to support the employers, they called themselves "Eurocommunists" and formed an open expression of treason.

In the 1990s, after the collapse of Soviet social-imperialism and the downfall of real socialism; the frenzy of the neoliberal policies of finance capital; the defeat of some revolutionary processes in progress, the collapse of socialism in Albania; and, in the course of the infamous anti-communist campaign unleashed by reaction and imperialism, an ebb in the revolutionary struggle took place. There was an ideological confusion and organizational dispersion of the workers' and trade union movement, the crisis of the revisionist parties sharpened, various revolutionary organizations of the petty bourgeoisie suffered the impact and dissolved or were seriously affected; our Marxist-Leninist parties also felt the onslaught, we suffered setbacks.

One of the elements that the events put forward in the debate within the movement of the workers and peoples, of the revolutionary organizations and parties, was the need for the existence and struggle of the revolutionary party of the proletariat, the communist party.

Those who accused the Communist Party of responsibility for the defeat of socialism were not lacking; from that assumption they concluded that to make the revolution there was no need for a political party, much less a communist party. Some directed their blows at what they called "Stalinist" schemes, at the character and nature of the party, at democratic centralism, at the "absence of democracy and the domination of authoritarianism", at the "elimination of individual initiative." From that premise they concluded that the party that would be able to make the revolution should be "a democratic, pluralist, multiclass party" that would recognize the new times and problems.

In the first years of the new millennium the old theses of "the new left," of "21st century socialism," of the "peaceful revolution," of the "new actors of the revolution," reappeared. Supported by the electoral victories of the progressive and advanced forces in Venezuela, Bolivia, Ecuador and other countries, they decreed the end of the communist party, of what they called "class reductionism" and proclaimed the emergence of "left and revolutionary" parties labelled as multiclass, that is, as representatives of the interests of the various "revolutionary" classes. In fact, the PSUV (Venezuela), the MAS (Bolivia), Alianza País (Ecuador) are political parties that proclaim themselves revolutionary and socialist but in reality they support the capitalist system, the sacrosanct right of private ownership the means of production. They are political organizations that represent the interests of a section of the ruling classes.

The Marxist theory of political parties

For bourgeois political science a political party is the sum of people organized in a stable manner with the purpose of gaining power and from there concretizing their proposals for the social and state organization.

All political parties have an ideology that characterizes them and endows them with some common purposes, which are embodied in doctrines and theories, in platforms, programs and slogans.

There have always existed groups and organizations that sought to hold power, that carried out activities, actions and struggles, but only in the second half of the 18th century, as a result of the liberal revolutionary processes, they began to form what were called political parties and, in the 19th century, they basically acquired the conditions that characterize them.

The Marxist theory of political parties fundamentally takes up these concepts, developing them to the point of defining the objectives and purposes of political parties as expressions of the class interests of their representatives and leaders. It emphatically points out that the decision to organize as a political party is not due to to moralist positions but, mainly, to the defense of their material interests and the willingness to take political power from there to defend these interests.

Independently of the integration into the political parties of hundreds and thousands of people coming from the working masses, from the oppressed peoples and nationalities, the nature of the ideology, programs and proposals of the political organizations correspond to the economic, social, cultural, military and political interests of the class or sector of the class to which the main core of its leadership belongs. In the conservative and/or liberal parties, in the reactionary and fascist parties that have existed and continue to exist, the bulk of their members and militants come from the working classes and social strata, who make up the rank and file, who are indoctrinated in the ideology, proposals and thinking professed by the leadership and who, fundamentally, consciously defend their proposals and militancy. This situation does not mean that this or that bourgeois party, because it is organizationally made up of people belonging to the working classes, represents their interests and defends them, even less that it carries out these interests when in power. Clearly, when a bourgeois political party, independently of its ideology, fights for power and eventually forms the government, it works to maintain and broaden its social base, its adherents, its voters. Therefore, they propose and develop programs and activities that respond to the yearnings and aspirations of the masses, promote material achievements that allow the voters to look upon them and accept them as "good rulers," concerned about the people, at the service of the country and the nation.

Generally, the bourgeois political parties hide their true economic interests behind a democratic, patriotic phraseology; they proclaim freedom, democracy, the defense of sovereignty but these refer to their particular and group interests, to the class sector to which they belong. For this reason, it is pertinent to recall the wise popular saying that people, political parties and particularly their leaders must be recognized for what they say and what they do, but mainly for what they do, for the way they act.

With the advent of capitalism, of bourgeois society and of one of its highest and newest expressions, representative democracy, the political struggle for power (the most important expression of the class struggle, under these conditions) is expressed fundamentally in the existence and confrontation of political parties.

In capitalist society the bourgeoisie, the holder of power, expresses its interests through the existence and struggle of various political parties, all of them representatives of class interests, of those general interests of the capitalists and imperialists, private property, the right to competition and the accumulation and concentration of the wealth created by the workers. In all capitalist countries the existence of various bourgeois political parties is evident, each of them besides representing and defending the general interests of the big business owners and bankers, of the monopolies and the imperialist countries, also embodies the specific interests of each of the different sections of the bourgeoisie, of the big economic and monopoly groups.

The confrontation among the bourgeois political parties for power is a question that is relevant in all circumstances; it is expressed in elections, in parliament, in local governments. At certain moments it can be expressed in uprisings, in coups d'état, even in civil wars. In all conditions the supposed pluralism that should take place, according to capitalist ideologists, in the existence of diverse bourgeois parties, comes into play. None of the bourgeois parties share their specific objectives with other such parties; they even contest them tooth and nail. This confrontation among the various political formations of the bourgeoisie expresses in reality the inter-bourgeois contradictions, among economic groups, among sections differentiated by different economic interests. In certain circumstances the various capitalist groups reach agreements, enter into alliances, together face some special situation without any of them renouncing their own interests.

Populism is one of the political forms of certain segments of the bourgeoisie that is taken up in order to win the support of the working masses in the name of the people. Bourgeois political science identifies populism as the immediatist version of power, as the management that squanders the country's resources without taking into account a medium and long term economic and political project.

The various forms of populism occupy a wide spectrum: there are those who proclaim themselves defenders of order and openly oppose change, identifying the social fighters, the workers' organizations as enemies of society, as representatives of evil. There are populist positions that claim to be nationalist and patriotic, raising the banners of independence in order to win the support of the masses. There are populist positions that openly proclaim defense of freedom and democracy, that disparage the ruling circles as oligarchies, the privileged ones; they use the popular dissatisfaction to gain followers. In short, the different varieties of populism do not change the essence of its nature and purposes; they try to take political power to shore up the capitalist system from those positions, taking advantage of those circumstances for the benefit of the sector of the ruling classes that they represent. In its political history, populism emphasizes a charismatic personality who unveils his proclamations before the people, uses his histrionic qualities to establish himself as a caudillo. Populism awakens illusions, it can organize very active political movements, even important levels of political organization, through trained cadres.

Some of the populist expressions have taken power, generally through elections, although they can also gain come to power through popular uprisings, even insurrections. From power, populism seeks to affirm and prolong itself. It continues its demagogic work, develops the discourse of promises and identifies enemies that it must continue to confront with the support of the voters; it puts into effect a good part of its proposals through welfare programs; it seeks to create works that shine brilliantly.

Essentially, populism is a bourgeois option that exists at certain moments and circumstances, which is developed in the great majority of countries. In special situations it is an ideal instrument to divert the mass movement and the youth from revolutionary policies. In Latin America there are typical expressions of populist regimes: Peronism in Argentina, the long history of the PRI in Mexico, Goulart in Brazil, Velasquez in Ecuador, among others.

Political parties of the petty bourgeoisie

As is known in capitalist society, in addition to the class of capitalists and the working class there are other secondary social classes and strata, the so-called middle classes and strata, which in reality correspond to the different strata of the middle bourgeoisie and the urban and rural petty bourgeoisie that also take part in the political contest, organizing political parties that represent them. In general, the various political parties that express the interests of the middle sectors and strata of the population are conservative political formations, defenders of social peace, order and private property (let us bear in mind that these social sectors aspire to accumulation, to individual economic growth, to share power with those above, to climb the economic and social ladder). A good part of the phraseology of these political parties is developed by appropriating for themselves the interests of the people, of those from below, in order to use them as a platform to maintain and increase their electoral base.

In some countries and in certain circumstances, the political parties that defend the interests of the middle classes and strata take on an air of opposition to the capitalist system, they take up patriotic positions in opposition to imperialist plundering, democratic proposals that oppose authoritarianism and the abuse of the ruling classes. Some of them even take up revolutionary programs and positions, they become involved in the revolutionary armed struggle, they lead heroic actions, they proclaim freedom and socialism. These various political expressions take place in different countries and, in general, we proletarian revolutionaries have to take up united positions towards them, to work so that they join the struggle for socialism through a correct united front policy.

In the dependent countries of Asia, Africa and Latin America some processes for independence and national liberation have been led by petty bourgeois and bourgeois political formations and have even won victory, but they have not been able to lead them in a consistent manner and carry them through to the end with the objective of achieving independence, as happened in Iraq, Algeria and Nicaragua among others.

Political parties in Ecuador

In Ecuador, the conservative party and the liberal party, which became the main political parties in the 19th century, historically represented the interests of the feudal lords and the bourgeoisie, respectively. These parties were the leaders of an intense and acute political struggle for power, the conservatives to maintain and perpetuate the interests of the landowners, the liberals to defend and impose the interests of the bourgeoisie. As we know, these struggles took the form of palace conspiracies, elections, revolts and military uprisings, in a long guerrilla struggle, in civil wars, and ended with the defeat of feudal obscurantism and the imposition of the interests of the merchants, with the victory of the bourgeois revolution and the formation of the liberal state. The existence and activity of the conservative and liberal parties continued until the 1980s.

With the rise of the working class, the socialist party was also born in the 1920s and later the communist party.

Today, various political parties representing the interests of different sections of the ruling classes are evident on the political scene. The old forms of the partyocracy are on the scene and new faces of the bourgeoisie are appearing, seeking to get in tune with the times, with the relation of social and political forces, the Social Christian Party, the Democratic Left, among others. There are also some political formations from among the petty bourgeoisie that seek to get involved, to gain the favor of those at the top and to participate in the political struggle. Although the old forms of populism are in crisis, it is not possible to deny the possibility of the emergence of new experiments and experiences.

In Ecuador in recent years, Rafael Correa's party, Alianza País, has existed and been playing a decisive role in the political development of the country. We have maintained that it is a party at the service of the system, of the international monopolies, of the big business owners and bankers. The conduct of Alianza País from the government, the political events, the nature of the interests it proclaims and defends, its demagogic and populist policies, its attacks against the trade union and popular movement, against the indigenous movement and its rabid attacks on the revolutionary left are a clear demonstration of what class interests Alianza País and President Correa represent. In this as in all cases, things are judged by what they say and proclaim, but, fundamentally, by what they do.

Some analysts who act as leftists and even as revolutionaries talk about the existence and vanguard role of what they call multi-class parties. In arguing these ideas, they refer to the PSUV (Unified Socialist Party of Venezuela), the MAS (Movement towards Socialism of Bolivia) and Alianza País. According to these fabrications that try to theorize about current political science, they are organizations made up of the working class, peasants, self-employed workers, "the class of intellectuals" who have developed a revolutionary program that represents those interests and those of the nation and the country, that would play from within the government the role of vanguard of the revolution and of socialism. (They are always careful not to speak of the proletarian revolution and instead mention the "Bolivarian revolution." the "democratic and cultural revolution," the "citizen's revolution," 21st century socialism which according to them is the negation of Marxist-Leninist socialism, it constitutes the tool for liberation.)

Evidently these parties and the governments they have formed have received an important degree of support from the workers of the city and the countryside, from the most impoverished social sectors and from the middle strata. Through their discourse, demagogy and important material achievements, they continue to enjoy this support.

Their ideological, political and programmatic proposals, as well as the conduct of these governments, are far from representing and serving the interests of the working classes, of social change, of putting an end to the expropriation of their wealth by the capitalists, of the elimination of the privileges of the big business owners, bankers and landowners. In spite of their patriotic speeches, in reality they shore up their dependence on the imperialist system, on Yankee imperialism, trying to disguise it by creating ties with other imperialist countries, especially China and Russia.

It is clear that the social revolution has not taken place, that capitalism continues to rule, that the workers, peasants and indigenous people continue to be at the bottom, exploited and oppressed; that Venezuela, Ecuador and Bolivia continue to be under the iron rule of dependence. They are therefore not a revolutionary party, much less a socialist political organization.

The integration into these parties of a good part of the working classes does not mean that they (the working classes) lead them. In each of these political formations, in the leadership, there is a layer of politicians coming from the bourgeois parties, from the revolutionary organizations of the petty bourgeoisie, from renegades to the revolution and socialism. At the top, in the decision-making bodies, there is a small circle that holds the privileges and is at the service of capitalism and imperialism.

This means that the existence of a multi-class party is nothing more than a fiction, a smokescreen to hide the truth, capitalist domination.

The Marxist-Leninist party is the party of the class, of the working class.

In today's world there are various parties that claim to be communist. These are the parties that were founded in the heat of the revolutionary struggle of the first half of the 20th century, which later became revisionist formations. They are the followers of Khrushchevite revisionism; to a large extent, these parties have unmasked

themselves, they have renounced the dictatorship of the proletariat, revolutionary violence, they have become opportunist and reformist parties.

There are parties that call themselves communist and keep their distance from the traditional CPs, they recognize part of the Marxist literature, but, in practice, they develop a reformist policy that seeks "benefits" for the working class while renouncing the organization of the revolution.

In Ecuador the revisionist party goes from bad to worse. In the 1990s its leadership decided to dissolve and merge with the socialist party. Later a group of its members reformed the "communist party". Currently they are divided into at least three forms that differ from each other by the degree of support to the Correa government and by the positions they are given.

What we have just stated must be taken into account in order to return to our initial idea, that political parties must be judged by their proposals, their program and their social practice.

The revolutionary party of the proletariat was formed in Ecuador in the 1920-30s. It played a excellent role in the course of the class struggle, contributed to organizing the workers of the city and the peasantry and youth, it participated actively in the national political life. At the end of the 1950s it succumbed to the revisionist barrage coming from the leadership of the CPSU in the USSR, it became an opportunist and reformist party.

Rescuing Marxism-Leninism, the tradition of struggle of workers and peoples, of the youth there arose the new Communist Party of Ecuador, which demarcated ideological, political and organizational positions with the old party and understood the need to put Marxism-Leninism in its name. Thus emerged the Marxist-Leninist Communist Party of Ecuador, PCMLE.

In the Declaration of Principles of the PCMLE it is expressly stated: **"The Marxist-Leninist Communist Party of Ecuador is the political Party of the Ecuadorian working class, its conscious vanguard, its highest detachment of class organization". And "The Marxist-Leninist Communist Party of Ecuador is independent of all forms of capital, of all the policies of imperialism and of the class of capitalists."**

These formulations show that the PCMLE is a political party, that is, it was organized to seize power and not only for the struggle of the unions and associations.

The PCMLE takes up the responsibility of placing itself at the head of the economic and political demands of the working class, to make its best efforts for the organization of the workers and youth, for their political education, to direct the daily struggle towards the objectives of overthrowing capitalism and seizing popular power. These characteristics of the party make it the vanguard of the working class; however, the role of vanguard is not established by decree, by calling itself Marxist-Leninist; it is won in the midst of social practice, immersed in the torment of the class struggle. The communist vanguard of the working class is trained in its adherence to Marxism-Leninism, in its elaboration of a correct policy, in its consistency in pushing forward that policy, in the role of organizer of the unions and the strike struggle, in the leadership of the struggles developed by the peoples and youth, in fully taking up the responsibilities of organizing and making the revolution.

The PCMLE in its political line and revolutionary practice is independent of any of the forms of capital. It adheres to the positions put forward by Marx, Lenin and Stalin on the need to be an independent party in all its aspects. The social practice of 50 years confirms this view; the PCMLE has never placed itself at the tail of any sector of the bourgeoisie, it has never taken up the banner of the lesser evil to underhandedly support a sector of the ruling class, it has never conciliated with the class enemy.

Fundamentally, the class nature of the party of the proletariat is expressed in that it defends and fights for the immediate, medium-term and strategic interests of the working class. Its program, policies, proposals and slogans directly correspond with the interests of the working class. They are openly anti-capitalist and anti-imperialist, they propose to abolish private ownership of the means of production, to overthrow the bourgeoisie and bury imperialist plundering. It fights for the working class to make the decision to become the ruling class, to establish the dictatorship of the proletariat, and from power to build a new society, the society of the workers, built by themselves for their own benefit, socialism, to abolish social inequality, all kinds of privileges, to eliminate social classes, to establish the society of abundance, communism on the face of the earth. Their final objectives converge in the emancipation of humanity.

The working class lives by the sale of its labor power, it directly takes part in production, it is grouped in large concentrations, it is linked to the chain of development of industry, it is in contact with the most recent advances in science, technique and technology, it is subject to the discipline of the working day. The material situations of the experiences of the working class allow it to have a disposition for organized work, a practical spirit, a significant degree of collective consciousness, of fraternity and solidarity. The material conditions, the social practice of the working class allow it to relatively quickly take up the class consciousness for itself, to appropriate the revolutionary theory, Marxism-Leninism if the communist party works tenaciously for that purpose.

In the struggle against capital, as the Manifesto of the Communist Party states, the working class "has nothing to lose but its chains, it has a world to win." The working class, in possession of its own ideology and with the leadership of its party, is the class best equipped to lead the other laboring classes in the struggle for emancipation.

In today's Ecuador, the current interests and objectives of the working class coincide with the interests of the other laboring masses of the city and the countryside; they cannot be fully resolved without the victory of the social revolution. This situation allows us to state with certainty that the working class genuinely represents the interests of the self-employed workers, the peasantry, the teachers, the youth and the peoples of Ecuador. By taking these interests as its own, the working class places itself at the head of the struggle to resolve them, it becomes in fact the vanguard of the liberating process, of the revolution and socialism.

The social composition of the communist party is one of the fundamental pillars of the class character of the party. As clearly indicated in its statutes, the members must be workers, agricultural wage earners, poor peasants, employees or revolutionary intellectuals; that is, members of the laboring classes. These postulates have been largely fulfilled; the great majority of its members come from these laboring classes and social strata. There is no place in the party for people who live off the labor of others.

Clearly, the ideology of the working class, the programmatic proposals, the slogans, the policies are contained in the programmatic documents of the party. Within the party, the members who come from the other laboring classes, from the progressive intelligentsia, fully take up those ideological and political postulates, which means that they renounce the economic, political and ideological interests of the social classes from which they come. The communist militant who comes from the poor peasantry adheres to the cause of the revolution and socialism, accepts the Political Line, the Declaration of Principles, the Program and Statute; he or she leaves aside the immediate aspirations of the poor peasantry to win the land to work it for their personal and family benefit, and takes up the determination to continue that battle for the land to the seizure of power, the fulfillment of the achievements demanded by all the workers, the peoples, the nation and the country, the determination to fight for the overthrow of the capitalists and imperialism and the building of people's power and socialism, he or she becomes a fighter for communism. This is the essential condition; the communist militants are proletarian revolutionaries.

These circumstances substantiate the Marxist theory on political parties; in theory and in practice they mean that the Marxist-Leninist Communist Party is a class party, it is the party of the working class.

If one starts from the idea that the members of the revolutionary party of the proletariat come from different laboring classes and one goes on to say that therefore it is a multi-class party, one is stating a falsehood, one is misrepresenting the facts and its nature. The question of the class character of a political party is expressed, fundamentally, by the ideology, policy, program and activity of that party.

The leading nucleus of the Marxist-Leninist party has the responsibility to train itself in theory and practice in the genuine expression of the revolutionary principles of Marxism-Leninism, of the immediate, medium-term and strategic interests of the working class, the laboring masses and the peoples; It must be capable of integrating socialism into the workers' and popular movement. This activity is fulfilled through the formulation of the general policy and the concrete orientations for the workers, for the situation of society and the country, and above all in taking up the leading role in the party, in the workers' and popular movement, in the leadership of the social and political struggles developed by the working masses and the youth. If the leadership of the party, the Central Committee takes up these responsibilities in the field of deeds it contributes to consolidating the class character of the party; if it does not do so or develops it in a defective way, it can help to divert the party from the revolutionary policy of the proletariat, from its class nature, from being an instrument of the working class to acquire the objectives of other social classes, of the petty bourgeoisie or even of the bourgeoisie. This means that the leadership of the party, its composition and its practice constitute a fundamental pillar of its class nature.

The revolutionary party of the working class adheres to and is guided by the revolutionary principles of Marxism-Leninism.

The doctrine of the working class is Marxism Leninism; the political party of the working class takes it up as its ideology and policy, as its philosophical conception, as its economic and social program.

Marxism Leninism emerged as a consequence of the theoretical abstraction of the organization and struggle of the workers, as the development of materialist philosophy, of historical materialism, of political economy, as a result of the analysis of the nature of capitalism. Its creators were immersed in the organization and struggle of the workers, in the ranks of the International Association of the Workers, they were fighters and union leaders, organizers of the communist party. They elaborated the science of the revolution; this science has been and is proven in social practice, in the struggle of the working class in each country and on an international scale, in the victory of the October revolution and of the other socialist and national liberation revolutions. It is the revolutionary thought, the most advanced political doctrine elaborated by humanity throughout its extensive historical journey; its revolutionary principles have universal validity, they are valid in all countries; obviously, their application takes into account the concrete situation. Marxism-Leninism is a living doctrine, a doctrine in development; each of the victorious revolutions contributed to its development; the various struggles of the working class and the work of the communists in all countries are a contribution to this advancement.

Marxism-Leninism is not a dogma; it is a guide for action, it is a philosophy to interpret the world but, fundamentally, to transform it.

The PCMLE was born in defense of Marxism-Leninism, in opposition to the traitors who tried to revise it and vulgarize it; it has been fighting with its orientations, it strives to apply it with initiative and audacity in the changing situations of the country and the world; it will persist in its principles to carry the revolution through to the end.

The central objective of the party is the seizure of power.

The policy, programmatic proposals, platforms and slogans follow in that direction. The struggle for power is waged every day, on the concrete terrain of society, in the heat of the class struggle.

The class struggle develops independently of the will of individuals, of political parties; it is expressed in the confrontation between the workers and the bosses, between the laboring classes and the bourgeoisie, between the peoples and imperialism. In certain conditions the class struggle becomes acute, it takes on great magnitudes, it involves the working class, the other laboring masses, the peoples, the ruling classes, and it could lead to a political crisis. At other times this confrontation is of lesser intensity, it unfolds in isolated social combats, it is dispersed; at certain times it would even seem that things are calm, that there is social peace. In any case, the class struggle does not disappear, it has different connotations, forms and levels.

The leading role of the party of the proletariat is expressed in a specific way by leading the organization and struggles of the working class, the peoples and the youth in the struggle for the immediate economic interests, using them as a means to unravel the real causes of the situation of the working masses, to identify the immediate enemies as well as the holders of power, to educate them politically and to point out the road to power.

We communists are deliberately involved in the struggle for power that develops daily in the heart of society; we take sides for the cause of the workers, of the poor, the exploited and oppressed. We confront the institutions, we are against the anti-worker laws, in opposition to authoritarianism and repression, against the abuses of the judges, the police and the armed forces. Together with the rejection of the policies of the capitalists, we put forward programmatic proposals, proclamations, paths and slogans that allow us to promote the policies of the working class, so that the workers, peoples and youth, but also society as a whole can take hold of them. Essentially this is the revolutionary policy of the party of the proletariat; it is expressed every day, in all circumstances and places. Clearly, in capitalist society, at certain moments the political struggle for power intensifies, the confrontation to settle accounts between the different segments of the ruling classes in general are resolved through the elections of representative democracy; suddenly political crises arise. These events involve the whole of society, all the social classes, the class sectors; objectively, no one sits on the sidelines. In all these events the PCMLE has been taking part with its own voice, from the interests of the working class and the peoples, from the positions of the peoples and the nation, from the objectives of development of the country.

The capitalist class, like the ruling classes of the past, ascended to power and works daily to maintain and perpetuate itself. The power of the bourgeoisie is based on force, on the role of the police and the armed forces; it defends itself through coercion and reactionary violence. However, in order to sustain and develop its power, essentially the class of capitalists works for the legitimization of its domination.

It justified its rise, the use of violence and terror by raising the banners of "freedom, equality and solidarity," proclaiming the freedom of the serfs, the emancipation of the slaves. It advanced to elaborate legislation proclaiming equality before the law, the law of universal suffrage, the alternation in the exercise of government, the existence and relevance of parliament, of representative democracy. In the stage of imperialism it declares itself the guardian of peace and freedom, of democracy, and proclaims its readiness to intervene in any country where these principles are violated. According to their suppositions and all the developments that are taking place in these times and events, the world is reaching its highest levels of development, of democracy and peace thanks to individual freedom, to competition and free trade. The workers take part in this society, they are involved in this democracy, they must be the leaders in the incessant development and beneficiaries of what is due to them, a salary to subsist and reproduce themselves.

With the advent of capitalism, the industrial working class arose, the proletariat that makes possible the creation of wealth, the transformation of nature's resources into commodities, into material goods that make life and its incessant development possible. Clearly, the wealth produced by the workers is expropriated by the owners of the private property of the means of production, by the class of capitalists turning them into wage slaves.

This situation places the main classes of capitalist society at opposite poles: the workers and the bourgeoisie.

When it overthrew feudalism, the bourgeoisie established a new, revolutionary world; it gave a great impulse to science, technique and technology, it permanently revolutionized the instruments of production, creating great quantities and also a great concentration of wealth. This new world was built on the foundations of the exploitation of the wage labor of billions of human beings, on their social and political oppression, on the plundering of the natural resources of all countries. This was marred from its beginnings by the reasons for its aging and disappearance. This new world is now an old, rotten, decaying world.

The class of the capitalists, by basing itself on the exploitation and oppression of millions of human beings, became a giant with a weak and vulnerable base; as it grew it transformed the former serfs into "free" workers, it multiplied them in numbers and spread them to all the ends of the earth, it placed them in direct relation with the advances of science and technology, it trained them as social subjects who were acquiring the consciousness of their role as gravediggers of the world of capital, the forgers of a new world, the society of the workers, socialism.

The bourgeoisie and the proletariat are the adversaries in capitalist society; they are in permanent struggle for the dominant role. For now, the capitalists are in power, but the workers are struggling to overthrow them, to bring them down and become the new ruling class; that struggle will continue until finally the proletariat will definitively win and social classes will disappear; the material and subjective conditions for the elimination of social classes, including their own disappearance as a class, for the advent of communism.

The ideological struggle between the proletariat and the bourgeoisie exists in all situations and moments of the class struggle. It is expressed in the struggle of the revolutionary new against the reactionary and outdated old; between the tradition of struggle of the working class and of the revolutionary movement, and the new and reactionary elitist; between "individual freedom", individualism and egoism against collective interests and solidarity; between bourgeois democracy that justifies the oppression of the working masses and the repression of the trade unionists and revolutionaries, and proletarian democracy, the right to speak, to decide and carry out great achievements for the benefit of the great majority, direct democracy, the democracy of the masses; between representative democracy and the revolutionary government that will take up the great achievements of socialism.

The Communist Party is the consistent standard-bearer of the great ideals of the proletariat; it participates decisively in this ideological contest, raising the principles of the revolution and socialism, of people's power and the dictatorship of the proletariat.

In opposition to the bourgeois dictatorship we fight for the dictatorship of the proletariat.

Society divided into classes from its beginnings formed the State as an expression of its institutions, as an instrument for the exercise of power, to subordinate and exploit the laboring classes and social strata.

The capitalist State does not escape these conceptions; it is the instrument of the class of capitalists and imperialism for the exercise of economic power, to safeguard, preserve and develop their interests. It is organized for the subordination of the working class and the other laboring classes; it becomes the guarantee for the perpetuation of their domination. The bourgeois state, regardless of its form, regardless of the level of social and political rights won by the workers and peoples, despite the formal declarations, constitutional dogmas and laws in force, **is an expression of the domination of the bosses, of the dictatorship of the class of capitalists** that proclaims freedom and democracy for the powerful, and institutionalizes exploitation and subordination for the workers.

Representative democracy, military dictatorship, authoritarian governments, fascist regimes or reformist governments are forms of the dictatorship of the bourgeoisie, expressions of the supremacy of privileges for the few and poverty and oppression for the vast majority.

The working class and its party cannot take over the bourgeois State and with its content and purposes carry out their class achievements; they must destroy the state machinery established by the exploiters and on its foundations, raise up the People's Power, the State of the Workers which will take on the essence of the Dictatorship of the Proletariat, assuming various forms according to the concrete historical circumstances. This will always be the expression of the broadest democracy for the workers and of dictatorship for the capitalists and other reactionaries. Historical experience has shown various forms of the dictatorship of the proletariat, and in the future the workers and the peoples, without a doubt, will find the most valid forms to exercise the power of the proletariat and the other laboring classes over the former exploiters, over the forms of capital within the country and to defend themselves from the attacks of reaction and counterrevolution at the national and international level.

We recognize revolutionary violence as the midwife of History.

The liberation of the slaves was the result of their rebellion, of great revolts and revolutions that broke their chains and gave rise to a new stage of development of human society, to the autocracy of the feudal lords, to absolutism, and to the serfdom of millions of peasants who as "free men" were chained to serfdom. Obscurantism was eradicated by the revolution of the artisans and peasants which was taken advantage of by the bourgeoisie in order to gain access to political power and establish the capitalist system. The repeated attempts of the feudal aristocracy and reaction to restore their privileges also made use of violence, but they were defeated again and again by the revolutionary violence wielded by the bourgeoisie, counting on the workers and peasants as their troops. The bourgeoisie in power uses violence to preserve its interests, to increase and perpetuate them; imperialism affirms its economic and political domination with wars of aggression, with the establishment of puppet regimes, with occupation troops. The first victorious proletarian revolution, the Paris Commune, established the first workers' government, the first expression of the dictatorship of the proletariat by an armed insurrection of the workers; it defended itself until it succumbed to the superiority of the capitalists through revolutionary violence. The Great October Revolution was born of the armed insurrection of October 25, 1917; it resisted the counterrevolutionary offensive and defeated it after a bloody civil war, counting on the Red Army, on the workers and peasants armed and fighting for their destiny. The Albanian revolution, the Chinese revolution, the war of liberation in Vietnam and all the revolutions that seized power and then formed the great socialist camp were the consequence, the result of revolutionary warfare, of guerrilla warfare, of insurrections.

The liberation of the workers, true independence can only come with the organization and victory of the revolutionary armed struggle. We Marxist-Leninist communists declare ourselves in favor of revolutionary violence; we strive to organize it under the concrete historical conditions.

To conceive of revolutionary violence as the form of struggle that leads to power presupposes for the proletarian party the use of all the other forms of struggle: the economic struggle, the struggles of trade union and associations, the democratic struggles of the people, the company strike and the general strike, the popular uprisings, the street struggle, the marches, sit-ins, seizures of highways and land, the participation in the elections of representative democracy. The capability of the party of the proletariat develops to the extent that it can resort to all forms of struggle, can use them to accumulate forces, to contribute to the organization of the workers and youth, to educate them politically, always having in view the power and victory. To use all forms of struggle, to combine them correctly, to subordinate them to the revolutionary armed struggle will allow the working class and its party to fulfill the first stage of the revolution, the seizure of power, and then the exercise of its rule and the realization of the great task of building socialism.

The ideology and politics of the proletariat are expressed in the Leninist organization of the party.

The communist party is radically different from each and every bourgeois and petty bourgeois party in the first place by its aims and objectives, by the interests that it defends, by the way it conceives and carries out the struggles for their achievement; it is also a different party by the way it is organized.

It is a centralized party, with a single leadership and a single will of action. This organizational conception conceived by Lenin has democratic centralism as its backbone. Democratic centralism is expressed in the equal rights of members and leaders; in the participation with voice and vote in the discussion and elaboration of the Political Line, the Declaration of Principles, the Program and the Statute of the party; in the right to elect and be elected for leadership positions; in the right to criticize the policy, members and leaders of the party, that is, in the broadest democracy in the party. And it is affirmed in a centralized leadership, in responsibilities and obligations to be fulfilled without restriction. Democratic centralism means the unity of opposites: freedom and discipline, right and duty, collective discussion and individual responsibility, decision making by majority, subordination of the members to the leadership at the different levels and of the whole party to the Central Committee.

Those who attack democratic centralism, misrepresenting it as an expression of the coercion of individual freedom, are in reality advocating an amorphous organization in which personal freedom is supposedly expressed. Those elements who sincerely criticize democratic centralism are wrong; personal freedom becomes a living expression when it is concretized in collective opinions and decisions.

When it is expressed in a voluntarist manner it has no political effect; it is only a manifestation of an idea, of a desire. Those who attack democratic centralism from reactionary and opportunist positions are not right; they wield fallacies on purpose. In the bourgeois and petty bourgeois political parties, without exception, there is no individual freedom, the voices are not heard and even less are they taken into account for decisions. It is in those parties where authoritarianism is evident, the expression of the will of a small core of leaders and in some of them the decision of a single person, the caudillo or the boss of the party.

The Leninist character of the party is expressed in the organization of cells, in the obligation to be a member of one of the organizations; the party does not consider sympathizers as members but works tenaciously to attract them to its ranks.

The communist party organizes its cells at the enterprise level, in the factories, farms and mines, on the territorial level with the aim that the social base of each organism is formed by a concrete sector of the masses in which the cell fulfills the leading role of the party, all its tasks and responsibilities.

Marxism Leninism is the philosophy of praxis, it is the unity of theory with practice. The political decisions of the party are taken from the positions of the working class, with the guidance of the Political Line; they take into account the concrete situation. They are correct to the degree that represent the interests of the working masses and project them to the political struggle, to the extent that they are taken up by the masses and converted into material force by their social and political struggle.

Criticism and self-criticism, the ideological struggle are tools that allow one to affirm the class character of the party, purifying it of erroneous conceptions, eradicating the wrong ideas and correcting errors and overcoming difficulties. The PCMLE strives to make revolutionary use of these tools.

Proletarian internationalism

The revolutionary party of the working class expresses in its policies and activities the validity of proletarian internationalism.

Capitalism and imperialism exploit the workers throughout the earth; the wealth created by billions of workers goes into the coffers of the big international monopolies and their allies, the bourgeoisie in each country. These conditions make the working class an international class, a social subject exploited and oppressed by the same bosses, by the same system; but at the same time, they endow it with ideological and political characteristics common in all countries.

The material situation of the working class, the capitalist exploitation and oppression demand the same position, the same policy; they give the proletarian revolution an international character, give the working class in each country and the communist parties internationalist obligations. Historical experience corroborates these conceptions, the Great October Revolution took place at a turning point in the imperialist capitalist system and formed a base of support for the international revolution.

Proletarian internationalism does not eliminate the Marxist conception that the working class stands as the ruling class in its own country; therefore, the socialist revolution took and will take place in each country, it will be, fundamentally, the result of the struggles of the workers and youth of that country, but also of the contribution of the international workers' movement, of the internationalist work of the communist parties.

In the epoch of imperialism, it is urgent, in the dependent countries, to take up national banners, the struggle for national liberation together with the struggles for social liberation, for the abolition of capitalist exploitation. In the imperialist countries, it is necessary to fulfill the tasks of the socialist revolution while condemning the imperialism of one's own country that accumulates wealth and power in the dependent countries.

The communist party is internationalist and simultaneously it is the most consistent fighter for national liberation, for the building of the New Homeland.

Ecuador, November 2014

France	Communist Party of the Workers of France – PCOF

A New Issue of our Journal *Rupture*

The Successive Crises Show that this System Has Had Its Day

The second issue of our journal *Rupture* is about to be published. It studies the ongoing changes in the productive apparatus of the capitalist system. Just as the first issue of our journal, published in January 2021, it relates articles of analysis and experiences of struggle with always the same purpose: to show that without a rupture with capitalist imperialist system, none of the crises of the system – economic, climate, health crisis or others, can be solved.

In order to try to overcome these crises, the big capitalist imperialist powers are radically transforming their apparatus of production through automation that is available through technical progress. **These transformations seek to generalize the automation of the productive processes and processes of circulation of commodities, through computerization and the interconnection of the instruments of production.**

These changes aim to reduce the times of production, mobilizing the physical and intellectual capacities of the producers of wealth to the maximum; that means increasing the productivity of labour and hence, extort more surplus-value. These transformations also seek to reduce the time of circulation of the commodities in order to accelerate the realisation of the surplus-value and hence, the circulation of capital and accumulation of profits.

This document also deals with the question of climate change and the responsibility of fossil fuels (coal, oil, gas) for the production of greenhouse gasses. The consequences of global warming are already striking millions of people, especially in the dependant countries. "Green capitalism" is the ideological, political and economic response that the capitalist-imperialist system is developing for its own interest, because fossil resources are not unlimited. They are also a means of pressure in the hands of the countries producing them, as we can see today in the imperialist war of redivision which is taking place in Ukraine, and also in 1973. This "green capitalism" deeply influences the choices of energy resources and in means of energy production.

As for the **"health crisis"** provoked by the coronavirus pandemic, it has highlighted the importance of the production of commodities and the weaknesses of the international division of labour, with the particular role played by China which has become the "workshop of the world". This crisis has also highlighted the degree of interdependence between monopolies and imperialist states in

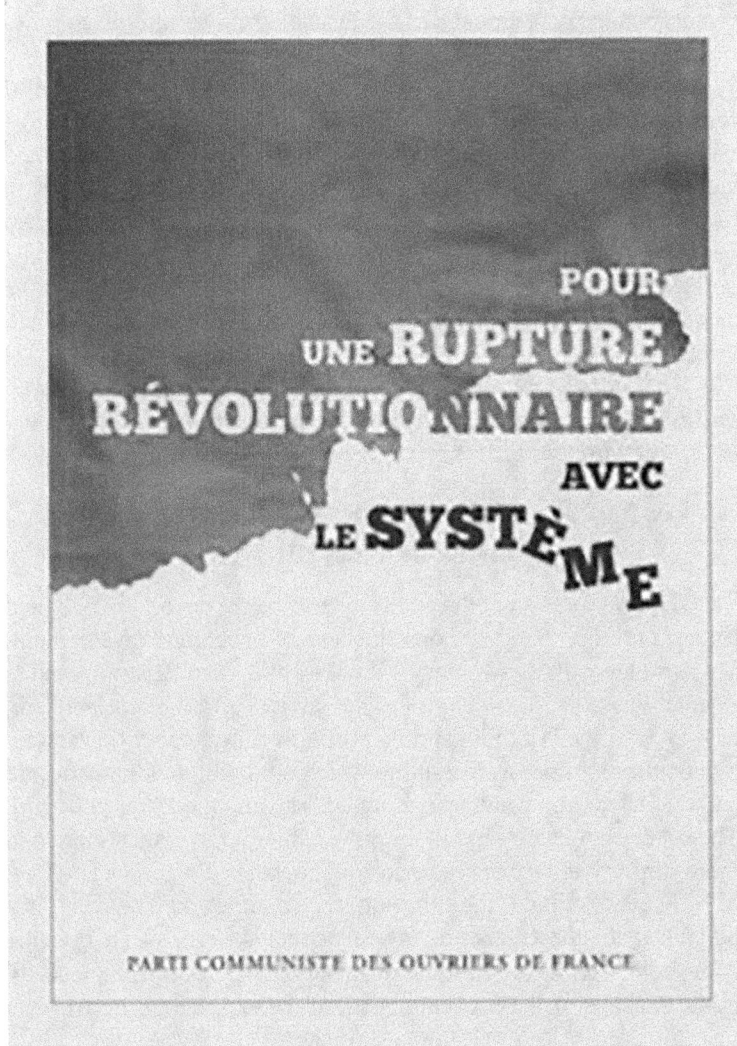

many sectors and the subsequent changes in the balance of power (especially the tremendous weight of GAFA [the internet giants Google, Apple, Facebook and Amazon]). The rupture in the delivery of indispensable parts and the degree of dependence towards certain monopolies specialized in their production have also been brought to light. That crisis has also accelerated and amplified great changes in the field of commercialization of commodities; from the big companies such as Amazon, down to the bike delivery workers. It is one of the consequences of the combination between computerization in all sectors and the development of the technological abilities in communication.

In a document issued in 1997, our party studied the question of **technique under the capitalist system** from a theoretical point of view that helped us to analyze the development of transportation and communication, as well as the place and the role of the workers in these industries. For the second issue of our journal *Rupture*, we have based ourselves on that work, recalling certain fundamental Marxist notions in order to understand the changes taking place today in the capitalist apparatus of production along with their economic and social consequences.

We publish here one of the articles that will appear in the second issue of our journal, an article that synthesizes the different questions raised in it.

A worn-out system cannot be reformed: it must be overthrown!

The deterioration of the environment and the devastating climate changes are no "natural" consequences of economic development. This development is governed by the laws of the capitalist-imperialist system: laws that also determine the choices and the researches in technology. The law of maximum profit, frenetic competition among monopolies in order to determine which ones will dominate, decide and drag along the whole economy, eliminating the lesser powerful. The super-exploitation of labour power, in order to extract more and more surplus-value, even in periods of crisis.

The plundering of the subsoil of the countries dominated by imperialism, for the control of raw materials, sources of energy; the "rare earth" elements and strategic metals, are concentrated precisely in the subsoils of these countries, all at the expense of the workers and peoples. Conflicts and even wars of redivision of spheres of influence, of markets, as we can see today in Europe, but which have been occurring for years and years in Africa, the Middle East, Asia, etc. The monopolies dominate the State and its instruments of coercion, of means of control, of indoctrination, etc. in order to maintain their power and domination over society.

All this leads to insoluble contradictions, as long as the very foundations of the system remain the same. One of these contradictions is between the technological level achieved in many fields and the permanence and even aggravation of the difficulties that the broad masses are confronting, first of all the working class, the working masses, the popular masses. It means unemployment, the continual worsening of working and living conditions, misery for more and more families, women, youth, lack of perspective especially for the youth.

"Green capitalism" remains capitalism and the "ecological transition," which is first of all an "energy transition", serves as justification for frenetic production and consumption of electricity, of electronic and computing devices, for more automation, more means of communication, etc. without calling into question the social relations of production: without calling into question the search for maximum profit, which is cornered by the monopolies and imperialist States that are dominating these areas of production and markets.

The technical and technological advances can exert a certain fascination. We must always think about their true social utility and their power to influence and manipulate ideologically and politically the monopolies that control them. It is also important to become aware of their costs for the workers, the masses and the peoples. It is important to share this awareness. It is the same for environmental questions, the damages and the risks associated with climate change.

The "solution" consisting in increasing the production of electricity by means of nuclear power plants – big or smaller ones – or by multiplying the number of mines for rare minerals, indispensable to these new technologies, are leading to protests and demonstrations that we must support.

More fundamentally, it is necessary to be aware of the accumulation of crises which the capitalist-imperialist system is driving us to: an economic crisis which has no end in sight and which continues to destroy productive forces on a large scale. An environmental crisis which is threatening hundreds of millions of people, particularly through the rise of the sea level. A health crisis with a pandemic that has affected 288 million people in the world, causing 5.4 million deaths. In addition to that, there are the anti-worker and anti-people consequences of the measures taken by the States to "save the system," shutdowns for several weeks[1]. And today, we are confronted with a war of redivision in Europe.

From all this, we come to the conclusion that the capitalist-imperialist system has had its day and that it is time to work to overthrow it.

April 2022

Addition

The first issue of our journal, which appeared in January 2021, was about "education in the capitalist system." That choice was necessary for two main reasons. First, this is a sector which has been the object of different counter reforms in the last years, provoking massive mobilizations of high school students, university students, teachers and national education staffs. Secondly: the pandemic and the almost total lockdown in in the spring of 2020, have made evident, to all of society, the paramount role of education. The articles link the training of the wage-labour force and the valorisation of capital: this is one of the angles with which we deal with the question.

---

[1] The International Organization of Labour (ILO) places at 255 million the number of jobs destroyed in 2020, due to the pandemic and the stoppage of production.

India

Vijay Singh
Revolutionary Democracy

Some Questions of the Dictatorship of the Proletariat and the People's Democracies

"Only he is a Marxist," said Lenin in *State and Revolution*, "who *extends* the recognition of the class struggle to the recognition of the *dictatorship of the proletariat.* This is what constitutes the most profound difference between the Marxist and the ordinary petty (and even big) bourgeoisie. This is the touchstone on which the *real* understanding and recognition of Marxism is to be tested."

The origins of New Democracy and People's Democracy are rooted in the experiences of the international communist movement after the coming to power of Nazism in early 1933. The Seventh Congress of the Communist International of 1935 sought to cognise, combat and crush the rise of fascism. It helps us to situate the political developments in the people's democracies in the late Stalin period and afterwards.

There was a sharp turn in 1935 with the Seventh Congress of the Communist International forging a new approach to the international revolutionary process. The coming to power of Nazism had compelled an initially defensive strategy and tactics in the fight against fascism and imperialism. Under the leadership of Stalin, Dimitrov and the Comintern the communist parties began their new orientation. The Comintern suggested to the CPC from 1935 that there be non-Soviet democratic approach to the national revolutionary process in the struggle against Japanese imperialism. In Spain the military assault on the Spanish Republic, backed by Hitler and Mussolini, required a wide popular front of all the anti-fascist forces in Spain. The Communist Party of Spain under the leadership of Jose Diaz argued from 1937 for the establishment of a new type of democratic parliamentary republic in which feudalism and the financial oligarchy would be destroyed during the course of the national liberation struggle.(1) Historians have stressed the birth of 'People's Democracy' in the communist movement in the Spanish revolution in the period 1931-1939 where a new type of parliamentary republic would lead to a state form where political power would be founded on the coalition of anti-fascist forces which would include the 'left section of the bourgeoisie' in the national front.(2) In China the need to counter Japanese imperialism led the Soviet Union and the Communist Party of China to seek a united front with the Kuomintang. It came into fruition after the Sian incident in 1936. In the 'New Stage', written in 1938, Mao recognised Chiang Kai-shek as the 'highest leader' of the united front against Japan. He argued for long term unity of the Communist Party and the Kuomintang for which the first step was formation of political democracy through the People's Political Council. Mao wrote of the need for 'new bourgeois-democratic revolution' which would constitute an anti-imperialist and anti-feudal revolution of the broad masses of the people under the leadership of the proletariat in 1939 directed primarily against Japanese imperialism. The projection from January, 1940, of New Democracy by the CPC is well-known and was marked by the united front between the Communist Party and the Kuomintang in which Mao and other leaders of the party participated in the Chinese government. New Democracy continued as the demand of the CPC in the period after 1945.(3) Later when the possibility of a united front with the Kuomintang clearly did not exist and when the CPC was in a strong position, Mao initiated the call for People's Democracy.

The new states established in Central and South-Eastern Europe after the defeat of Nazism were initially known as the New Democracies. After the defeat of the pro-fascist and pro-landlord forces and the beginnings of the orientation towards socialism, the perspective opened of People's Democracy in these countries. In his Political Report to the Fifth Congress of the Bulgarian Workers' Party in December 1948, Georgi Dimitrov extensively discussed the question of People's Democracy in the country, where he propounded the necessity of establishing the dictatorship of the proletariat in Bulgaria and constructing socialism within the framework of people's democracy.(4) And a few months later, prior to the victory of the revolution in China, in July 1949, Mao published the work 'On People's Democratic Dictatorship'. It replaced the earlier theses on New Democracy which were now outdated.(5) Stalin made significant observations on the differences between the People's Democracies in Eastern Europe and China during his discussions with Soviet economists on 22nd February 1950. He pointed out that European People's Democracies were carrying out the functions of the dictatorship of the proletariat while in China this was not yet the case. There the people's democratic state was akin to the democratic dictatorship of the proletariat and the peasantry.(6)

People's Democracy in the East, in China, Korea and Vietnam, was understood as passing through two stages: initially it began as an anti-imperialist and anti-feudal revolution and then in the second stage the question of carrying out the functions of the dictatorship of the proletariat and development towards socialism was posed. This understanding was derived from the experience of People's Democracy in the European countries.

In Central and South-Eastern Europe the revolutionary process began as an anti-fascist, anti-imperialist one which was intertwined with the anti-feudal movement. The People's Democracies did not establish the full dictatorship of the proletariat immediately or fight directly for socialism in these countries as the principal task was to ensure the defeat of fascism, attain national independence and democratic liberties; end the serfdom and slavery introduced by the Nazis; liquidate the consequences of Nazi rule and terminate the survivals of feudalism. In the initial period of People's Democracy the middle bourgeoisie participated in the state power in a number of countries.(7) At a certain stage from 1948-49 in these states the dictatorship of the proletariat and the peasantry began to develop into the dictatorship of the proletariat having the objective of the construction of socialism. This was in accordance with the Leninist understanding of the need for the uninterrupted transition from the democratic revolution to socialism. The middle bourgeoisie began to be a hindrance in the onward march to socialism and had to be exposed before the masses and removed from state power. In this manner the second stage of People's Democracy, that of socialist revolution was inaugurated.(8)

In the second phase the economics of the European countries of people's democracy were not considered socialist but were of a transitional character in which there were three forms of property:

> "...nation-wide socialist ownership of the means of production; co-operative ownership which in the main is socialist; private ownership of the means of production, which is of two kinds: ownership by the working peasantry, handicraftsmen and artisans, based on private labour; and capitalist private ownership, based on exploitation.... In each of these countries there are three basic social-economic structures: socialist, small-

commodity and capitalist. The Socialist sector has become the dominating structure in industry and is dominant in the national economy. Finally, an important characteristic feature of the economy of the transitional period is that in the countries of people's democracy there still exist exploiters (bourgeoisie, kulaks)..."(9)

These relations of property remained such in the European people's democracies right through till the close of the Stalin period.

The countries of the European people's democracies, although they were stated to be dictatorships of the proletariat, were not considered to be socialist nor were their economies thought to be socialist as some exploiting classes, the middle bourgeoisie and the rural bourgeoisie, were still extant. The people's democracies were considered as transitional economies which had barely embarked on the construction of socialism.

These countries were categorised as democratic states allied to the socialist Soviet Union. Thus, Zhdanov spoke of the 'Soviet Union and the democratic countries' in his speech on the international situation at the inaugural meeting of the Communist Information Bureau in September 1947.(10) This characterisation was confirmed at the November 1949 meeting of the Communist Information Bureau.(11) Following in this line of thinking G. Malenkov in 1952 distinguished

between the socialist Soviet Union and the camp of people's democracy in his speech at the 19th Congress of the CPSU (b).(12)

In 'Economic Problems of Socialism in the USSR' in 1952 Stalin argued that a socialist camp had arisen in opposition to the camp of imperialism:

"China and other, European, people's democracies broke away from the capitalist system and, together with the Soviet Union, formed a united and powerful socialist camp confronting the camp of capitalism."(13)

Stalin was speaking of the formation of a socialist economic market; he did not imply that any of the people's democratic countries of either the west or the east had become socialist states; they remained within the democratic fold.

This is evident from Malenkov's Speech at the 19th Congress of the CPSU (b). He referred (a) to the breaking away of the people's democracies from the capitalist system, their linking up with the Soviet Union to form a single camp of peace and democracy in opposition to the camp of imperialism; and (b) to the formation of a parallel economic market to that of world imperialism which was composed of the market of the countries in the camp of peace and democracy:

"...China and the People's Democracies in Europe broke away from the capitalist system and, with the Soviet Union, formed a single and mighty camp of peace and democracy confronting the camp of imperialism...

"The economic consequences of the formation of two opposite camps was, as Comrade Stalin has pointed out, that the single, all-embracing world market disintegrated and two parallel world markets were formed: the market of the countries in the camp of peace and democracy, and the camp of the countries in the aggressive imperialist camp. The breakup of the single world market is the most important economic result of the Second World War and of its economic consequences."(14)

Soviet writers under Stalin such as A.I. Sobolev continued to draw a distinction between the socialist Soviet Union, the western people's democracies which had formed the dictatorship of the proletariat and had embarked on the path of socialist construction and the people's democracies of the east where there existed dictatorships of the proletariat and the peasantry, allied with national capital, where dictatorships of the proletariat had yet to be established and the path of socialist construction had yet to be inaugurated. These distinctions were to be blurred after the 20th Congress of the CPSU in 1956.

II

"But whereas bourgeois democracy is the dictatorship of capital, of an exploiting big business minority over the great majority of working people, the people's democracy fulfils the functions of the dictatorship of the proletariat in the interests of the overwhelming majority of working people and realises the widest and most complete democracy – socialist democracy." (Dimitrov)

The transition from the dictatorship of the proletariat and the peasantry to the dictatorship of the proletariat as well as the transition from the anti-fascist, anti-imperialist and anti-feudal stage of people's democracy to the stage of the introductory steps of the construction of socialism was not entirely peaceable. This is evident from the case of Yugoslavia which withdrew from the united socialist front of the Soviet Union and the democratic states. The economic basis for this was the fierce resistance of the Communist Party of Yugoslavia to the nationalisation of capitalist elements and the liquidation of the numerically largest section of the bourgeoisie, the kulaks, which was the necessary condition for the formation of the collective farms of the poor and middle peasantry. In the correspondence of the CPSU (b) to the CPY, signed by Stalin and Molotov, these questions were raised. In their letter of 27th March, 1948 they stated:

"The spirit of class struggle is not felt in the CPY. The increase of capitalist elements in the villages and cities is in full swing, and the leadership of the Party is taking no measures to check these capitalist elements. The CPY is being hoodwinked by the degenerate and opportunist theory of the peaceful absorption of capitalist elements by a socialist system, borrowed from Bernstein, Vollmar and Bukharin."(15)

The CPY denied these charges in the letter signed by Tito and Kardelj dated 13th April 1948. Stalin and Molotov continued their line of argument in their letter of 4th May, 1948 where they contrasted the experience of the Soviet Union with that of Yugoslavia, pointing out that the Yugoslavs were not accepting the Marxist-Leninist theory that the class struggle intensified in the transition from capitalism to socialism. Stalin and Molotov cited Lenin:

"...In 1920-21 Lenin stated that 'while we live in a country of small-holders there is stronger economic basis for capitalism in Russia, than there is for communism', since 'small-scale individual farming gives birth to capitalism and the bourgeoisie continually, daily, hourly, spontaneously and on a mass scale'...

"It is no accident that the leaders of the CPY are avoiding the question of the class struggle and the checking of the capitalist elements in the village. What is more, in the speeches of the Yugoslav leaders there is no mention of the question of class differentiation in the village; the peasantry are considered as an agrarian whole, and the Party does not mobilise its forces in an effort to overcome the difficulties arising from the increase of the exploiting elements in the villages."(16)

Stalin and Molotov stressed that there was no room for complacency as in Yugoslavia the land was not nationalised; under the conditions of private property in land, it was concentrated in the hands of the kulaks who used hired labour. Class struggle could not be glossed over if socialism was to be built.(17)

In response to the criticism of the CPSU (b) and other parties the CPY now embarked upon a series of ultra-leftist measures to end capitalist elements and the rural bourgeoisie. These were of a demagogic character as no preparatory measures were taken prior to 'collectivisation', such as manufacturing and supplying agricultural machinery, so that the policies could not have been successful. (18) The CPY created a new agrarian formation where 'collective farms' were formed not of the poor and middle peasantry as in the Soviet Union but included the rural bourgeoisie, the kulaks. (19)

In its resolution of 1949, the Information Bureau stated on the question of the situation in Yugoslavia:

"The 'producer cooperatives' forcibly set up and run by kulaks constitute a new form of exploitation of the working peasantry. Kulaks who possess agricultural implements exploit the labour of poor peasants in the so-called cooperatives far more ruthlessly than on their own farms."(20)

The agricultural machine stations had owned the instruments and means of production in the agrarian sector in Yugoslavia. They were abolished by decree in 1950 on the ground that the means of production should belong to the producers themselves. The tractors and other machinery of these stations were handed over to the cooperatives for permanent use. This expanded the sphere of commodity circulation in the country. This action became the precedent for the Soviet Union and People's China in 1958. Yugoslavia presented a model of 'socialism' in which capitalist elements could exist alongside kulak co-operative farms and the 'self-administrative' industries engaging in commodity production.

As for the Yugoslavian kulak dominated collective farms they were wound up partly in 1951, and more substantially by the Decree of Property Relations and the Reorganisation of Peasant Work Co-operatives of March 28, 1953. By the end of the year in 1953 only 1258 'peasant work co-operatives' remained in Yugoslavia. (21)

Yugoslavia represented a people's democracy which refused to uninterruptedly advance to socialism and which re-established the capitalist path of development. The Cominform pointed out in 1949 that the system of people's democracy was liquidated in that country. In such conditions the functions of the dictatorship of the proletariat could not be sustained.

III

'The capitalist forces are striving to freeze the present relation of class forces, pending conditions more advantageous to them. They want stabilisation, they want to preserve the people' democratic system at least with its present opportunities for the capitalist elements". (Bierut)

If Yugoslavia serves as the major, spectacular, and successful example of revisionism in state power of the people's democracies of the Stalin period it must be remembered that there were analogous trends of the right deviation in the other countries in Central and South-Eastern Europe. In Poland the major right deviation was that of Gomulka, who resisted the uninterrupted transition to socialism which perforce was directed against the middle capitalists and the peasant bourgeoisie. In the western territories of Poland, Gomulka and his group, contrary to Marxism, created large kulak farms and diminished the role of the poor peasantry in the party organisation in the countryside. The developments in Yugoslavia encouraged the Gomulka group in its pro-kulak policies in the rural areas and it now called for the postponement of the transition to socialism in the countryside. The nationalist perspective of the group of Gomulka was manifested in its hostility to the establishment of the Information Bureau as well its understanding of the developments in Yugoslavia.

The Marxist-Leninists in the Polish party were headed by Bierut. They rejected the view that people's democracy in Poland was to represent a 'harmonious compromise' of capitalism and socialism. Bierut pointed out that 'People's Democracy is not a form of synthesis or solid co-existence of two different social systems, but a form of a gradual pushing-out and in the long run liquidation of the capitalist elements and at the same time a form of development and strengthening of the basis of the future socialist economy'. The Gomulka-Spychalski group were defeated, temporarily, in 1949. This permitted the continuation of the building of socialism against the remaining capitalist elements and the struggle against the strong remnants of bourgeois ideology in people's minds. By the 1st of April 1953 there were constructed 7000 agricultural production co-operatives involving 146,500 households. After the 20th Congress of the CPSU and the death of Bierut, Gomulka came to power. Collective farming was never completed in Poland, the peasant bourgeoisie was carefully preserved so that the country was never able effect the transition to a socialist society.(22)

Similarly, in Rumania the right-wing deviation of Vasile Luca retarded the laying of the foundations of socialism, aided by the conciliationist attitude of Ana Pauker and others. The policies of Luca, as those of Gomulka, echoed those of Tito and Kardelj. He opposed the development of industry which produced the means of production thereby slowing down socialist industrialisation; hindered the activity of the state farms and the collective farms and undermined the creation of peasant associations for the joint cultivation of the land; and assisted capitalist speculative trade by fixing prices of purchasing and contracting on the basis of open market prices. Ana Pauker was charged with neglecting the formation of collective farms; tolerating the activities of kulaks in the development of socialist agriculture; and displaying a lack of concern in the establishment of the Machine Tractor Stations.

Rightism on questions of agriculture had one interesting feature by which the kulaks were buttressed in Rumania. A large number of them were categorised as 'middle' peasants and helped in this way to evade state deliveries and the taxation policies of the state. Though the kulaks were estimated to be 6% to 10% of peasant holdings merely 2.5% of them were placed in that class. The raising of the prices of agricultural products in an unlawful manner created conditions for the enrichment of kulaks and profiteers as the prices for certain manufactured goods earmarked for the countryside were below cost of production. (23) The exposure and defeat of the right deviation in Rumania ensured the uninterrupted transition of the first stage of people's democracy to its second stage, that of beginning the advance to socialism. The advent of Khrushchev was to retard and reverse this process in Rumania and the majority of the people's democracies.

IV

"In China there exists a democratic dictatorship of the proletariat and the peasantry, something akin to what the Bolsheviks talked about in 1904-05." (Stalin, 1950).

Where did matters stand in terms of the stage of development of the People's Democracies in Asia: in China, Korea and Vietnam? The views of Mao and Stalin in the period 1949 and 1950 are instructive on this question.

Stalin, during the course of his discussions with Soviet economists on the 22nd of February 1952, made a clear distinction in the nature of the people's democracies of Central and South-Eastern Europe, exemplified by Poland, and those of Asia, such as China. He argued that in the people's democracies of Europe, political power lay in the hands of the proletariat; industry was nationalised; the Communist and Workers Parties played the guiding role; and the construction of socialism was taking place not just in the towns but also in the villages. In China the dictatorship of the proletariat did not exist. In its place there was a democratic dictatorship of the proletariat and the peasantry. The nationalisation of industry was not complete and there existed a bloc between the communists and the national bourgeoisie. He considered that the special feature of the Chinese revolution was that the Communist Party stood at the head of the state. Stalin concluded that there was in China a People's Democratic Republic which was only at the first stage of the development of people's democracy. (24) This analysis extended to the examples of Korea and Vietnam.

The comments of Stalin to the Soviet economists apropos of China illumine Mao's publication, 'On People's Democratic Dictatorship'. In this work, Mao argued that state power in China constituted a people's democratic dictatorship which was directed against imperialism and feudalism and its local allies 'the landlord class and the bureaucratic capitalist class, i.e., the monopoly capitalist class' which had to be eliminated. (25) Political power in China was founded on the alliance of the workers and the peasants. As Mao said: 'Who are the people'? At the present stage in China, they are the working class, the peasantry, the petty bourgeoisie and the national bourgeoisie'. (26) This corresponded to what Stalin had described as the democratic dictatorship of the proletariat and the peasantry. And what of the future transition of the people's democracy from the first stage, the anti-imperialist and anti-feudal phase to the second stage of socialism? What did Mao have to say about that? This was a contentious question as the case of Yugoslavia had shown in a striking manner. Mao was writing in July 1949, midway between the first resolution of the Information Bureau of June, 1948, and the second resolution of November, 1949. Mao did not mention the necessity of the rapid and uninterrupted transition of the democratic dictatorship of the proletariat and peasantry to the dictatorship of the proletariat. Indeed, he did not, no doubt for correct tactical reasons just three months prior to coming to power, mention the categorical political imperative to carry out in future the functions of the dictatorship of the proletariat in China, implying as it did, the ejection of the national bourgeoisie and its political parties from state power. It was the moment that every effort needed to be made to win over sections of middle capital away from the monopoly capitalist sections of the bourgeoisie centred around Chiang Kai-shek. This had been a major recommendation made by Stalin to the leadership of the CPC which initially had considered the establishment of a state without the participation of any section of the national bourgeoisie

Regarding the national bourgeoisie, Mao considered the cardinal need to educate and reform this class both prior to the establishment of socialism, which was predicated upon their elimination, and after the nationalisation of their enterprises. He argued that once the work of the people's democratic dictatorship was accomplished:

> "Then there will remain only the national bourgeoisie. In the present stage a great deal of suitable educational work can be

done among them. When the time comes to realise Socialism, that is, to nationalise private enterprise, we will go a step further in our work of educating and reforming them. The people have a strong state apparatus in their hands, and they do not fear rebellion on the part of the national bourgeoisie."(27)

This passage evokes great interest as in the post-1954 period the assertion that the private enterprises of the national bourgeoisie would be nationalised under socialism, was deleted from the editions of this text. The national bourgeoisie was never to be removed from the National People's Congress or economically liquidated in the economy of People's China.

In the article by Yu Huai 'The National Bourgeoisie in the Chinese Revolution' which was published in 'People's China' in January 1950, the author argued on the lines of Mao on the need to incorporate the national bourgeoisie in the first stage of people's democracy. But he recognised that:

"Of course, this is not to say that there exist no contradictions, and consequently no struggle, between the state-owned economy of a socialist nature and the private-operated economy of a capitalist nature. No, contradictions do exist, and so struggle is inevitable, and it will be further sharpened.

"But since tremendous changes have already taken place in the relative strength of the various classes in China, and since the powerful state apparatus is now in the hands of the people, and since the growing state-owned economy having a socialist nature together with the co-operative economy having a semi-socialist nature will become the leading components of China's economy, this kind of contradiction and struggle need not be solved by further bloodshed, but can be solved, to a considerable extent, by means of education and reform."(28)

While the contemporary writings of the CPC leadership tactically omitted mention of the need for a rapid and uninterrupted transition from the dictatorship of the proletariat and the peasantry to carrying out the functions of the dictatorship of the proletariat no such concession needed to be made by the CPSU (b) and the Cominform. Both continuously reiterated the position of Stalin and the CPSU (b) that the people's democratic dictatorship in China had yet to fulfil the tasks of the dictatorship of the proletariat. Thus, by way of example, on the first anniversary of the Chinese revolution, the journal of the Cominform wrote that:

> "State power in China is not the dictatorship of the proletariat, and in this it differs from the state power in the European countries of People's Democracy where this democracy fulfils the functions of the dictatorship of the proletariat...
>
> "The nature of the people's democratic state power in China is defined by the conditions in this recently colonial country. At present the working people of China are not confronted directly with the task of building Socialism, the instrument of which is the dictatorship of the proletariat. (29)

The question of the uninterrupted transition to the dictatorship of the proletariat and socialism was to be posed once production was rapidly restored to the pre-war levels and successes had been scored in the anti-imperialist and anti-feudal tasks of the people's democratic revolution.

The nationalisation of imperialist interests and the property of the Chinese compradore bureaucratic bourgeoisie, which had close ties with the foreign imperialists took place and the state took over their factories, mills, banks and commercial enterprises in China while the completion of the agrarian revolution which was carried through on the principle that the land should belong to the tillers, destroyed the economic basis for the existence of the landlord class. That class was abolished and the peasantry was freed from the annual rents paid to the landlords. All this meant that the anti-feudal and anti-imperialist tasks of the revolution had been largely achieved by 1952. The People's Republic of China stood on the brink of the establishment of the dictatorship of the proletariat and the uninterrupted transition to socialism.

In these circumstances Mao, on June 6th 1952, argued that the principal contradiction in China was between the national bourgeoisie and the working class:

> "With the overthrow of the landlord class and the bureaucrat-capitalist class, the contradiction between the working class and the national bourgeoisie has become the principal contradiction in China; therefore the national bourgeoisie should no longer be defined as an intermediate class."(30)

This implied that People's China would begin the change-over to exercising the functions of the dictatorship of the proletariat and inaugurate the process of transition to socialism.

A.I. Sobolev confirmed this understanding:

"Whereas the Korean People's Democratic Republic and the Democratic Republic of Viet-Nam are in the first stage of the development of People's Democracy, the Chinese People's Republic has already passed through its first stage, *the stage of the democratic revolution, and now has entered a new stage, that of realizing the tasks of the socialist revolution.* The popular democratic regime in these countries is a revolutionary power carrying out the functions of the dictatorship of the proletariat and the peasantry."

Further he argued with reference to China that:

"The successful solution of anti-imperialist and anti-feudal tasks ensured the *direct* growing over of the general-democratic revolution into a socialist revolution. *At present the Chinese people under the leadership of the working class with the Communist Party at its head set to realize the tasks of the socialist revolution and of the socialist transformation of society.*"(31)

The necessity of converting the democratic dictatorship of the proletariat and the peasantry to the dictatorship of the proletariat in China in the transition to socialism was implied rather than explicit in this statement.

V

'Between capitalist and communist society there lies the period of the revolutionary transformation of the one into the other. Corresponding to this is also a political transition period in which the state can be nothing but *the revolutionary dictatorship of the proletariat*'. (Marx).

After March 1953 the Soviet state did not fulfil the functions of the dictatorship of the proletariat. The termination of the proletarian dictatorship, a fundamental requirement for the retention of socialism and the uninterrupted transition to communism, was formally notified in 1961 by the CPSU so that the Soviet state now was officially considered to be 'the state of the whole people'.

In the period 1953 to 1958 a system of generalised commodity production was built in the USSR. Directive centralised planning by Gosplan to construct communism was terminated and replaced by a new system of 'co-ordinated planning' of the government departments of the central government and the Union Republics. Gosplan itself was reconstructed and divided into two organisations. The powers of the directors of the enterprises were expanded at the expense of Gosplan and they were required to operate the enterprises on the principle that the criterion of efficiency was profitability. The instruments and means of production in agriculture, the Machine Tractor Stations, were sold to the collective farms. It meant that a section of the means of production which was socialised property passed over to the group property of the collective farms, thereby becoming a part of the commodity sector. Under socialism the products of Soviet industry were allocated according to plan. After 1958 the products of Soviet industry were newly designated as commodities circulating in the state sector and a score of agencies were established under Gosplan to sell the products of Soviet industry. In such conditions the economic categories such as labour power, surplus value, profit and the average rate of profit were to appear once more.(32)

The ending of the dictatorship of the proletariat and the construction of capitalism in the Soviet Union had widespread ramifications for the people's democracies.

VI

"Only by advancing directly on the road to the achievement of socialism, can the people's democracy stabilise itself and fulfil its historic mission. Should it cease to fight again the exploiting classes, and to eliminate them, the latter would inevitably gain the upper hand, and would bring about its downfall." (Dimitrov).

The people's democracies of Central and South-Eastern Europe as we saw from 1947-48 had established dictatorships of the proletariat and embarked on the construction of socialism. The people's democracies of Asia were still at the first stage of people's democracy, that is the democratic dictatorship of the proletariat and the peasantry, and China was on the brink of beginning the uninterrupted transition to socialist construction, the *conditio sine qua non* of which was the dictatorship of the proletariat.

The Constitution of China adopted in September 20th, 1954 could have been an occasion to register the construction of the dictatorship of the proletariat. Mao in his speech 'On the Draft Constitution of the People's Republic of China' of June 14th 1954 asserted that the Leninist understanding of the dictatorship of the proletariat was by no means outmoded. He even described the 1954 constitution as one of a 'socialist type'. (33) Mao informed that the draft Chinese constitution had drawn upon the constitutions of the Soviet Union and the People's Democracies. (34) But Mao did not accept the understanding of Marxism-Leninism that the dictatorship of the proletariat was the necessary pre-condition for the transition to socialism. It was a question which had been posed to the CPC in the immediate past by Stalin, the CPSU (b) and the Information Bureau of the Communist and Workers' Parties. The preservation of the democratic parties in the National People's Congress in the Chinese constitution of 1954 and indeed in all subsequent constitutions to the present time confirms that the functions of the dictatorship of the proletariat were never performed in People's China. In essence the democratic dictatorship of the proletariat and the peasantry, including the national bourgeoisie, formed in October 1949 remained frozen throughout the Mao period and afterwards. In his seminal work 'On the Correct Handling of Contradictions Among the People' which is dated *February 27, 1957, Mao developed his arguments further. He elaborated that the national bourgeoisie was working for socialism in the concrete conditions of the country and that the political parties in the National People's Congress of the working class and the national bourgeoisie would engage in* 'long-term coexistence and mutual supervision'. In the course of their work the industrialists and the businessmen would 'remould' themselves. (35) Clearly Mao did not accept the Leninist understanding that the class struggle intensifies in the transition from capitalism to socialism. Lenin considered that the dictatorship of the proletariat was necessary for the struggle against the bourgeoisie: 'small-scale production is still widespread in the world, and small-scale production engenders capitalism and the bourgeoisie continuously, daily, hourly, spontaneously, and on a mass scale. All these reasons make the dictatorship of the proletariat necessary, and victory over the bourgeoisie is impossible without a long, stubborn and desperate life-and-death struggle which calls for tenacity, discipline, and a single and inflexible will.' ("Left-Wing" Communism: an Infantile

Disorder). But in the view of Mao it was possible in China for the bourgeoisie to help build socialism.

How did the CPC square its position and that of Marxism-Leninism on the need for the dictatorship of the proletariat? Given the open, public position adopted by the CPSU (b) and the Cominform between 1949 and 1953, that the dictatorship of the proletariat had yet to be built in China, it was a matter which could not be avoided. It was 'resolved' by simply asserting that the dictatorship of the proletariat had been established in 1949. This was the reasoning of the CPC:

> "After the founding of the People's Republic of China, a people's democratic dictatorship was set up, led by the working class and based on a worker-peasant alliance. **This state power was in essence a form of proletarian dictatorship**. Under the historical conditions of our country, it not only embraced the peasants and petty bourgeoisie but also the national bourgeoisie which expressed its support to the proletarian leadership."(36)

Essentially the democratic dictatorship of the proletariat and the peasantry established in 1949 remained stalled and did not develop into fulfilling the functions of the dictatorship of the proletariat.

It logically followed that the claim that People's China had embarked on the transition to socialism could not be correct. This is evident as the economic relations of socialism were not to be built in China.

The national bourgeoisie was not to be economically liquidated in People's China. The number of industrial enterprises run by national capital in 1949 was 123,165 and they employed over 1,640,000 workers. Commercial enterprises in 1950, including individual merchants, numbered about 4,020,000 employing 6,620,000 people.(37) The national bourgeoisie in the time of 'socialist transformation' was initially subjected to restrictions in the form of the state-private enterprises and was guaranteed a profit of 5% by the Chinese state. As production expanded the profit of the national capitalists declined proportionately in relation to that of the state. The rise in labour productivity at the same time meant that the national bourgeoisie drew more in terms of dividends and bonuses so that the proportion of their profit on capital kept rising.(38) At this time the national bourgeoisie had a considerable hold in the economy. The state capitalist sector in the first half of 1956 in industry constituted 32% of the gross output value of industry and in commerce it constituted 25.24% of the retail trade of China.(39)

The policy of 'state capitalism' was inspired by the New Economic Policy which had been followed by Soviet Russia when it was compelled to retreat and compromise with capitalism after setbacks to socialism at the close of 'war communism'. In contrast, state capitalism was taken up in People's China after the first phase of people's democracy was completed and the advance to socialist transformation was ostensibly taking place.

During the years of the cultural revolution the national bourgeoisie was further restricted by having its interest on capital frozen for 12 years. Mao went back on his statement of July 1949 that the enterprises of the national bourgeoisie would be nationalised. This had been consonant with the understanding of Dimitrov that as the people's democracy passed over to the second stage of socialism, the urban bourgeoisie which represented the last vestiges of the exploiting classes, would be liquidated. This was necessary as the roots of capitalism were not extirpated so that the capitalist vestiges persisted and would try to restore their rule.(40) In the period after the cultural revolution the blocked interest of the national bourgeoisie which had been frozen in their banks was restored to them.

The lack of the fulfilment of the functions of the dictatorship of the proletariat in People's China had clear implications for the policy adopted towards the kulaks and the landlords. Engels, in his work *The Peasant Question in France and Germany,* had confined the membership of the co-operative farms to the small peasants rejecting any possibility of compromise with the rich peasantry.(41) In the Soviet Union in line with the understanding of Marx and Engels the kulaks, the largest section of the bourgeoisie, were excluded from the collective farms. This is evident in the collective farm statute.(42)

In the interests of the restoration of the national economy and to isolate the landlords Mao had supported the policy of terminating the requisitioning the surplus land and property of the rich peasantry and every effort was made to preserve their economy as may be seen in the statement of June 1950.

"...there should be a change in our policy towards the rich peasants, a change from the policy of requisitioning the surplus land and property of the rich peasants to one of preserving a rich peasant economy, in order to further the early restoration of production in the rural areas. This change of policy will also serve to isolate the landlords while protecting the middle peasants and those who rent out small plots of lands."(43)

The original collective farms established in People's China after liberation were constituted of the poor and middle peasantry. After 1955 the collective farms included the kulaks. In this way there was a family resemblance between the post-1953 Chinese collective farms and those formed in Yugoslavia after the Cominform resolution of 1948, which had been subjected to criticism in the 1949 Cominform resolution. But in addition in China the former landlords were brought into the collective farms. During the course of the upsurge of agricultural cooperation most of the rich peasantry and the former landlords were taken into the cooperatives.(44) The reactionary social classes, the kulaks, and the landlords, were incorporated later on in the 'People's Communes'. These were distinct from the Communes of the Soviet Union as these were comprised in terms of their class composition of the working peasantry, and in which the instruments and means of production were socialised and were not a part of group property.

Many of the economic policies adopted by Khrushchev after 1953 in the Soviet Union were embraced in People's China. Engels had pointed out in 'Anti-Dühring' that commodity circulation in the economic communes was inevitably bound to lead to the regeneration of capitalism. For this reason, Stalin had opposed the proposal of Sanina and Venzher that the basic implements of production concentrated in the Machine Tractor Stations be sold to the collective farms.(45) In 1958 in the Soviet Union and People's China the basic implements of agriculture of the Machine Tractor Stations were sold to the collective farms. As a consequence, in both states an enormous quantum of the means of production now became a part of the sphere of commodity circulation. At the 19th Congress of the CPSU (b) in 1952 the proposal to engage in manufacturing on the collective farms was criticised by Malenkov as it was inefficient, relatively costly and a diversion from agriculture.(46) Under Khrushchev the realm of commodity circulation was extended in the Soviet Union by building power stations and industrial enterprises for processing food products in the collective farms.(47) In People's China thousands of rural industries were established in the People's Communes including modern fertiliser plants. Mao pointed out that 'In the communes not only land and machinery but labour, seeds, and other means of production as well are commune-owned. Thus the output is so owned.'(48) The fact that the People's Communes owned the basic means of production, the land, the basic agricultural machinery, and, also operated widespread commune-based industries meant that a 'gigantic' quantity of the means of production was outside the sector of state property which constituted the property of the whole people. It is apparent that in People's China, in the absence of the dictatorship of the proletariat, that a vast sector of commodity production and circulation existed in the state-private sector and in the People's Communes which was incompatible with the construction of socialism.

What was the response of the CPSU? Did they defend the Marxist understanding of the need for exercising the functions of the dictatorship of the proletariat in People's China as the decisive pre-condition for the transition to socialism and remonstrate that it was not possible to alter the basic laws on the transition period from capitalism to socialism which, as Dimitrov had said, was valid for all countries? No. On the contrary, the political and economic developments in People's China, which included the refusal to support the need to assert the functions of the dictatorship of the proletariat, and the rightist policies with regard to the national bourgeoisie, the rich peasantry, and the landlords after 1953, gained the approval of the leaders of the Soviet Union. At the 20th Congress of the CPSU Khrushchev noted that much that was 'unique' in 'socialist' construction was being done in the People's Republic of China:

> "Having taken over the decisive commanding positions, the people's democratic state is using them in the social revolution to implement a policy of peaceful reorganisation of private industry and trade and their gradual transformation into a component of socialist economy."(48)

The CPSU and the CPC despite differences of form clearly concurred on the repudiation of the views of Marxism-Leninism on the dictatorship of the proletariat and the construction of socialism.

VII

> "The regime of the people's democracy will not change its character during the carrying out of this policy which aims at eliminating the capitalist elements from the national economy. The key positions of the working class in all spheres of public

life must continuously be strengthened and all village elements rallied who might become allies of the workers during the period of sharp struggles against the kulaks and their hangers-on. The people's democratic regime must be strengthened and improved in order to render powerless and liquidate the class enemies." (Dimitrov)

On August 15th, 1945 Soviet troops, after defeating the Japanese Kwantung army, liberated Korea from the 36-year long rule of Japanese imperialism. Korea was the first colony to gain liberation after the Second World War. In these circumstances:

"The people, with the working class at their head, smashed the reactionary forces and established their own rule. People's Committees which took over full state authority sprang up throughout the country. Theirs was a revolutionary power carrying out the tasks of the dictatorship of the proletariat and the peasantry. In establishing their own power the popular masses won broad democratic rights and liberties. A new epoch of people's democratism began in Korea."(49)

Pak Hen En set about reorganising the Communist Party and became its General Secretary; a preparatory committee was organised for this purpose and a programme of action was worked out. The Communist Party became the centre of the democratic forces in the country. (50) In October, 1945, Kim Il Sung came to head the Orgburo of the Central Committee of the Communist Party.

Corresponding to the requirements of a New Democracy, Kim Il Sung at this time argued that Korea should take the road of progressive democracy which would give the people rights, freedom and full independence. Progressive democracy, he said, was distinct both from the democracy of the western countries and also from socialism: this new type of democracy would be both anti-feudal and anti-imperialist for the interests of the broad popular masses and the patriots and not just for one class. Accordingly there had to be formed a democratic national front of all the democratic and patriotic forces composed of the workers, the peasantry, the intelligentsia, the religious communities and the 'honest national capitalists'.(51) This alliance of classes and tasks correlated to the requirements of both new democracy and the first stage of people's democracy. Under this perspective, the property of landlordism, comprador capital, the pro-

Japanese elements was taken over by the state. Major industry was nationalised and the agrarian revolution was carried out. These policies ended the colonial and semi-feudal character of North Korean society. Capitalism was not ended completely. Private industry and trade remained in the towns and the largest section of the bourgeoisie, the kulaks, were in existence in the countryside.(52) By 1947 the state controlled 80.2% of industry with 19.8% remaining in the private sector.(53) By 1949 in industry the state sector and the co-operatives of the industrial enterprises comprised 90.7% of total industrial production. In agriculture the socialist sector was composed of the state farms, stock-breeding farms and the farm machine leasing stations constituted 3.2% of the agricultural section and rose to become the leading sector by 1955. By the end of 1956 agricultural co-operatives were established in 65.2% of total farm households. The first Machine Tractor Stations were built in 1950 with Soviet assistance.(54)

The Korean People's Democratic Republic had been proclaimed on 9th September, 1948. However, the US aggression on Korea between 1950 and 1953 made matters very complex for the uninterrupted transition from the first to the second stage of people's democracy, from the democratic dictatorship of the proletariat and the peasantry to the dictatorship of the proletariat, which was the basis for the transition to socialism. It was necessary to economically recover from the devastation caused by US imperialism.

In August 1958 it was argued that in the DPRK the socialist transformation in relations of production both in town and country had been completed so that socialism was firmly established.(55)

But the transition from the democratic dictatorship of the proletariat and the peasantry to the dictatorship of the proletariat did not take place in the DPRK. This would have required the elimination of the national bourgeoisie from the united front which ruled the state. Kim Il Sung asserted, writing in March 1956 - the month following the 20th Congress of the CPSU, that this people's power nonetheless constituted the dictatorship of the proletariat.

> "Some people say that our people's power is not one that exercises the dictatorship of the proletariat because it is based on a united front. This is entirely an erroneous view. Today our people's power is a state power that belongs to the category of the dictatorship of the proletariat. In the northern half of the Republic, now in the period of transition from capitalism to socialism,

the functions of the proletarian dictatorship of our people's power must be strengthened even more."(56)

The functions of the 'dictatorship of the proletariat' were necessary in a consolidated form it was said because there existed small commodity producers, private manufacturers, private merchants in the rural and urban areas and the tasks of the socialist revolution needed to be accomplished.(57) How did Kim Il Sung assert that there was a dictatorship of the proletariat in the DPRK when in fact it had not been established, when the democratic dictatorship of the proletariat and the peasantry actually still existed? This was done by arguing that the questions of the transition period and the dictatorship of the proletariat had to be decided not on the vantage point of Marxism-Leninism but on the basis of the Juche principles. It was necessary, said the Korean leader, to avoid 'flunkeyism' and 'dogmatism' by rejecting 'the thinking of other countries'. Marx examined these questions in the context of developed capitalist countries and Lenin too operated in a backward but still capitalist country. It was necessary to proceed from the practical experiences in socialist construction in Korea. (58) This effectively implied that it was not mandatory for a People's Democracy in a former colonial and semi-feudal country to oust the national bourgeoisie from the ruling united front or to economically liquidate the national bourgeoisie and the kulaks. The Juche principle did not accept that the principles of Marx, Engels, Lenin and Stalin were applicable to Korea. Stalin and the Cominform, on the contrary, were very clear that Marxist principles were applicable in the former colonial countries in the newly constructed people's democracies of the east.

The Korean Workers' Party expressed the understanding that after the successful revolution in a colonial revolution the country had to go through a transitional period to socialism. It was necessary for the people through people's democracy under the leadership of the working class to end the foreign and domestic imperialist forces, the feudal landlords, to nationalise the key industries and lay the foundations of an independent national economy. This would be done in the preparatory period which was known as the people's democratic revolution. This people's democratic dictatorship was led by the working class and was based on the worker-peasant alliance in alliance with the national bourgeoisie. (59) So far so good. But it was then considered that the people's democratic dictatorship performed '*essentially* the function of the dictatorship of the proletariat'. This argument obliterated the distinction between the people's democratic dictatorship and the dictatorship of the proletariat. It ended the difference between the two phases of people's democracy, between the class basis of the two stages of people's democracy and the distinct tasks of the two stages of people's democratic revolution. The outcome of this was to justify the non-establishment of the functions of the dictatorship of the proletariat in North Korea to avoid the necessity to economically liquidate the national bourgeoisie and the rural bourgeoisie. In place of elimination these reactionary bourgeois classes were 'to be educated and remoulded into socialist working people'. It was then later claimed that the capitalist ownership of the means of production was 'abolished completely'.(60)

The national bourgeoisie was composed of the manufacturing and merchant elements. In 1949 total industrial production in the state sector and the co-operative industrial enterprises constituted 90.7% and after the process of 'socialisation' had started in 1955 this increased to 98.3%.(61)

> "Capitalist trade and industry were transformed by way of organizing producers' cooperatives according to business lines in close combination with reorganization of handicrafts. There were three forms of producers' cooperatives The first form was an initial form of cooperative economy in which the production tools were not placed under common ownership and work alone was done on a collective basis. The second form was a semi-socialist form in which the means of production were under both joint and private ownership and both socialist distribution according to work done and distribution according to the amount of investment were applied. The third form was a completely socialist form in which all means of production and funds were turned into common property and only socialist distribution applied. The second form was popular in the cooperation of capitalist trade and industry. It was a rational form which was readily acceptable to capitalists because it applied the distribution according to the amount of investment while laying stress on the socialist principle in the ownership of the means of production and distribution. A considerable number of entrepreneurs went over to the third form through the second form."(62)

In the Soviet Union socialisation was founded on the basis of the nationalisation of private property which became the property of the whole people. In addition there existed in the Soviet Union the group property of the collective farms, industrial co-operative artels and consumer societies of the working peoples.(63) In North Korea this was not the case. The term 'socialisation' was utilised for the group property or the collective property of the middle bourgeoisie whose property was not expropriated. The formation of the group property of national capital converted them into 'socialist working people' it was speciously argued.(64) The national bourgeoisie would later be taken to communist society.(65)

It logically followed from this that the rural bourgeoisie would be incorporated into the 'collective farms' along the lines of the prior Yugoslav and Chinese practice. At the time of agricultural co-operation in Korea official statistics held that the poor peasantry constituted 40% of the rural population; the middle peasantry 59.4%; and the kulaks were categorised at an unusually miniscule figure of 0.6%. At the end of 1956, 80.9% of the rural households had joined the 'co-operatives'. Sections remained outside these institutions such as the well-to-do peasants, peasants engaged in trade and farming, peasants widely dispersed in the mountain areas and peasants in the newly-liberated areas. This movement for a 'socialist' agriculture was completed in August 1958. Parallel to the national bourgeoisie, the kulaks also underwent 'remoulding' in order for them to be converted into 'socialist working people'.(66)

There was one area where the North Koreans ran counter to the dominant international practice in the post-Stalin period of initiating commodification of the means of production. In the Soviet Union Machine Tractor Stations (MTS) had been established from 1928 to assist the collective farms in agricultural production. The MTS were a part of the socialised means of production which worked with and guided the working peasantry in the collective farms.(67) The collective farms represented a form of group property under socialism. In the Soviet Union and its allies in Europe (excluding People's Albania) and in People's China the MTS were ended in 1958 which strengthened the sphere of commodity circulation in the respective economies. Machine Tractor Stations were established in the DPRK in 1950 with Soviet aid introducing tractors and other machinery for use in the co-operative farms and helped to restrict the role of the kulaks in the rural economy. During the war period the farm machine hire stations were increased three-fold and between 1956 and 1960 their number nearly doubled further.(68) It is a matter of interest that in August 1958 Kim Il Sung privately criticised the dissolution of the MTS in the Soviet Union by Khrushchev and contended that the handing over of the state property of the people to the co-operatives was contrary to the need for the transition to communism.(69)

Lenin in *Economics and Politics in the Era of the Dictatorship of the Proletariat* argued that until the abolition of classes it was necessary to uphold the dictatorship of the proletariat.(70) He noted that the overthrow of the landlords and the capitalists was a relatively easy task. More difficult was the task of abolishing classes and abolishing the difference between the factory worker and the peasant and to make workers of all of them. Classes necessarily remained in the era of the dictatorship of the proletariat; without it, it was not possible for classes to disappear; the proletarian dictatorship would cease to exist only once classes disappeared. By the overthrow of the bourgeoisie the proletariat took the most decisive step towards the abolition of classes. In order to complete the process the proletariat must continue its class struggle, making use of the apparatus of state power and employing various methods of combating, influencing and bringing pressure to bear on the overthrown bourgeoisie and the vacillating petty bourgeoisie.

The collision between the CPSU (b) and the CPY arose in 1948 as Yugoslavia was reluctant to transit to the second stage of people's democracy – socialism. This necessarily required that the state of Yugoslavia exercise the functions of the dictatorship of the proletariat. It is no coincidence that Stalin and Molotov pointed to Bernstein, Vollmar and Bukharin in their correspondence with Tito and Kardelj. Bernstein was identified with the view that socialism would come about through capitalism itself. Vollmar belonged to the right wing of German Social Democracy, who during the development of the party's agrarian programme, defended the interests of the well-to-do peasants and asserted that the *Grossbauern*, the kulaks, could provide support for the socialist restructuring of the countryside. Bukharin had entered into opposition to the party policy of collectivisation of agriculture based on the working peasantry. His understanding was that it was possible to build socialism in the Soviet Union in co-operation with the kulak class; that it was necessary to industrialise on the basis of the kulak market. It became clear that the Yugoslav leadership were hostile to the economic liquidation of the rich peasant bourgeoisie. Even when they felt obliged to collectivise they included the kulaks in the 'collective farms'. This was to become a precedent for the Chinese and the Koreans after 1953. Such was the hostility of the Yugoslav leadership to internationalist socialism that they incarcerated its supporters in concentration camps such as at the notorious Goli Otok. The Cominform in its 1949 resolution concluded that the Yugoslavs had liquidated the People's Democratic system, gone over to the camp of US imperialism; while internally they had established a police state in which the social basis consisted of the kulaks in the countryside and the capitalist elements in the towns; the State sector had ceased to be the people's property as State power was in the hands of the enemies of the people.(71)

In the post Stalin period the question of upholding the dictatorship of the proletariat for building socialism and communism was no longer a desideratum for the majority of the communist and worker's parties holding state power. People's Albania remained an exception to this trend, and it progressed to being the only people's democratic state which established socialism. In general it was not regarded as imperative to distinguish between a socialist state and a democratic one. Khrushchev now referred to not one but a plurality of socialist countries at the Twentieth Congress of the CPSU in 1956. (72) He reversed the understanding of Zhdanov, Stalin and Malenkov of 1947-1952 on this question. In a similar way, Yugoslavia which had liquidated the people's democratic system, was now incorporated into the putative 'socialist camp'. There was now no necessity to demarcate between people's democratic states where there existed a dictatorship of the proletariat and those where state power was still at the stage of the democratic dictatorship of the proletariat and the peasantry. Nor was there now any pressing requirement to complete the collectivisation of agriculture or to socialise the means of production in agriculture to be considered a socialist country. The magnanimous formulations of Khrushchev and the CPSU elevated to the status of 'socialism' the people's democratic states in the west which were in the main in transition to the formation of market economies as well as the people's democracies of the east which declined to fulfil the functions of the dictatorship of the proletariat or economically liquidate national capital and the peasant bourgeoisie. The people's democratic states with felicity embraced the designation that they were now socialist states.

Endnotes

Jose Diaz, 'Organising for the Victory of the Spanish People', 'Communist International', May, 1937. Jose Diaz Archive, www.revolutionarydemocracy.org/https://www.revolutionarydemocracy.org/archive/diaz5-1937.pdf; Jose Diaz, 'Tres Años de Lucha', Ediciones España Popular, México, julio de 1942, 500 pp.

(2) T.V. Volokitina, G.P. Murashko, A.F. Noskova, 'Narodnaya Demokratiya: mif ili real'nost'? obshchestvenno-politicheskiye protsessy v vostochnoi evrope 1944-1948', Moskva, 'Nauka', 1993, C. 3.

(3) Mao Tse-tung, 'The New Stage', Report to the Sixth Enlarged Plenum of the Central Committee of the Communist Party of China, New China Information Committee, Chungking, 1938, pp. 21, 33-4, 42, 49, 50, 55; Interview Given by Mao Tse-tung to Mr. Wang Kung-Tah, Correspondent of the Associated Press, February 1938, in *Revolutionary Democracy,* Vol. XI, No. 2, September 2005; 'The Chinese Revolution and the Chinese Communist Party', December 1939, PPH, Bombay, n.d., 'China's New Democracy', People's Publishing House, Bombay, 3rd Edition, June, 1950, p. 5.

Georgi Dimitrov, 'Political Report of the Central Committee to the V Congress of the Bulgarian Workers' Party (Communists)',19 December, 1948. Georgi Dimitrov Archive. www.revolutionarydemocracy.org

(5) Mao Tse-tung, 'On People's Democratic Dictatorship', Mao Tse-Tung Archive, https://www.revolutionarydemocracy.-org/archive/MaoPPD2.pdf

(6) J. V. Stalin on People's Democracy in China, 22nd February 1950 https://revolutionarydemocracy.org/archive/pdchina.-htm

A. I. Sobolev, People's Democracy, a New Form of Political Organization of Society, Foreign Languages Publishing House, Moscow, 1954. https://www.revolutionarydemocracy.org/archive/sobolev.htm

This section is based on that headed 'Anti-Imperialist, Anti-Feudal Revolutions in Central and South-Eastern Europe'.

A. I. Sobolev, *loc. cit.;* 'Lenin and Stalin on the State Form of Dictatorship of the Proletariat'; D.I. Chesnokov in 'Communist' (Bombay), No. 2, February-March 1950.

A. Sobolev, 'Peoples' Democracy as a Form of Political Organisation of Society', *Bolshevik* No. 19, October, 1951. Printed in *Communist Review*, London, January, 1952, pp. 3-21. https://www.revolutionarydemocracy.org/archive/sobolev2.htm

. A. Zhdanov, The International Situation, Foreign Languages Publishing House, Moscow, 1947, p. 9.

'The Struggle for Peace, National Independence, Working Class Unity', Resolutions and Reports of the Meeting of Information Bureau of Communist and Workers' Parties held in Hungary in November, 1949, p. 2. https://www.revolutionarydemocracy.org/archive/cominform.pdf

G. Malenkov, Report to the Nineteenth Party Congress on the Work of the Central Committee of the C.P.S.U. (B.), October 5, 1952, Foreign Languages Publishing House, Moscow, 1952, p. 7.

https://www.marxists.org/reference/archive/stalin/works/1951/economic-problems/ch06.htm

(14) Malenkov, *op. cit.*, pp. 15-16.

(15) The Soviet-Yugoslav Dispute, Royal Institute for International Relations, London, November 1948, p. 16.

(16) *Ibid.*, p. 42.

(17) *Loc. cit.*

(18) Resolution of the Information Bureau Concerning the Situation in the Communist Party of Yugoslavia, 28th June 1948, *ibid.,* p. 66.

(19) 'Model Statutes of the Agricultural Artel', *Inprecor*, Vol. 15, No. 13, 23rd March, 1935, p. 370.

(20) 'Communist Party of Yugoslavia in the Power of Murderers and Spies', Resolution of the Information Bureau (1949), in 'The Struggle for Peace, National Independence, Working Class Unity', PPH, Bombay, 1950, https://www.revolutionarydemocracy.org/archive/cominform.pdf p. 62.

(21) Petro Rasic, 'Agricultural Development in Yugoslavia', Publicity and Publishing Enterprise Yugoslavija, Beograd, 1955, pp. 43, 46, 47.

(22) Boleslaw Bierut, 'Roots of the Mistakes of the Polish Party Leadership', (1948). *Revolutionary Democracy*, April 2019, pp.135-143; Frantsishek Yuzyak (Vitold), 'The Victory Over the Right-Wing Nationalist Group within the Polish Workers' Party Has Paved the Way Towards the Unity of the Working Class and Socialist Construction', translated from the Russian 'Pol'skaya Robochaya Partiya v borbe za natsionalnoe i sotsialnoe osvobozhdeniye, Moscow 1953, pp. 224-255, in *Revolutionary Democracy,* Vol. XXV, No. 1, October, 2019, pp. 165-191.

(23) 'Document Concerning Right Deviation in Rumanian Workers' Party', Rumanian Workers' Party Publishing House, 1952, in the section on People's Democracy, Rumania, Revolutionary Democracy Archive. https://www.revolutionarydemocracy.org/archive/

(24) J.V. Stalin, 'Five Conversations with Soviet Economists', *Revolutionary Democracy*, Vol. IV, No. 2, September 1998.

(25) 'On People's Democratic Dictatorship', 1st July, 1949, Peking 1950, p. 8. https://www.revolutionarydemocracy.org/archive/MaoPPD2.pdf

(26) *Ibid.*, pp. 6-7.

(27) *Ibid.*, p. 8.

(28) https://www.revolutionarydemocracy.org/archive/-huai.htm

(29) 'First Anniversary of the People's Republic of China', 'For a Lasting Peace, For a People's Democracy', organ of the Communist Information Bureau, September 29, 1950. https://www.revolutionarydemocracy.org/archive/china.htm

(30) 'The Contradiction Between the Working Class and the Bourgeoisie is the Principal Contradiction in China', Selected Works of Mao Tse-tung: Vol. V. https://www.marxists.org/reference/archive/mao/selected-works/volume-5/mswv5_21.-htm

(31) A.I. Sobolev, 1954, *op. cit.* Section headed Anti-Imperialist, Anti-Feudal Revolutions in the East. Emphases added.

(32) Vijay Singh, 'Stalin and the Question of 'Market Socialism' in the Soviet Union After the Second World War', *Revolutionary Democracy,* Vol. 1, No. 1, April 1995.

(33) 'Selected Works of Mao Tse-tung', Vol. V, Peking, 1977, p. 297.

(34) https://www.marxists.org/reference/archive/mao/selected-works/volume-5/mswv5_37.htm

(35) https://www.marxists.org/reference/archive/mao/selected-works/volume-5/mswv5_37.htm

(36) Kuan Ta-tung, 'The Socialist Transformation of Capitalist Industry and Commerce in China', Foreign Languages Press, Peking, 1960, pp. 127-8. Emphasis added.

(37) *Ibid.*, p. 24.

(38) *Ibid.* p. 82.

(39) *Ibid.* p. 56.

Georgi Dimitrov, 'Political Report of the Central Committee to the V Congress of the Bulgarian Workers' Party (Communists)', 19 December 1948. Georgi Dimitrov Archive: www.revolutionarydemocracy.org

(41) K. Marx and F. Engels, 'Selected Works', London, 1968, p. 645.

(42) 'Model Statutes of the Agricultural Artel', *Inprecor*, Vol. 15, No. 13, 23rd March, 1935, p. 370.

(43) Mao Tse-tung, 'Fight for a Fundamental Turn for the Better in the Financial and Economic Situation in China', June 6, 1950, in 'New China' Economic Achievements 1950-1952', Compiled by the China

Committee for the Promotion of International Trade, Foreign Languages Press, Peking, 1952, p. 6.

(44) Chi An, 'Agricultural Cooperation: A Record of Achievement', *People's China,* October, 1956, p. 13.

(45) J.V. Stalin, 'Economic Problems of Socialism in the USSR', Moscow, 1952, p. 101.

(46) G. Malenkov, 'Report to the 19th Congress on the Work of the C.C. of the CPSU (b)', Moscow, 1952, pp. 75-76.

(47) 'History of the CPSU', Moscow, n.d., Second revised edition, p. 670.

(48) Mao Tse-tung, 'A Critique of Soviet Economics', New York, 1977, pp. 144-5.

(48a) N.S. Khrushchov, 'Report of the C.C. of the CPSU to the 20th Party Congress', Moscow, 1956, p. 43.

(49) A. I. Sobolev, *op. cit.*

(50) F. I. Shabshina, 'Korea: After the Second World War', Colonial Peoples' Struggle for Liberation', Reports to the Joint Session of the Scholars' Council of the Institute of Economics and the Pacific Institute of the Academy of Sciences, USSR, devoted to the problems of the national and colonial movement after the Second World War, 1949. Published by People's Publishing House Ltd, Bombay, n.d., pp. 81-2.

(51) Kim Han Gil, 'Modern History of Korea', Foreign Languages Publishing House, Pyongyang, Korea, 1979. pp. 169-184.

(52) *Ibid.*, p. 191.

(53) Kim Byong Sik, 'Modern Korea: the Socialist North, Revolutionary Perspectives in the South and Unification, International Publishers, New York, 1970, p.37.

(54) 'E. Pigulevskaya, Koreyskiye narod v bor'be protiv imperialisticheskikh agressorov', Akademia Nauk SSSR, Institut ekonomi,' 'Uglublenie krisisa kol'onialnoye sistemy imperialism posle mirovoi voiny', Gosizpolit, Moskva, 1953, C.149. *Ibid.* p. 47.

(55) *Ibid.* p. 47.

(56) Kim Il Sung, 'On Juche in Our Revolution', Vol 1, FLPH, Pyongyang, 1975, in 'For the Successful Fulfilment of the First Five-Year Plan', March 6, 1958, p. 215.

(57) *Loc. cit.*

(58) 'On the Questions of the Period of Transition from Capitalism to Socialism and the Dictatorship of the Proletariat', May 25, 1967 in Kim Il Sung, 'Works', Vol. 21, FLPH, Pyongyang, 1985, pp. 228-232.

(59) Kim Byong Sik, *op. cit.* p. 78-79.

(60) *Ibid.*, p. 79.

(61) *Ibid.*, p 47.

(62) Kim Han Gil, *op. cit.* p. 387.

(63) 'Political Economy', A Textbook issued by the Institute of Economics of the Academy of Sciences of the U.S.S.R., (1955 edition), Lawrence and Wishart, London, 1957, p. 524.

(64) Kim Il Sung: 'The Democratic People's Republic is the Banner of Freedom and Independence for Our People...', in: 'Selected Works', Volume 5; Pyongyang; 1975; p. 151.

(65) 'Let Us further Strengthen the Socialist System of Our Country', in: 'Selected Works', Volume 6, Pyongyang; 1975, p. 317.

(66) Kim Han Gil, *op. cit.* pp. 383-5.

(67) 'Kratkiy Economicheskiy Slovar' Moskva, Gosudarstvennoe Izdat'elstvo politicheskoi literatury, 1958., pp. 169-70.

(68) Kim Han Gil, *op. cit.* pp. 243, 332. Kim Il Sung, 'On Juche in Our Revolution', Vol. 1, FLPH, Pyongyang, p. 252.

(69) 'The adored Kim Jong Il'. Official biography of the North Korean leader, Obarrao Publishing House, Milano, 2005, pp. 118-119.

(70) V.I. Lenin, Collected Works, Vol. 30, Progress Publishers, Moscow, Second printing, 1974, pp. 107-117.

(71) 'The Struggle for Peace, National Independence, Working Class Unity', PPH, Bombay, 1950, *op. cit.* p. 49. https://www.revolutionarydemocracy.org/archive/cominform.pdf p. 62.

(72) XX S'ezd, Kommunisticheskoy Partii Sovietskogo Soyuza, Stenograficheskiy otchet, Tom 1, Gosudarstvennoe Izdatelstvo Politicheskoy Literatury, Moskva, 1956, C. 13. Following this A. I Sobolev refers to 'the mighty socialist camp'. See: 'Some Forms of Transition from Capitalism to Socialism', Delhi, 1956. www.revolutionarydemocracy.org/archive/sob1956

	Communist Platform – for the
Italy	Communist Party of the
	Proletariat of Italy

Ecological Crisis, Capitalism and Scientific Socialism

The COP [Climate Change Conference] 26 summit held in Glasgow did not produce any joint agreement on the objectives of reducing greenhouse gases that feed the threat of climate change, on keeping the temperatures of the globe within 1.5° C degrees more than in the pre-industrial era (minimum target of the 2015 Paris Agreement) and on the time to pass from word to deeds. These questions continue to divide imperialist and capitalist countries, beginning with those that are the greater and historically responsible for pollution, because of their enormous economic, geopolitical, economic interests, rivalries and calculations to defend the privileges of a social minority.

Yet the "state of the Earth" leaves no room for hypocritical words, weak and generic commitments, or delays. According to the report of the Intergovernmental Panel on Climate Change (IPCC, a UN scientific forum), entitled "Climate Change 2021 –Its physical-scientific basis"), there are widespread, rapid climate changes that are intensifying with different impacts and modalities in the various regions of the planet. Many of these changes are unprecedented in thousands of years, and some that are already underway – such as the melting of the polar ice caps and the subsequent rise in the sea level – are irreversible over thousands of years.

The report, although drawn up by scientists selected by bourgeois governments, shows that greenhouse gas emissions are responsible for about 1.1° C of warming compared to 1860 and estimates with more than 50% probability that the 1.5° C of warming will be exceeded in the years immediately following 2030, thus in advance of what was estimated in 2018.

As a result, the report states that unless there are immediate, rapid and large-scale reductions in greenhouse gas emissions, the limit of warming by about 1.5° C, or even 2° C, it will be an impossible target.

It should be remembered that with 1.5° C of global warming, an increase in the number of heat waves, longer warm seasons and shorter cold seasons is to be expected. With a global warming of 2°

C, extremes of heat would more often reach critical tolerances for agriculture and health, and the process of climate change would no longer be stoppable.

Temperature is not the only element to consider. For example, climate change is intensifying the water cycle. This leads, in some regions, to heavier rains, hurricanes and floods; in other fragile regions and territories (including our country) it leads to extreme phenomena, drought, floods, landslides, fires, desertification, etc., while a continuous rise in the sea level is expected for coastal areas which will lead to more frequent and severe coastal flooding and coastal erosion. Further warming will intensify the melting of the permafrost, the loss of seasonal snow cover, the melting of glaciers and the polar ice cap, the loss of Arctic sea ice in the summer.

The changes in the oceans, such as warming of waters, more frequent sea heat waves, acidification of the oceans and reduction of oxygen levels in the sea, affect both marine ecosystems and humans that depend on them; these changes will continue at least throughout this century, with longer-term effects, some of which are unpredictable today.

Greenhouse gases and climate stabilization

In the coming decades, climate change is expected to develop in all regions. For the cities, some aspects of climate change can be amplified. These include heat waves (urban areas are usually warmer than their surroundings) and floods due to heavy rainfall and rising sea levels in coastal cities. Among the dramatic consequences of these changes are forced migration and the deleterious effects on human health, as well as the extinctions of thousands of vegetable and animal species.

If global warming continues at the present rate, a large part of the earth's surface (starting with the tropical regions) will become unlivable in a few decades for thousands of millions of human beings.

This is already a serious problem for the populations of the poorest and least equipped countries to face the effects of climate change. The highest price is paid by the peoples who have contributed least to the environmental catastrophe!

Several studies show that in scenarios with higher emissions, the proportion of CO_2 (carbon dioxide) absorbed by the land and ocean is reduced. This means that more CO_2 is emitted into the atmosphere, and the more the natural capacity of absorption is limited. In other words, less is absorbed in proportion to the heating. Air pollution and climate change are two sides of the same coin.

In order to stabilize the climate, society needs strong, rapid and constant reductions in greenhouse gas emissions, to reach CO_2 emissions equal to zero, as well as limiting other greenhouse gases and air pollutants, especially methane that comes from burning fossil fuels, intensive farms and landfills. Strong and steady reductions in emissions of CO_2 and other greenhouse gases (methane and nitrous oxide) can limit climate change, but it could take decades for global temperatures to stabilize. Without immediate, rapid and large-scale reductions in greenhouse gas emissions, it will be impossible to limit warming to 1.5° C.

To better understand the extent of the problem: the lockdowns that occurred in 2020 due to the Covid 19 pandemic produced a 7% reduction in CO_2 emissions globally, a figure that is unprecedented in the last 50 years. However, this was not associated with a reduction in CO_2 concentration and, consequently, no appreciable effect on the planet's temperature occurred. This data confirms that in order to combat global warming, large and sustained reductions in the concentration of CO_2 and other greenhouse gases [this has been repeated several times already] are necessary, up to complete decarbonisation.

Human activities and social relations of production

Scientific evidence reinforces the awareness that human activities are at the basis of the causes of climate change, the most evident expression of the global ecological crisis.

Human beings are a part of nature and cannot live outside of it. Since human beings are social beings, their interaction with nature is determined by social practice.

After the last ice age, about 12 thousand years ago, a relative climatic equilibrium was established, with stable global temperatures, which allowed the spreading out and historical development of the human species.

But in the last three centuries the scale of the economy has become so large, the development of the productive forces so high, the daily activities so harmful – such as the burning of fossil fuels and the consequent CO_2 emissions, the massive use of water, the agriculture and super-intensive livestock that dry up the soils, the destruction of forests, the irrational way in which consumption is induced that produces increasing quantities of waste – that they threaten the fundamental biochemical processes of the planet, affect the geological processes and modify the ecological equilibriums.

In such way climate stability was broken.

The "human activities", starting with the productive ones, do not take place outside society, but within certain social relations of production (with particular forms of ownership of the means of production) which together with the productive forces constitute a mode of production with its fundamental economic laws.

This means that the cause of the current environmental problems lies in the specific socio-economic system which has entered into an antagonistic contradiction with the natural system, causing "an irreparable break in the coherence of social interchange prescribed by the natural laws of life " (Marx, *Capital*, Vol. 3, chap. 47).

From the industrial revolution of the late 1700s to today, the predominant mode of production on the planet has been capitalism. The ruling class, except for a few decades in some socialist countries, is the bourgeoisie, a minority of society that owns the means of production, and the largest part of the socially produced wealth.

Undoubtedly, capitalism and the bourgeoisie are the main culprits of the global ecological crisis. The inability to recognize this historical and social fact characterizes the environmentalists linked to the ruling classes and prevents them from seeing the solution to the problem.

No serious measures to avoid the catastrophe

Can the bourgeoisie slow down and stop climate change by carrying out a massive, coordinated and planned transformation of the entire economic structure, of production, agriculture and consumption, without undermining the conditions of existence of the current mode of production?

Is it possible to continue to hope in the "world leaders" who speak of the ecological crisis from summit to summit while remaining in fact immobile or proposing unrealizable or insane solutions that serve only to secure the existence of capitalism and the bourgeoisie as the ruling class?

The answers are there for everyone to see. Means and measures to avoid the ecological catastrophe are not taken because their implementation would prejudice the profits of a handful of omnipotent capitalist monopolies. As a result, climate change proceeds with increasingly serious consequences: 2021 is ranked in second place for the highest increase in emissions ever recorded.

The vague commitment to "zero emissions around the middle of the century" and the maximum temperature increase set within 2 degrees, contained in the final declaration of the G-20, are a death knell for residual climatic equilibriums.

According to the Climate Action Tracker, with the commitments to decarbonisation made by the States participating in the COP26 in Glasgow, by 2030 greenhouse gas emissions will be double those needed to stay within 1.5 degrees of warming, and the increase in temperatures by 2100 will be 2.4 degrees.

The voracious interests of States and monopolies (such as those of oil), the unhealable contradictions between imperialist and capitalist countries (in particular between USA and China that are fighting for hegemony), between imperialism and the dependent countries that are suffering the most from the consequences of climate change, prevent the adoption of urgent and effective measures to prevent the catastrophe.

In the joint declarations between imperialist powers, such as the one recently signed between the US and China on the climate, strategic and geopolitical reasons are predominant. Behind the so-called "green turn" there are the interests of the monopolies to renew constant capital and crush their competitors with new forms of protectionism, as well as to renew the market for individual and business consumption.

The international summits convened by the imperialists are meant to convince the peoples that the solution of the problems depends on the great powers and their agreements. But the "masters of the world" are interested in maintaining the system based on the private ownership of the means of production and obtaining the maximum profit at any cost and in the shortest possible time. On the other hand, the anarchy inherent in capitalism prevents any planned action.

The effect of the "Green Deal" will not be the overcoming of the environmental crisis, but the redefinition of relations between great powers, in particular for the availability of the energy supply system.

The result: capitalism will continue to destroy the environment, work, health, placing the consequences of its crises on the shoulders of the workers and peoples.

Environmental conditions will therefore worsen in the coming years, bringing humanity closer to the ecological precipice, after which all the processes of climate and environmental change will become irreversible and disastrous.

Capitalist accumulation and nature

The question to ask is: what is the underlying reason why capitalism cannot stop the destructive course of the ecological crisis?

It is not a moral problem, of "good" and "bad" capitalism. The problem is that the fundamental laws of capitalism prevent it, entering into conflict with the laws of nature; like the general law of capitalist accumulation, discovered by Marx, which derives from the very development of capitalism.

This law, besides causing the impoverishment of the proletariat and the enrichment of the bourgeoisie, with its incessant rush to amass ever greater capital (which requires greater consumption of energy, raw materials and generates ever greater waste), determines the progressive and unstoppable degradation of the environment under capitalism.

Capital is nothing more than value that must be self-valued on an unlimited scale through the exploitation of human beings and nature.

Capitalism cannot survive without the ever-expanding reproduction of capitalist relations. Hence the increase of the proletariat and capitalists on the one hand; the extension of the exploitation and increase in the production of commodities that incorporate value and surplus-value on the other hand; consequently, increasing emissions into the atmosphere and release of waste into the environment. The mechanisms of competition and capitalist accumulation cause the increase of the different material elements of capital, including the mass of means of labor, the raw materials to be consumed and commodities to be sold. Therefore, the more capitalist accumulation increases, the more the ecological space of the human species is reduced.

Capital does not care if the production process and the sales of commodities have harmful consequences for human beings and nature. What matters are not human needs and the natural equilibrium, but the growth of capital itself, or the "accumulation for the sake of accumulation" (Marx), the condition of existence of capitalism itself.

Without indefinite expansion, the capitalist system cannot survive. Zero growth, stagnation or decrease in growth are in contradiction with the laws of this mode of production. The economic crises are in fact only a moment of the capitalist cycle that must renew itself in the long run. But if the tendency of capital is to unlimited expansion, the Earth is limited, it has finite resources and delicate ecological balances. From this it follows that there can be no sustainable capitalist development.

Capitalism in its monopoly stage is an unsustainable system for mankind and nature. The failure of COP26 indisputably proves that any attempt to make capitalism "ecological" is made impossible by the nature of this system, by its fundamental laws. The only way to stop climate change is to overthrow capitalism.

The ecological crisis aggravates the general crisis of capitalism

The unbridled rush of capitalist accumulation has led to a deep ecological crisis, whose main phenomenon is climate change, with all its destructive consequences.

The ecological crisis is a multidimensional aspect of the general crisis of the capitalist system, which overlaps and intertwines with its other aspects: economic, political, ideological, social, energetic, military, health, cultural, moral, etc.

The general crisis of capitalism, which embraces an entire historical period, expresses the ever more advanced decomposition of this world system which has exhausted its historical role.

Every aspect and phenomenon of the general crisis of capitalism is interdependent and reacts on the other aspects (e.g., climate change, as well as the pandemic, aggravate economic crises), which intersect and condition each other, aggravating the general crisis itself.

The contradiction between the capitalist-imperialist system and nature are worsening together with the other fundamental contradictions of the epoch.

Today's world has entered a prolonged period of deep economic crises, political instability, environmental devastation, cultural decay, health emergencies, rampant corruption, and intense imperialist struggle for a re-division of the world and spheres of influence.

The increase in military spending and the arms race, the tendency to lead the economy onto the war path, determined by the worsening of the inter-imperialist contradictions, constitute a further threat to the biosphere and the future of mankind, due to the destructive force of the enormous arsenals of war and the exploitation of mineral resources and raw materials, of enormous energy capacities used to produce means of mass destruction.

The large military bases of the imperialist and capitalist countries, the continuous military exercises, the "demonstrative" use of conventional, chemical, bacteriological and nuclear weapons and the ongoing wars are producing serious pollution and increasingly harmful consequences for the biosphere and the peoples.

The working class and peoples are forced to fight against the bourgeoisie on all fronts, including the struggle for the protection of the environment, to defend their living and working conditions, to emancipate themselves from wage slavery.

It is increasingly difficult to separate the struggles that are developing on one front from those that are developing on the other fronts. The convergence of the struggles is produced by the closer interrelation between the different aspects of the general crisis of capitalism. For example, the intensive exploitation of labor power and the destruction of the environment go hand in hand.

This means greater possibility for the working class to forge alliances under its leadership with the popular strata that are involved in the struggle against capital.

The ecological crisis thus provides an objective ground for the development of the class struggle on a world level, both in the imperialist countries and in the plundered and oppressed dependent ones.

The bourgeoisie is aware of this dynamic and therefore acts to calm the masses with the "ecological transition", diverting the movements of struggle onto the dead end of petty bourgeois ecologism, which does not raise any social question and has no other political strategy than the illusory appeals to bourgeois leaders.

Despite the efforts of the ruling class to maintain its rule and avoid mass revolts by adopting the strategy of the "green, digital, sustainable and inclusive revolution", in the coming decades it will be the class struggle that determines how the general crisis of capitalism and with it the ecological crisis will be resolved.

Future scenarios

The class struggle does not develop under conditions that we desire but in those historically given. The analysis of reality tells us that we are at the beginning of a phase of the sharpening of class antagonisms, of economic, social and environmental upheavals.

What are the possible scenarios for the next decades?

a) The many-sided crisis will lead to a new accumulation and concentration of capital and the bourgeoisie will be able to maintain its power by preventing social revolution; in this case the socio-environmental catastrophe will be inevitable and with it "the common ruin of the contending classes" (Marx, Engels, *Manifesto*).

b) The exacerbation of all existing contradictions will lead to the world proletarian revolution to eliminate the rule of the bourgeoisie: this is a process that will not be simultaneous, but will mean the progressive detachment of the weak links from the imperialist chain, made more rapid by the maturation of objective conditions in the totality of the system.

This will pave the way for the victory of socialism first in some countries, or initially in one country, that will awaken and hasten the revolution in all countries, to move to a complete economic restructuring that will ensure the basic needs of the workers, with high technological development and high productivity of social labor determined by the material relations between labor and renewable resources.

Only scientific socialism will be able to achieve a conscious organization of social production in which the material exchange between human beings and nature will be rationally regulated.

To implement this regulation and reach climatic stabilization "requires a complete revolution in our hitherto existing mode of production, and with it of our whole contemporary social order." (Engels, *Dialectic of Nature*).

In socialist society, well-being will not be measured by consumerism, but by the social and environmental quality of the processes of production and of the goods socially produced; by their use value in terms of satisfying the real and fundamental needs of the working masses, eliminating waste and luxury; by reducing the amount of energy needed to produce the goods; by the sharp reduction in working hours, guaranteed employment, free and high-quality social and health services, poly-technical and humanist education, early and dignified pensions and safety at work; by less pollution, traffic and stress; by libraries, cinemas, theaters, science, art, sport and mass recreation; by the total protection of the environment and cultural heritage, etc.

The new socialist societies that will arise will have to solve problems that the first experiences of socialism did not face, or faced in a different way, due to the high cost that capitalism will leave on the environmental level. They will have to create the necessary social structure within which workers can unite and mobilize their forces to avoid environmental catastrophe.

Depending on the environmental conditions that will exist when the new social order will be established, we cannot exclude a period of drastic and rapid socio-economic measures with a decisive, sustained and socially just reduction in emissions of CO_2 and other greenhouse gases, campaigns of labor on various fronts (industrial, agricultural, hydro-geological, forestry, marine, etc.) and severe sanctions for the ravagers of nature, aimed at avoiding the worst, including for generations to come.

However, we cannot discard the hypothesis that "the movement that abolishes the present state of things" will delay its development and socialism on a global scale will triumph in a period in which ecological degradation will be completely irreversible and there will be great environmental catastrophes and a quantitative reduction of mankind. Its task will then be to adapt society to the effects of climate change, for a long time carrying out strong and profound transformations of the model of production and consumption, raising technology to the maximum, coordinating efforts at a planetary level, strengthening solidarity between the peoples and safeguarding the best and most important achievements of human civilization.

In this respect, scientific socialism will be the evolutionary novelty of our species.

The ruling class cannot "rewrite history" and it is not in a position to restore the ecological equilibrium it has broken.

It is therefore a question of writing a new history, within a different and superior social order that has at its center the real well-being of the workers and is able to achieve a rational regulation between human society and nature.

The proletariat, the class alienated from nature and its own labor, always fighting against harmful conditions in the workplace and in the territory, is the only class that can lead humanity to the overthrow of capitalism and the construction of socialism, seizing political power as soon as possible and carrying out its world dictatorship, its program of struggle for communism.

January 2022

Mexico	Communist Party of Mexico (Marxist-Leninist)

The Struggle of the Masses towards Their Sovietization, A Task on the Order of the Day

* The Soviets, A Historical Experience

The soviets, assemblies of workers, peasants and soldiers, also known as Workers' Councils, were an experience born in the struggle of the proletariat in Russia in the revolution of 1905. They were essential for the triumph of the October Revolution of 1917. The soviets became part of the building of scientific socialism, of the functioning of the State of the proletariat with the participation and effective leadership of the proletarian masses. The soviets were the form adopted by the dictatorship of the proletariat to maintain the political and economic power of the workers and poor peasants over the means of production expropriated from the bourgeoisie and to develop production for their collective benefit.

The assembly or soviet, the form of struggle adopted by the working masses, were the most democratic and revolutionary form to resolve their needs and aspirations, where decision-making was analyzed, discussed and organized, first against the Government of the Tsar Nicholas and later against the provisional revolutionary government led by Kerensky.

The soviets functioned on the principle of democratic centralism, which guaranteed the participation of all workers; from the bottom up and the top down. Once the issues were analyzed, discussed and defined, decisions were made that represented the interest of the majority, of the collective established in assemblies.

The soviet was the most advanced expression of the proletarian class, the action of the immense majority that established an identity with its interests. It was and is the result of the daily struggle of the masses and was developed as a fundamental form of organization, decision-making and mobilization of a people in arms, to confront and defeat their enemy, and to exercise the power of the majority. It was not an invention of the Bolsheviks; they systematized it and deepened it, and Marxism-Leninism used it as a guide, enhancing its operation and defending it.

The assemblies of the masses of the Russian proletariat and of other nations, their active and decisive participation, allowed the first socialist power in the world to be set in motion and founded the Union of Soviet Socialist Republics, based on the unity of interests of the class of proletarians. In each nation there was a soviet from which a head of state or president was chosen. From all these assemblies sprang the Supreme Soviet, that is, a true representation from below that led to the Council of People's Commissars. That body, converted into will, made it possible to show that scientific socialism is the higher form and content of socialism, following immediately after capitalism, whose development is achieved with unexploited laboOr, cooperation, solidarity and common benefit.

The Soviet Union, as its name indicates, was a union of assemblies, of councils, a power based on the unity of the assemblies of the workers, poor peasants and soldiers. It represented and was the real power of the proletariat, which modern revisionism later deformed and degenerated. to reestablish capitalism.

* Importance and Relevance of the Soviets

It seems necessary to us to raise the importance and relevance of the soviets, because this practice of the Russian proletarian masses and of other nationalities that formed the USSR, who developed it, left teachings that must be rescued and enriched:

1. They are assemblies, broad meetings where the vast majority of the population participates. They do so in an organized manner from their workplace and/or association of their productive activity and the place where they live.
2. It is a permanent democratic collective formation that works from the bottom up and the top down. Here the individual and the collective coexist and interrelate, subordinating the individual to the conscious collective and individualism to collectivism. That is, each individual represents the synthesis of the collective and the collective to the individual.
3. The assembly is a form of organization and collective participation that is being perfected more and more, where the problems and their solutions begin to be resolved from the base committee to the higher structure, through a process of analysis, discussion and decision-making that favor the majority and that are carried out.
4. It becomes the form of government, in which the power is in the hands of the majority (a power that rests on the control and

leadership of the means and instruments of production in the hands of the workers).

5. The assembly is a gain and is exercised through its daily practice. This is opposed to caudillismo, presidentialism and other forms of bourgeois and petty-bourgeois individualism.

6. The representatives, chiefs or leaders, are elected in these base committees, factory assemblies, workplaces and associations and have a temporary and specific function that is carried out without profit. They only receive salaries based on the average salary of the working population.

7. The highest office is chosen and exercised by conviction, disposition, will, degree of responsibility, honesty, ranking of offices held and experience, who represents the interest of the collective and is an expression of the will of the majority.

8. The offices are assigned and exercised without distinction between women and men; without religious or cultural distinction and even less by the color of one's skin. There is no discrimination and they can be recalled.

9. Women and men are trained and educated to serve, hold office and not take advantage of them, as the community or collective demands; These offices are accounted for in an open and permanent manner.

10. Women hold positions of responsibility and leadership, from the base to the higher structure.

11. Power and government are given to the collective, not to individuals; these only represent it as long as the organized collective determines.

12. The soviet or assembly is an exercise of democratic and revolutionary dictatorship of the majority of the working class, which guarantees the defense of the interests of this working majority, of its possession of the means and instruments of production and its permanence in power. It is a body that favors education based on unexploited labor, on the socialization of production and collective appropriation of wealth, which is also supported by peaceful or violent force against the remnants of capitalism.

13. The soviet or workers' assembly is the organ of insurrection, of the exercise of revolutionary class violence; it is the people in arms, to guarantee or preserve the interests of the majority above the parasitic minority.

These are some basic elements that were developed and that in general some movements, classes, class sectors and indigenous communities experienced and practiced, as a result of their historical past or their context of class struggle.

This broad expression of the masses or assemblies is as old as the existence of human beings living in society, which evolved in the primitive community and receded with its disappearance, that is, with the appearance of private property. Now, as a result of private property, the result of the contradiction between the social production of wealth and its private appropriation, they re-emerge and adopt other forms that will develop with the appearance and functioning of collective property. These assemblies with the soviets and under socialism reached a higher level of development, which finally did not continue because of the degeneration caused by revisionism after Stalin's death.

* Contemporary Struggles in Mexico That Have Adopted the Form of the Assembly Similar to the Soviet Form

For us it is important and necessary to bear in mind the experience of the soviets in the USSR, as well as the experience of the movements in our country, where assemblies or councils have developed naturally or through learning from the experiences of others. The various contemporary struggles in Mexico where assemblies have been developed have not reached the level achieved by the soviets of the USSR; however, they have had the same basic principle of functioning and organization. In this regard, we will present some examples that have taken place or are currently functioning with those elements that must be studied in depth in order to develop them into soviets.

The CRAC-PC (RCCA-CP)

This arose in 1995, from the initiative of several communities to confront the violence of delinquency or paramilitarism. The Regional Coordinator of Community Authorities – Community Police (CRAC-PC for its initials in Spanish) is made up of indigenous communities from the state of Guerrero, which came together and created a Community System of Security, Justice and Reeducation of detainees through community work, without the intervention of lawyers.

They are organized in houses of justice and liaison committees, and their representatives attend the general assembly. The houses of justice have the objective of guaranteeing security and the administration of justice; they aim to reeducate those who have committed crimes through community work. San Luis Acatlán, Espino Blanco, El Paraíso, Zitlaltepec and De Las Juntas Caxitepec are some of the little more than 200 communities that function with a regional assembly as the highest decision-making body.

The houses of justice are made up of three coordinators (judges) who administer justice according to their jurisdiction. They have a certain number of commanders and their respective community police (these exercise vigilance and arrests of those who harm community or collective interests).

The highest governing body is the regional assembly, made up of coordinators, commanders, commissioners and delegates.

This experience continues with difficulty; the paramilitaries, the local and national agrarian bourgeoisie are continuing to act directly against the CRAC-PC in order to eliminate it, since it hinders bourgeois control, exercising autonomy and its own democratic government by the peasant-indigenous masses themselves.

The experience of the Zapatistas of the EZLN (ZANL)

They became publicly known in 1994, when the Zapatista Army of National Liberation (EZLN) rose up in arms. They are a political-military organization concentrated in the state of Chiapas, which from its origin developed the autonomy of the communities where they have a presence; autonomy with respect to the Mexican bourgeois state, organizationally, politically and economically. In 2003 they began to expand and with them formed the Zapatista rebel autonomous municipalities that gave rise to the Good Government Boards (JBG), which are the representation of each autonomous municipality. Each municipality brings together communities that form the Autonomous Councils, which in turn are part of each Caracol [a conch shell, regional organization of autonomous communities – *translator's note*], whose members are rotated and recallable as decided by the assemblies. This organizational structure is directed by the Clandestine Revolutionary Indigenous Committee – General Command of the EZLN, which is governed by the principle of commanding by obeying.

This political and organizational form attends to, monitors, develops and directs its internal life and its relations with the outside; it is different or separated from the political-military form of the EZLN, because the former is civilian, but under the political-ideological leadership of the EZLN. The EZLN states that it exists as an army to defend, not to govern.

The organizational base of this democratic exercise from below is based on the popular indigenous system that they were building. This building takes into account not only local and national coordination but international coordination as well, because they are understood as a global inclusive process of the indigenous and the non-indigenous.

The territories where they govern have reduced or eliminated the trafficking of drugs, arms and wood; they control alcohol and other basic consumer commodities and relations between people, communities and municipalities; they govern on the basis of reason and understanding, meeting the needs of the majority. It is also supported by an educational program called: "Organization for the New Indigenous Autonomous Education for Peace and Humanity", where Production, Political Education, Art Education, Culture, Literacy, Health, Sports, Mathematics, History and Languages (Spanish and mother tongues) are studied.

The Zapatistas are an expression of autonomy that functions on the basis of consultation, on collective civil decisions related to the military.

APPO

The Popular Assembly of the Peoples of Oaxaca (APPO) emerged in 2006, triggered by the repression of the state government against the democratic teachers of Section 22 of the National Coordinator of Education Workers (CNTE) of the National Union of Education Workers (SNTE), the official body of the teachers' union.

The response of the teachers to the repression due to their eviction by the state government of the PRI was to call on the Oaxacan people to retake the Zocalo and remove the riot police who had occupied it. This objective was achieved due to the broad popular participation that joined the action of the teachers.

Once the Zocalo was retaken, the plantón [officially a sit-in, but one in which people set up tents for protestors with signs explaining their demands – *translator's note*] was reestablished but now with the participation of other working masses, who were immediately called upon to provide organization, continuity and expansion of what had begun as a struggle of the teachers but went beyond that and became a teachers' and popular struggle against repression, for the departure of the state governor and other democratic changes in the state. A mass assembly was called of the representatives and organizations that were involved and coincided in that need. The action itself led to the formation of APPO, which became the highest authority of the popular movement and de facto governed the state for approximately six months.

The formation of APPO led to a change in the state movement that developed a broad unity and raised its forms of struggle and organization. APPO synthesized the demands of the masses and particularly the demand for the removal of the governor in office. From the plenary assembly came the organization of assemblies in other places in Oaxaca and in different class sectors, as the basic forms of functioning, representation and decision-making that would emanate from the bottom up and the top down, all subordinated to the general assembly that met periodically.

The APPO organization exceeded the importance of the governor and his government, who was forced to flee the capital and try to rule from another place; this came about from the movement's rejection of him and the demand for his resignation. The state Chamber of Deputies was also made powerless; it could not legislate because it was overtaken by the popular movement and it was also rejected because it was on the side of the governor.

The repression that the governor unleashed against the movement as a whole, since the beginning of his term led to its unity in

confronting him, but it was the violent eviction of the teachers from their plantón that accelerated the broad process of the masses and the formation of APPO.

APPO was a popular uprising whose rejection of the governor and his government changed it, in fact, into a form of parallel popular government, which for just over six months acted like a commune, like a soviet. The economy was paralyzed and there was practically a general strike in the state, so the local bourgeoisie was forced to negotiate a solution to the conflict with APPO, worried about its economic losses.

The masses built barricades located mainly in the city, later organized by APPO, in order to repel the attack of the bourgeoisie and its State. The takeover of public radio stations served as a tribune and a means of propaganda to organize and guide the masses in the struggle.

APPO exercised its government from the state capital; it did not occupy the few existing factories, nor did it expropriate land. Its government did not spread, nor did it consolidate its control throughout the state; it neutralized the army of the military region, but it did not incorporate it to form part of it.

APPO did not have the perspective of a revolutionary or socialist struggle, and our Marxist-Leninist party was not strong enough to bring to it the perspective of the proletarian revolution. The working class was not organized as such and its diminished role in the struggle also influenced its inability to develop the worker-peasant alliance.

Finally, the violence of the financial oligarchy and its State defeated APPO with an action that exceeded its immediate and medium-term ability to respond; its force was weakened until it disappeared.

APPO was a popular uprising, an exercise in popular-democratic government, a commune, and close to a soviet. It was based on the general assembly as the highest decision-making, governing and organizational body. It was one of the great experiences of struggle not only of the Oaxacan people, but of the whole country. We Marxist-Leninists were a leading part of it, but our limitations did not let us deepen it and turn it into a soviet.

The town of San Francisco Cherán, Michoacán

Cherán is an indigenous community located in the Purépecha Plateau of the state of Michoacán, as the municipality is also called.

Its main activity is agriculture and it manufactures shoes. It has a population of just over 16 thousand inhabitants. A large part of its population has emigrated to other places, due to poverty, unemployment and lately the violence unleashed by paramilitaries dedicated to drug trafficking.

The illegal exploitation of its forests, the assassinations and frequent disappearances of residents of Cherán by criminals, with the complicity of the municipal, state and federal authorities, forced the population to confront them. In 2011 this situation exploded with a response by the population, led by women, who repelled the attack of the illegal forest loggers, who are criminals; this induced the rest of the population to stop their actions. This response of the population led to the organization and participation of the majority in vigilance committees, security patrols, barricades and checkpoints to control people who enter or leave the municipality. From this urgent action, the town assembly was organized, in fact surpassing the formal municipal authority; this was also rejected because it had been involved with crime.

The Cherán town assembly appointed new authorities, organized self-defense and community security; it expelled the bourgeois parties from the municipality, prevented the return of criminals to the community and the participation of the state and federal authority in the protection of the criminals. It prevented any interference in the organizational, political and economic decisions that were being adopted to develop a functioning democratic government, making decisions from the bottom up and the top down.

The pressures of the paramilitary-criminals, political and economic pressures of the bourgeois institutions, legal and illegal, sought to reject this form of popular assembly democracy and make it fail.

Here the people in arms prevailed and established an open and effective form of organization and participation, which is sustained by the real involvement of the majority of the population. They have established a government and a democracy emanating from the popular will, represented by people who sum up the true interests of the people, who have authority over them to represent them. The salaries of the officials or representatives of the people, like the offices, are defined by the conviction of service to the people, by the responsibility of looking after the collective interests of the entire community, by trust and experience in the tasks of the community. This government, essentially ruled by the people's assembly, ordered and collectivized the various productive, commercial, transportation activities, etc., which are decided on and supervised for the collective use of the population.

From 2011 to date, Cherán has been a living example of how assembly life can be built and sustained, how without declaring or defining it, they are close to the soviet form of organization, participation and political leadership.

Its organizational structure is made up of a Major Council (12 people) and indigenous councils (made up of 3 people per neighborhood), also ruled by the system of functions. Only people with social prestige can join the Major Council, based on honesty, service, disposition and interests of the population and the decision to defend the collective interests of the community, above private or individual interests. Everyone is accountable for their responsibility and the offices also include the participation of women.

The highest authority is the community assembly, where men and women participate, community members have the right to speak and vote, with personal and direct representation. The Major Council is the governing body in between assemblies, which executes agreements and monitors their compliance for three years and can be removed from office if so decided by the community assembly, which in turn depends on the neighborhood community assemblies.

The changes in the system of government from the previous one to this one were approved by all the peoples and they continue to support it.

The women who started the movement that led to the assembly government have little participation in the offices, but they are not excluded from them.

The majority of the working people of Cherán, organized and conscious, define the course of their existence, outside of the bourgeois institutions, advancing in a situation where these institutions are seeking to weaken and eliminate it, limiting and preventing its expansion. But it seeks to serve as amodel of good government and the power of the people that needs to be expanded and strengthened in more communities and also in large cities, as a means for the democratic and revolutionary transformation of society as a whole. Its defense and strengthening are necessary because the siege and attacks do not stop.

Another case, Ayutla de los Libres

Ayutla de los Libres is a town located in the state of Guerrero. It is heterogeneous in composition, and different indigenous peoples converge and coexist in the same territory. Since 2017, it took them three years to formalize and exercise it, they have developed a government of uses and customs, an assembly, where the participation of bourgeois and petty-bourgeois parties was prohibited and they have been recognized institutionally.

Here the process was conceived as a movement against the corruption of the municipal authorities and the political parties that represented them, as well as against insecurity and violence. Therefore, they promoted and achieved a change in the government system, in which there was an internal resistance led mainly by the political parties that represent the interests of the local bourgeois bosses.

This process of democratic government through an assembly of the people, is given by recognizing the representation of indigenous languages and culture in the governing body. The change of the government system was by the majority, with resistance from the caciques, the local bourgeoisie, the paramilitaries and the federal government. The population was divided; however this process is continuing its course, where the majority is imposing itself against strong resistance from the parties of the bourgeoisie in the community, the local and national bourgeoisie.

The growth of violence, which was one of the causes of the movement, has slowed down, but it haunts the periphery of the community or communities where paramilitarism has penetrated or where they are controlled by the parties of the state bourgeoisie.

Other examples in Oaxaca

Most of the communities in the state of Oaxaca are governed by indigenous uses and customs formally recognized at the state and national levels. Of the 570 municipalities, 427 are governed by the electoral system, by political parties of the bourgeoisie.

Constitutionally, uses and customs or customary practices are recognized at the local and national levels, where there are indigenous communities. However, that is not a guarantee that they will be carried out and respected.

It is assumed that the uses and customs are a different form of government, democratic, officially recognized at the national and state levels. These are based on the election of their authorities through assemblies by show of hands or ballot box; they are elected.

Much of these uses and customs are tainted by the participation of political parties of the financial oligarchy or the petty bourgeoisie, who use the community assemblies to continue degrading these processes and maintain their positions as caciques. They distribute money, alcohol, use official programs and even threats to impose themselves. In Oaxaca, few community assemblies have a truly democratic function.

In indigenous communities where uses and customs are applied, that is, through town assemblies without being tainted by bourgeois parties or local or state caciques, or despite them, the government system is different, officially recognized and implemented. The government and the offices that exist in the communities are exercised through service in positions, without payment, demanding and embodying responsibility, honorability and experience. They are elected through a show of hands or direct and secret ballot. Some examples of those indigenous communities of Oaxaca that exercise the democracy of the masses are the municipalities of Río de las Peñas, Municipality of Putla, Tiltepec, Nochixtlán; Santo Tomás Ocotepec, in the Mixteca and Santa María, Yucuti, among others. Although these are small towns, they are examples of the practices that we need to expand, apply, develop and defend there.

Other movements with assembly experiences

In the country, in these times, more struggles have developed and will continue to develop that adopt assemblies as essential mechanisms or methods of participation, discussion, decision-making and organization.

Thus, we have had notable movements such as the 1999 student strike, led by the General Strike Council at the National Autonomous University of Mexico (UNAM), which lasted almost 10 months. It was repressed by the army with the seizure of the UNAM. The Strike Council managed to undo the reforms that sought to increase school fees, reduce student enrollment through exams and registration, etc., which were part of the neoliberal measures in education in general and higher education in particular. In this, the role of unity, the decisions of the assembly were decisive in achieving their demands. The street mobilization and the organization oriented by the assemblies achieved part of the demands raised.

In 2006, the mining workers of the Lázaro Cárdenas-Las Truchas Municipality, Michoacán, rose up in the face of the repression exerted by the State to end the strike they had undertaken against the steel company. This struggle became a worker-popular uprising since some of the residents of the municipality also participated. The company violated the collective agreement of section 271 of the National Miners' Union, ignored the leaders of that section, which were democratically elected in their assemblies, and violated the right of association. The violence by the army and the state police caused two deaths and several injuries. The workers and people responded by defending themselves, developing a heroic resistance of just over 10 hours, which made the repressive force withdraw. This prevented the objective of the capitalists, extending the strike for more than five months, winning a salary increase of 40% and 100% of lost wages.

The agricultural workers of the San Quintín Valley, in Baja California, are another remarkable movement that broke out in a strike in 2017, against the capitalists in the countryside. Their assemblies stopped production for two months until their main demands were resolved. The day laborers produce fruit and vegetables for the United States; approximately 70,000 workers in these fields stopped work. Immediately the violence of the State tried to destroy this legitimate and just movement that demanded the most basic rights, better working conditions, social security, salary increase and new union representation, which gave rise to its new National Democratic Independent Union of Agricultural Workers. Although many of the demands were won, the bosses have not complied with all of them and continue to violate the gains obtained.

Other struggles exist in the history of the class struggle, which have shown the ups and downs of these movements for the future of the exploited and oppressed. In this sense, we emphasize the resistance of the Mexican Union of Electricians, who fought and are continuing to fight against the unfair and arbitrary dismissals carried out by the Mexican State represented by Felipe Calderón Hinojosa. More than 44 thousand workers were violently dismissed, using the army, from the company Luz y Fuerza del Centro, as part of the privatization. The workers are still fighting to get their jobs back.

The National Coordinator of Education Workers is another great contingent of struggle that preserves the democratic and assembly organizational forms that have allowed it to win important demands. It is still one of the most active and lasting unions in the country that have triggered teachers' and popular struggles. at the national level and in the states where they have a strong presence.

* The Need for Soviets as a Form of Struggle for Proletarian Emancipation

Proposing to apply and develop soviets in the current process of mass struggle in our country, such as what developed in the USSR, is not a mechanical transfer of that experience to the present situation. It is the need to develop this form of elemental and universal exercise of direct democracy and mass assembly in order to resolve their immediate, long-term and definitive liberation needs. A Soviet government and power begins with these elementary assembly and organizational forms under democratic centralism that can be developed, adopted and adapted according to the concrete conditions of power and government.

The people's assembly is the basic and fundamental path for the establishment of the soviets, for their propagandization and implementation where the masses confront the bourgeoisie and imperialism. The soviets are a central element of scientific socialism, of Marxism-Leninism that can be developed by raising the consciousness of the masses. The right to independence and free self-determination of peoples is a requirement for unity with others, on the basis of the interests of the exploited and oppressed, in order to build the unity and voluntary integration of peoples with respect for the sovereignty of the collective, where autonomy is used not to divide, but to promote the unity and brotherhood of peoples.

Where the contradiction between capital and labor governs the development of society, it is necessary to build the soviets as the solution in the proletarian perspective, where the working class, poor peasants and soldiers establish the government and the power of the people, politically but also economically, with the control and direction of the means and instruments of production.

It is in this sense that we propose the formation of the Assembly of the Proletariat and Peoples of Mexico as the form of sovietization of the struggle of the masses, as part of the Marxist-Leninist tactics and strategy.

March 2022

Morocco	Democratic Way

The Situation in Morocco

The situation in Morocco is essentially characterized as follows:
• On the economic and social level:
The crisis of the dependent and rentier economy aggravated by the pandemic and due to the continuation of neoliberal policies despite their failure and the drought.

Serious social repercussions: pauperization, endemic unemployment, increasing precariousness of the working masses and part of the middle classes, further dismantling of public social services, in particular education and health. Young people from the working classes are the most affected.
• On the political level:

1. The regime:

Increased despotism and tightening of the police grip under the pretext of fighting the pandemic.

Increased dependence on imperialism, especially U.S. imperialism, reflected, among other things, in the normalization of relations with the Zionist entity, joint military maneuvers and total alignment with the positions of Western imperialism.

Attempts by the regime to overcome the economic crisis through anti-popular measures (austerity to the detriment of the working classes and benefits of all kinds to the bloc of ruling classes, consequent increases in the prices of basic commodities and energy), the super-exploitation of the working class, the generalization of precariousness and the opening of investment opportunities for Moroccan monopoly capital in Africa.

The search for social peace at the expense of the working class and the toiling masses by using the question of the Western Sahara, by elaborating a so-called alternative development model which is, essentially, nothing more than a rehash of the stale recipes of the imperialist economic and monetary institutions, by organizing elections boycotted by the overwhelming majority of the Moroccan people, who have understood that the institutions that emerged from them have no real power that could have a beneficial effect on their situation, and by maintaining the illusion of social dialogue with the unions and of total social protection.

2. Political and social forces:

The right-wing and social-democratic forces are integrated into the system and merely decorate the political scene.

The left-wing forces are weak, divided and weakly rooted in the people.

The left, which is betting on the elections, is in crisis and its attempts at unification failed on the eve of the legislative elections of September 8, 2021, where its results were catastrophic.

The Marxist left is divided, but it is present in the majority of the popular struggles.

The Islamist movement has experienced a resounding failure during the last elections, with its Justice and Development Party and its opportunist line of tailing the regime-. This will further widen the gap between it and the more radical Justice and Benevolence organization in its opposition to the current regime.

The trade union movement suffers from a low rate of unionization, its fragmentation (more than 20 federations) and bureaucracies.

The Amazigh [Berber – *translator's note*] movement is characterized by the weakness of the democratic current within it.

The human rights movement is relatively developed and active. But the human rights organizations, in particular the Moroccan Association for Human Rights, which has the most consistent line and is the most established and the most combative in Morocco, are the target of increasingly aggressive attacks by the regime.

The class struggle is currently characterized, for the most part, by the struggle of marginalized regions (the Rif, Jerada, [Berber region of northern Morocco, region of northeast Morocco, respectively – *translator's note*] etc.) for economic and social demands, the struggle of social sectors (teachers under contract, medical students, etc.). These struggles were violently repressed. The workers' struggles are limited and purely defensive and solidarity is often lacking, even within the same sector.

3. Democratic Way:

Democratic Way is focusing its efforts on advancing four intimately linked and interdependent processes:

3.1. The process of building the party of the proletariat:

We consider this process to be the most important and decisive.

Within this framework, we give top priority to preparing the conditions for the announcement of the creation of the party of the proletariat at our next national congress by :

- clarifying and enriching our political and ideological line based on Marxism-Leninism, as a method of analysis and theory of revolutionary change, of which Marx and Engels laid the cornerstone and which Lenin enriched in an essential way and opened to the contributions of great Marxist leaders, a method and theory that is enriched in the light of scientific development and the lessons of revolutionary struggles.
- developing and concentrating our propaganda work (weekly newspaper, website, bi-monthly electronic newspaper aimed at the working class and the toiling masses, television channel, etc.) on the situation of the working class and the necessity for it to build its tools of struggle (union and party) independent of the bourgeoisie.
- making known as widely as possible our project of formation of the party of the proletariat (public conferences in the cities, videos, distribution of leaflets in the popular districts, etc.),
- reorienting our trade union work so that it targets the working class, in particular those in the big factories and mines, aiming to

develop its class consciousness and to attract its most advanced elements into our ranks,

- urging our activists working in the field of human rights to focus their action on the defense of the social and economic rights of the workers, those working in popular neighborhoods in order to target the neighborhoods where the working class lives, etc.
- urging our women's and youth organizations to pay the greatest attention to young workers,
- developing and carrying out a plan to train workers to raise their class consciousness and enable them to take on the leadership of Democratic Way,
- having a dialogue with the Moroccan Marxist activists about the project of formation of the party of the working class and proposing to them to contribute to the realization of this project.
- studying similar experiences in some countries of the south.

3.2. The process of development of the militant organizations and the convergence of their struggles:

Since its creation, Democratic Way, drawing the lessons from the failure of the building of socialism in the U.S.S.R., has given great importance to the independent organizations of the popular masses, and at their head the working masses, and to the defense of their independence, even towards the party which has to defend, within them and democratically, its visions, positions and proposals.

This question is of great topicality in Morocco, which is experiencing a flowering of organizations of all kinds (popular movements in marginalized regions such as the Rif, coordination of teachers under contract in the public sector, etc.) with well-established structures and programs. Some of these have led and/or are leading long-term struggles, many of them refusing to have any relationship with political, trade union and associative militant forces, and isolated from each other, wrongly believing that this would allow these struggles to succeed. This situation made their repression by the regime easier and led to failure or to weak gains, despite the great sacrifices made. If this situation continues, it will lead to despair and demobilization.

Also Democratic Way has not ceased:

- to call for the convergence of the struggles and public dialogue between the militant forces,
- to fight the policy of the regime to divide and rule (Islamists against secularists, Amazighs against Arabs, etc.),

- to begin the creation of certain organizations or contribute strongly to the creation of others (Social Front, Moroccan Front of Support to Palestine and against the normalization with the Zionist State, various trade-union organizations, federations of human rights organizations in Morocco and in the region, etc.)
- To point to those in power (makhzen [the monarchy, nobles, big landowners and other members of the elite – *translator's note*]) as being, currently, the obstacle to any progress before there can be any development for the benefit of the people and to call for the union of the popular forces to get rid of them.

3.3. The process of building of the front of the popular classes:

Morocco, like other dependent countries, is going through the phase of struggle for national liberation from imperialism and the bloc of ruling classes (bourgeois agents of the colonial multinational companies and big landowners). In order to achieve the tasks of this phase and lead to socialism, the struggle must be led by the party of the proletariat and supported by the front of popular classes whose backbone is the worker-peasant alliance.

The building of the front of the popular classes, as a strategic front, requires time and demands the building of tactical fronts gathering, at a given time, all the classes, strata and social sections that are victims of the domination of those in power (the makhzen), and at its head the predatory and repressive makhzen mafia.

In this framework, Democratic Way fights for the formation of a democratic front as large as possible and a front of struggle gathering all the militant forces, whatever their ideology and their class position, except for the reactionary, fascist and takfirist [referring to a form of Islamic fundamentalism – *translator's note*] forces.

4. The process of building a Marxist international:

The current situation is characterized by the failure of capitalism on the economic level (a persistent crisis since 2008), ideological level (failure of liberalism and of the different theories of the end of history and ideology, of post-modernism, etc.), social level (increase of social inequality, unemployment, precariousness and pauperization, etc.), political level (deep crisis of bourgeois democracy), environmental level (accelerated destruction of life on our planet) and moral level revealed, in particular, by the pandemic. This failure is creating the objective conditions favorable for the development and struggle of the anti-capitalist forces, and at their head the Marxist forces.

But the following subjective factors hinder this development:

- the media hegemony of imperialism, which prevents the peoples' awareness of the dangers of capitalism for the survival of the human species.
- the absence of a socialist alternative that could give hope for a more just world after the collapse of the USSR.
- the deep divisions of the forces claiming to be Marxist, and more generally of the anti-capitalist forces.

The building of the Marxist international will not take place, for the most part, through discussions among the Marxist forces, but in the common struggle of the Marxist and anti-capitalist forces (anarchists and ecologists having become aware of the fundamental antagonism between environmental protection and capitalism, etc.) against capitalism.

In this framework and given that the consciousness of the peoples that U.S. imperialism is their principal enemy is developing, the formation of a world front against U.S. imperialism, the spearhead of imperialism and capitalism in the world, can contribute to the maturing of the subjective conditions for the building of a Marxist international.

March 2022

Serbia	Revolutionary Alliance of Labour of Serbia

Is the War in Ukraine Only an Inter-Imperialist between the USA and Russia or Is It Also a National-Liberation War of the Ukrainian People?[1]

(Serbia, April 2022)

We are witnessing that the modern revisionists and parts of the Left are taking a pro-war, social-imperialist and social-chauvinist

---

[1] On the question of the war in Ukraine, there is a difference between the approach of the declaration of the Coordinating Committee and our Conference in general on the one hand, and the article of our Serbian comrades for the latest issue of *Unity and Struggle*.

The article of the Serbian comrades differs with its emphasis on two wars in Ukraine. It would be better if that were the case, but unfortunately there is only one war, and it is between the imperialists and reactionaries themselves: that is, Russia with China's backing on one side, and the US and UK on the other, with the European imperialists joining them as partners in a short time.

It is most probable that the majority of the people of Ukraine have hostile feelings against the Russian invaders. However, they are not waging a war against them. The only war against Russia is being waged by the Ukrainian government backed by western imperialists. Moreover, one cannot suppose that the pro-imperialist Ukrainian government is waging a liberation war.

It is true that the Ukrainian government distributed weapons to the people, and some Ukrainians certainly used their weapons against Russia. However, the reality now is that these weapons are not being used for the interests of the people or for their liberation struggle, but only for the interests of the pro-imperialist government.

The Leninist principle is to turn the imperialist wars into civil wars, and one needs to have this perspective. This is not the situation now, but it should be aimed to have a national liberation war against the Russian invaders, separate from that of the governments, and this national liberation war should not and cannot rely on the western imperialists. And not now in practice, but in the future, it should be united with a civil war, a struggle of social liberation against the reactionary bourgeois government.

Coordination Committee, ICMLPO

stand on the war in Ukraine, or, "in better cases", the social-pacifist stand that is presented as opposition to the imperialist war, that they are "not choosing sides", but are calling for "peace" and are playing naive. This "neutral" and "pacifist" stand is trying to avoid to take a firm revolutionary anti-imperialist position and is actually just an appendix to a pro-war imperialist stand.

The core of this question lies in the characterization of the present war in Ukraine and in general the approach towards imperialist war, which from a Leninist perspective is to be changed in character on the course of the revolutionary people's struggle.

Are imperialist "superpowers" Gods, or is it the might that lies in the revolutionary people's struggle that can change the world?

Let us look at characterizations of the First and the Second World War by Lenin and Stalin:

"The conversion of the present imperialist war into a civil war is the only correct proletarian slogan, one that follows from the experience of the Commune... it has been dictated by all the conditions of an imperialist war between highly developed bourgeois countries."

– Berne Conference of the Bolsheviks, February 1915

"In the present war the national element is represented only by Serbia's war against Austria (which, by the way, was noted in the resolution of our Party's Berne Conference). It is only in Serbia and among the Serbs that we can find a national-liberation movement of long standing, embracing millions, "the masses of the people", a movement of which the present war of Serbia against Austria is a "continuation". If this war were an isolated one, i.e., if it were not connected with the general European war, with the selfish and predatory aims of Britain, Russia, etc., it would have been the duty of all socialists to desire the success of the Serbian bourgeoisie as this is the only correct and absolutely inevitable conclusion to be drawn from the national element in the present war...

*"...A sudden change in the mood of the masses is not only possible, but is becoming more and more probable... We cannot tell whether a powerful revolutionary movement will develop immediately after this war, or during it, etc., but at all events, it is only work in this direction that deserves the name of socialist work. **The slogan of a civil war** is the one that summarises and directs this work..."*

– Lenin, The Collapse of the Second International, June 1915

"A distinguishing feature of the second imperialist war is that so far it is being waged and extended by the aggressor powers, while the other powers, the "democratic" powers, against whom in fact the war is directed, pretend that it does not concern them, wash their hands of it, draw back, boast of their love of peace, scold the fascist aggressors, and... surrender their positions to the aggressors bit by bit, at the same time asserting that they are preparing to resist.

"This war, it will be seen, is of a rather strange and one-sided character. But that does not prevent it from being a brutal war of unmitigated conquest waged at the expense of the poorly defended peoples of Ethiopia, Spain and China."

– History of the C.P.S.U.(b) (Short Course), 1939

"We do not approve of German expansion in the Balkans. But that does not mean that we are deviating from the pact with Germany and veering toward England."

– Zhdanov and Dimitrov, April 1941 (Dimitrov's Diary)

"The war of the Greek and Yugoslav people against imperialist aggression is a just war, there are no reservations."

– Stalin to Zhdanov, April 1941 (Dimitrov's Diary)

"It would be wrong to think that the Second World War was a casual occurrence or the result of mistakes of any particular statesmen, though mistakes undoubtedly were made. Actually, the war was the inevitable result of the development of world economic and political forces on the basis of modern monopoly capitalism. Marxists have declared more than once that the capitalist system of world economy harbors elements of general's crises and armed conflicts and that, hence, the development of capitalism in our time proceeds not in the form of smooth, and even progress but through crises and military catastrophe.

The fact is that the unevenness of development of the capitalist countries usually leads in time to violent disturbance of equilibrium in the world system of capitalism. That group of capitalist countries which considers itself worse provided than others with raw materials and markets usually makes attempts to alter the situation and to repartition the "spheres of influence" in its favor by armed force. The result is a splitting of the capitalist world into two hostile camps and war between them.

Perhaps military catastrophes might be avoided if it were possible for raw materials and markets to be periodically redistributed among the various countries in accordance with their economic importance, by agreement and peaceable settlement. But that is impossible to do under present capitalist conditions of the development of world economy.

Thus the First World War (1914-18) was the result of the first crisis of the capitalist system of world economy, and the Second World War (1939-45) was the result of a second crisis.

That does not mean of course that the Second World War is a copy of the first. On the contrary, the Second World War differs materially from the first in character. It must be borne in mind that before attacking the Allied countries the principal fascist states—Germany, Japan, and Italy—destroyed the last vestiges of bourgeois-democratic liberties at home, established a brutal terrorist regime in their own countries, rode roughshod over the principles of sovereignty and free development of small countries, proclaimed a policy of seizure of alien territories as their own policy, and declared for all to hear that they were out for world domination and the establishment of a fascist regime throughout the world.

Moreover, by the seizure of Czechoslovakia and of the central areas of China, the Axis states showed that they were prepared to carry out their threat of enslaving all freedom-loving nations. In view of this, unlike the First World War, the Second World War against the Axis states from the very outset assumed the character of an anti-fascist war, a war of liberation, one aim of which was also the restoration of democratic liberties. The entry of the Soviet Union into the war against the Axis states could only enhance, and indeed did enhance, the anti-fascist and liberation character of the Second World War...”

– Stalin, Origin and the Character of the Second World War,
February 1946

From the writings of Lenin and Stalin, we can see that saying the war is inter-imperialist is not the same as the politics of "non-interference".

It is in the aggressor's best interest to picture the present war in Ukraine as a war of Russia with NATO. Actually, this is what the Putinists propagate. They do not recognize the right of a sovereign nation to exist, nor the struggle of its people to defend it.

What is more, this "non-interference" position actually does not see the imperialist character of the coming war from the Marxist position of the general world capitalist crisis, but is actually influenced by reactionary "geopolitical" theories, in which the main actors of history are the superpowers and not the peoples. This position is scared of the "superpowers" as of almighty Gods. It serves to hide in the bush, to wash Pilate's hands and not do anything against aggressive powers and thus help the imperialist warmongers and imperialist war. Instead of the resolute and dialectical Leninist slogan "turn imperialist war into a civil war", these social-pacifists give empty reformist phrases such as: "No war between nations, no peace between classes" (as if any of this is possible in capitalist world). This is their cover for passivity and cowardness, for a "left-wing" appendage to the imperialist aggressors. This position, if we not fight to unmask it, can put communists not on the forefront, but only on the slopy tail of historical developments.

That is why we fight the modern Kautskyian, revisionist and actually pro-imperialist position that is predominating, and make the efforts that the Leninist, revolutionary position on the present war in Ukraine be more clearly shaped among Marxists-Leninists. In this sense, we are presenting the revolutionary anti-war platform that we outlined for the proposition of the anti-war movement in Serbia and in the Balkans...

Stop the war in Ukraine
(platform against the war)

Stop the War in Ukraine!
Russian Occupiers, Get Out!
NATO and Putin Are Not Factors of Peace and Freedom,
But of Fascism and War!

1. We condemn the Russian imperialist invasion of the sovereign country of Ukraine and the homes of Ukrainian people and families. The Ukrainian people, like all nations in the world, have the right to "exist" (which the Great Russian chauvinists and aggressors openly and loudly question), have the right to self-determination, as well as the right to defend their homeland from the occupiers. We demand the urgent withdrawal of Russian troops from Ukraine. We stand in solidarity with the Ukrainian working people, who are fighting with

a rifle in hand, as well as with all Ukrainian refugees who have been forced to leave their homes.

2. Although the war in Ukraine is part of the general inter-imperialist struggle between NATO countries and Putin's Russia in Eastern Europe, it is at the same time a national-liberation war of the Ukrainian people to defend their country and homes from the Great-Russian occupiers. Ukraine is not fighting with the Russian occupiers over some imperialist "sphere of influences" but to defend its own country. Actually, the national-liberation war of the Ukrainian people is reducing the danger of the general inter-imperialist war and is a factor of world peace. To the degree that the Putinist occupiers are driven away from Kiev, to that degree is the world far from the nuclear military catastrophe.

We believe that the struggle of the armed Ukrainian people in the liberation war, which stands in the middle of imperialist plans, is a brave and impressive example to all nations of the world in today's historical conditions - that it is possible to resist the imperialist nuclear "superpowers", which push the world into a new general imperialist war and militaristic catastrophe, and to spoil their vicious plans. The resistance of the generally armed people once again shows that "all imperialists are paper tigers!"

While we unconditionally support the national liberation war of the Ukrainian people against Putin's Great Russian occupiers, we also support the isolation of sectarian chauvinist elements and other imperialist agencies in the Ukrainian national liberation movement, which are imposing the course of its development. Such elements can only compromise the just struggle of the Ukrainian people for

liberation from the Russian White Guards, morally strengthen the illegal Russian invasion, push Ukraine even more into the arms of Western imperialists and thus, finally, threaten any Ukrainian sovereignty and independence...

We call on the international working-class movement and the peoples of the world to fulfil their internationalist duty and support the national liberation struggle waged by the armed Ukrainian working people, and thus significantly help them isolate anti-people's and treacherous elements who seek their chance in the chaos of war.

3. We support *the friendship of the people* and condemn the attempts of Russian chauvinists to present their invasion as a fratricidal struggle between Russians and Ukrainians, using for these purposes the so-called "People's Republics" in Donbas. Ukrainians and Russians together and unitedly are resisting the Great Russian imperialists in defence of their homeland, Ukraine. The Russian people are fighting on the streets of Russia in support of their Ukrainian brothers. Putin's crude propaganda, although he does not try too hard to hide his imperial goals, is also trying to use the red flag of victory over fascism to justify his invasion. In the words of Alexander Batov, a representative of the Russian United Front of Labour (Rot Front): there is no more insolent provocation than that! Vlasov's white army is trying to enter Kiev, not the red one!

It is no coincidence that in his speech that prepared the attack on Ukraine, Putin attacked Lenin and Stalin in a revisionist manner, as symbols of principled national policy and the right of peoples to self-determination, using theses from Khrushchev's "secret speech". The logic of the development of the new Russian Pinochetist and now monopolistic bourgeoisie, which after the collapse of the USSR, like interwar Germany, found itself humiliated in order to rise with the investments of Western monopoly capital – leads to the renewal of old tsarist, Cadet and Menshevik imperialist and revisionist social-imperialist ambitions, in rising ambitions for redistribution of the world and world markets. The flags of the USSR on Putin's tanks in Ukraine with the infamous semi-swastika "Z" do not represent Lenin-Stalin's anti-imperialism and anti-fascism, but the traditions of Khrushchev-Brezhnev-type social-imperialism, i.e. neo-tsarism.

4. We condemn the policies of all imperialist "superpowers", which are pushing the world into a new general imperialist war. We condemn NATO's imperialist military alliance, as aggressive as Putin's imperialist war machine – which has dared to threaten a world

nuclear war. We condemn the hypocritical imperialist policy of NATO and the EU, which, on the backs of the Ukrainian people and the peoples of Europe and the world in general, are making their own imperialist plans for their Russian, Chinese and other imperialist rivals. We condemn the false portrayal of NATO and EU imperialists and monopolists as defenders of "democracy" and "national independence", as well as the cynical portrayal of Putin's imperialists as "anti-fascists" and "anti-imperialists". We believe that monopolists-imperialists from the west and the east cannot have any "liberating" role, that they are not mutual ideological enemies as they try to present themselves and thus try to deceive the peoples to support them in the imperialist wars of conquest. This is not a war for "liberation", but for a new division of the world and world markets. We stand in solidarity with the Russian anti-war movement, the rebellion of the Russian people and all imprisoned anti-war activists in Russia. We also stand in solidarity with all sincere and consistent anti-imperialists in Western countries. "A nation that oppresses another nation is forging its own chains."

5. We stand for the complete economic, political, military and national independence of Serbia, as well as all Balkan countries, from the imperialist powers. We are fighting against Serbia's accession to NATO and the EU; against the domination of Western, Russian and Chinese monopoly capital in our country, as well as the severance of any military-political ties with the imperialists of the East and the West, the enemies of the peoples of the Balkans and the world. We support all consistent anti-imperialist movements in the Balkans. We call for a revolutionary alliance of the Balkan peoples and a joint international struggle against the capitalist crisis, fascism and imperialist war.

6. In addition to clearly refusing to join the camp of social chauvinists and liberal nationalists who side with Russian or Western imperialist powers, we also refuse to join the camp of social pacifists and liberal pacifists as their appendage. Pacifist slogans and appeals to the imperialists to stop the war can only accelerate the preparation of a new inter-imperialist war, the only logical result of the general capitalist crisis, and lull the peoples toward the revolutionary tasks that await them. Only the overthrow of the power of the imperialists and the instigators of war can stop the coming imperialist war and bloodshed among nations. Instead of pacifist slogans, we call on the working class and the peoples of the Balkans, Europe and the world

to fight the war with strikes and demonstrations and take the Lenin's slogan and prepare *to turn the imperialist war into a revolutionary one*.

7. We refuse to pay for the crisis and die in the imperialist war to save the rotten corpse of capitalism. We believe that the black clouds of the general imperialist war looming over us are an expression not of the "geopolitical" crisis between the USA and Russia, but of the capitalist crisis in both USA and Russia and the rest of the capitalist world. This crisis is not only of economic, not only political, not only health and social, but a general world capitalist crisis, which primarily threatens the working class but also other working and non-monopoly urban and rural layers of the people.

We believe that only a united working class can gather and lead the people in a consistent and complete liberation struggle, reverse the course of the crisis and save the country from social and national catastrophe. We are fighting for the unity of the working class and the gathering around it of a broad popular front against the capitalist crisis, fascism and war – against the state power of the instigators of war and imperialist and chauvinist agents in our country and in the Balkans.

Independence, democracy, socialism!
Not with Putin, not with NATO, not with the EU!
Against submission to the imperialists!
Fight against the imperialist occupiers, instigators of war and their criminal policies!
All to the people's front against the capitalist crisis, fascism and imperialist war!

Balkan resistance movement!
Revolutionary Alliance of Labor[2]

Revolutionary Alliance of Labour of Serbia
savezrada.org
April 2022

---

[2] A platform presented at a meeting of nominally anti-war organizations in Belgrade, March 13, 2022.

Spain	Carlos Hermida Communist Party of Spain (Marxist-Leninist) – PCE(ml)

The Intellectuals and Communism

1. The Reasons for a Rapprochement (1917-1945).

Communism has undoubtedly been the most influential ideological and political movement of the 20th century. Regardless of the sympathies or fears it arouses, it is undeniable that communism and communists have been present in all areas of life during what historian Eric Hobsbawm called the short 20th century: 1914-1991.

Since the triumph of the Bolshevik revolution, a very large section of the working class has identified itself with the project of building a socialist society and the communist parties have become fundamental elements of political life practically throughout the world. It will not hurt to remember, now that we live in an era of historical revisionism and the rise of fascism, that between the above-mentioned dates a good part of humanity lived under political systems led by communist parties; systems that transformed very backward countries into modern, industrialized societies, with universal and free public health-care and education systems, and all this in a short space of time. The case of Russia are China are examples of this change. Moreover, these processes of transformation took place in extraordinarily difficult historical contexts, when the new revolutionary governments had to face brutal imperialist aggressions and, in many cases, forced to wage long wars of national liberation.

Communism not only became a reference point for workers and peasants, but also influenced sectors of the middle classes and, in a very special way, on the intellectuals. When we talk about intellectuals, we do not refer only to writers, artists, philosophers and historians, that is, to what is generally known as high culture, but we include teachers, professors, scientists, etc. In short, an important sector of the world of Culture, in a broad sense, saw in communism the possibility of transforming the world.

There are several reasons that explain this attraction. One of them, a fundamental one, is the scientific character of Marxism. Faced with ideologies of a utopian nature, which spoke of equality and social harmony, but which did not carry out a thorough analysis of reality, consequently, they were not able to explain it, nor did they propose the means for the transformation of the world. Marxism provides the theoretical and conceptual instruments that allow one to explain reality and understand historical evolution. At the same time it defines the means to overcome the capitalist order and establish a new social, political and economic model that will make it possible to eliminate exploitation and the division of society into classes. Through historical and dialectical materialism, Marx and Engels, whom we can define as revolutionary intellectuals, unraveled the historical development of humanity, they provided a coherent explanation of material reality by analyzing its contradictions, and clearly established that the proletariat was the class that was called to establish a classless world through revolutionary action. The innumerable writings of Marx and Engels, through an immense documentary apparatus, show that another world is possible. This scientific character of Marxism, which unravels the contradictions of the economic and social order established by the bourgeoisie, necessarily had to attract a section of progressive intellectuals who sought an alternative to capitalism.

When the Bolshevik revolution put into practice what until then was only a revolutionary theory established in the works of Marx, Engels, Lenin and other Marxist theorists; when the Bolshevik party embarked on the gigantic task of building a socialist society, and philosophy became praxis, many intellectuals decided to participate actively by joining the communist parties that were formed from 1917 onwards. It was the first time that the workers and peasants took power in a country and began the construction of an alternative model to capitalism, where the words solidarity, fraternity, dignity and freedom were the basis of life. For this reason, the events of October were echoed throughout the world, crossed oceans, crossed mountain ranges, and reached the villages of China, the Andalusian farmhouses, the mines of South Africa, etc. making the workers enthusiastic and plunging the bourgeoisie into the worst of their nightmares. The concerns of those intellectuals who sought alternatives to an unjust order now found in Soviet Russia an exciting project. Moreover, the Bolshevik government, composed largely of revolutionary intellectuals, beginning with Lenin himself, gave priority attention to education and culture, aware that it was impossible to build socialism without raising the cultural level of the popular masses. Poetry, art, cinematography, culture and science in general, experienced an extraordinary boom after the October Revolution. New pedagogical experiments were tried out in schools, while vanguard writers and artists proposed innovative conceptions in poetry, painting and theatre. It stands to reason that many intellectuals around the world perceived the October Revolution as a challenge in which they should participate.

But the meeting between intellectuals and communists was not easy and was not without problems and polemics. The vast majority of intellectuals came from the petty bourgeoisie and the so-called middle classes and their incorporation into proletarian parties was not easy. While for the workers the discipline of the party and democratic centralism was never a problem, as they were accustomed to the discipline of factory work, the intellectuals had to get used to an activism that was alien to them and required them to integrate into structures where the collective was above the individual. On the other hand, they became organic intellectuals, in Gramsci's words, within a party that constituted the vanguard of the proletariat, which meant stripping themselves of their spirit of superiority in relation to the manual workers and putting aside their petty-bourgeois vision of the world. Some intellectuals served under communism throughout their lives and paid with their lives for their loyalty to the revolutionary cause, while many of those who joined the party did so temporarily and in many cases traumatic ruptures occurred. There were not a few who, after abandoning militancy, adopted openly reactionary positions. In many cases the rupture was disguised as insurmountable ideological differences when in reality what was at stake was simply that many of these intellectuals were not able to adapt to a militancy that demanded enormous sacrifices, especially when the communists were in hiding and suffered harsh persecution. This does not mean that in some cases the abandonment was not due to real political differences honestly defended.

But, undoubtedly, other factors, beyond the class origins or personal attitudes, influenced the disagreement between the intellectuals and communism.

2. The Disagreement (1945-1991)

The victory of the USSR in World War II and the decisive role that the Communists played in the struggle against the fascist occupier, both in Europe and in the countries invaded by Japan, raised the prestige of the Soviet Union and the Communist parties throughout the world. The establishment of socialism in Eastern Europe, the coming to power of the Communists in China in 1949 and the struggles for national liberation in the European colonies of Africa and Asia were episodes that showed with great clarity the decline of the capitalist system. To prevent this, the United States, which had emerged from the world war as a world superpower, began a policy that aimed to consolidate the capitalist system on a world scale, to stop the expansion of the communists and destroy the USSR. Thus began the so-called Cold War, in which, except for a direct confrontation between the United States and the Soviet Union, the great U.S. power used all strategies – economic warfare, propaganda warfare, military interventions to overthrow progressive political regimes, massive support for the military dictatorships of Latin America, etc. – to weaken the USSR and fight communism. The allies in the war were again the great enemies and the fascists became useful elements in the new U.S. strategy.

The enormous successes of the USSR in all fields – let us remember its successes in the space race surpassing the United States – exerted an immense attraction on the intelligentsia that was channeled not only through militancy, but in participation in international organizations and associations directly influenced by the Soviet Union or openly sympathetic to it. This participation of the world of culture in the communist project has been belittled by bourgeois propaganda, which has presented post-war intellectuals as "fellow travelers" or simple puppets manipulated by communism. Nothing could be further from the truth. Those who approached the communists from militancy or collaboration did so convinced by an incontestable reality. The countries ruled by the communists from 1945 onwards experienced enormous economic, cultural, social and scientific advancement.

The anti-communist propaganda of the Cold War, together with the repressive measures used against communists or suspected sympathizers with communism, negatively influenced many intellectuals, but undoubtedly the most devastating blow came from the Soviet Union itself.

One of the problems that the Bolsheviks had to face from the beginning was the development of the bureaucracy. The Soviet state was forced to use officials of the Tsarist regime in order to function, and as the state came to control the economy, a communist bureaucracy also emerged. Lenin was always seriously concerned about this question and tried by all means to ensure that this bureaucratic stratum was at the service of the workers and not placed above them. In fact, the Commissariat for the Workers' and Peasants' Inspectorate, headed by Stalin until 1922, had the objective of ensuring the proper functioning of the administration and avoiding bureaucratic deviations. In his last writings, Lenin recommended that 50% of the members of the Central Committee be workers who had not had a long period of management in the Soviet apparatus.

The introduction of the planned economy since 1928, with the state management of the entire economy, increased the dimensions of the bureaucracy and forced greater revolutionary vigilance. Although we cannot say this with absolute certainty, we consider that a part of the political violence exercised by the Soviet state between 1936 and 1939 was due to this attempt to control a state apparatus in which conspiracies were organized to end the building of socialism and to remove Stalin from the leadership of the Party. All these attempts failed and socialism became a reality, transforming the USSR into a great economic and scientific power. Stalin's successful policy was proven during World War II, when the Soviet Union played the pivotal role in the defeat of Nazism.

However, bureaucratic deformations did not disappear from the Soviet state and, on Stalin's death in 1953, came to light. The political and ideological struggle that began from that date marked the triumph of a revisionist bureaucracy that abandoned the principles of

Marxism-Leninism, although in the face of the Soviet people fidelity to the teachings of Marx, Engels and Lenin was maintained.

The first act in the enthronement of revisionism was the 20th Congress of the Communist Party of the Soviet Union (CPSU), held in 1956. During a closed session, between February 24 and 25, Nikita Khrushchev, general secretary of the Party, read the so-called Secret Report, in which he made a brutal criticism of Stalin's management without evidence or documentation, accusing him of innumerable crimes, of violating Soviet law, of promoting the cult of personality, etc. in short, a catalogue of accusations that turned the Bolshevik leader into little less than a monstrous tyrant. This Report not only demoralized millions of communists around the world, but provided ammunition to the bourgeoisie in its anti-communist campaigns. Khrushchev carried out a criminal act and began a path that would end up destroying the USSR in 1991.

The intellectuals felt the impact that Khrushchev caused with his accusations and many abandoned communist activity. Instead of carrying out an in-depth analysis of the Report, demonstrating its inconsistency and misrepresentations, many adopted the pose of disenchantment and disappointment, often adopting reactionary and openly anti-communist positions.

Because of the gap opened by the so-called Secret Report, the bourgeoisie launched a great ideological offensive against communism. Disguised with a leftist language in some cases, post-modernist intellectuals appeared in the 1970s who systematically dedicated themselves to fighting Marxism in all areas and trying to banish it from the University. When the USSR disintegrated in 1991 and capitalism was fully re-established in the country and throughout Eastern Europe, the bourgeoisie won an immense triumph not only over the working class, but over all the progressive social forces of the world. Intellectuals turned away en masse from the communists and sought more comfortable places, especially from the economic point of view. Many found accommodation in the different "isms" that were already proliferating at the end of the last century: environmentalism, feminism, etc.

3. The Long Journey through the Desert (1991-2022)

The disintegration of the Soviet Union in 1991, which dragged down all the European countries of so-called "real socialism", produced a tremendous shock in the communists of the whole world and in all the popular classes. The USSR was a reference point for the workers and its disappearance caused an enormous political vacuum through which the ideological artillery of the bourgeoisie entered the watershed, ready to definitively bury communism and turn Marx and Engels into bibliographic relics. And it was not long before the purpose was achieved. Communist parties of enormous prestige and with a considerable social presence, such as the Italian one, disappeared and thousands of communists ceased their activity due to discouragement or frustration, while others passed over to the class enemy.

In these circumstances it is logical to ask a question: are communist parties necessary?

First of all, it is necessary to remember that it was never easy to be a communist. Imprisonment, torture, shooting, repression in short, formed and are part of the daily life of tens of thousands of militants in many areas of the world. At certain times, communist men and women found themselves in more difficult circumstances than the present ones. Think of the long night of Francoism. And they did not give up or surrender because they were very clear that they were part of a long process of struggle that would end in the final victory of the proletariat, even if they would not be around to see it.

Throughout history there were always men and women who questioned exploitation and aspired to social equality, but for centuries the weak development of the productive forces prevented the building of a society capable of satisfying the needs of the entire population. Now, at the beginning of the second decade of the 21st century, this is possible. We have the technical and scientific basis capable of making the Marxist slogan a reality: from each according to his ability, to each according to his needs. What prevents the materialization of this new society is the capitalist system, a mode of production characterized by anarchy in production and periodic crises that cause unemployment, misery and despair. Only the revolutionary overcoming of capitalism will bring true democracy and the disappearance of exploitation. And this is where the need for the Communist Party appears. No matter how extensive the social movements are, no matter how much indignation is built up, social protest will be sterile if it is not accompanied by political leadership and defined objectives. The Communist Party is the instrument capable of leading the revolutionary struggle of the working class insofar as it has a tool for scientific analysis of social reality (Marxism-Leninism) and an organizational model (democratic centralism) that is absolutely effective in the struggle against capital. The triumphant socialist revolutions throughout the 20th century are the empirical proof of what we say.

The Communist Party is as necessary in the 21st century as it was in the previous one.

And one must recreate a politics that appeals to intellectuals. It is necessary to approach those thousands of professors, teachers and university graduates who have precarious jobs and low wages. They constitute an intellectual proletariat which is fundamental to winning for the cause of socialism. But we can only do this if we are able to develop an appropriate tactic, to create spaces in which these intellectuals can collaborate and become active in our parties.

We need intellectuals for the struggle against capital. The unity of the working class and the world of culture is indispensable for victory over capitalism. The technical, scientific and humanist knowledge of intellectuals is necessary to raise the cultural level of the proletariat.

The parties that make up the ICMLPO must make a deep reflection in this sense and work intensively with the aim that the workers of culture see in Marxism-Leninism the instrument of their liberation; so that the intellectuals can once again understand that there is only one alternative: socialism or barbarism.

Madrid, April 2022

Tunisia	Mortadha Labidi Workers' Party of Tunisia

Address of the Central Committee to the Activists of the Party on the Situation Prevailing in the Country

Dear comrades,

Warm communist greetings. You are receiving herewith the April correspondence that we have devoted to the follow-up of the evolution of the general political situation in our country, which includes the summaries of the deliberations of the Central Committee held on March 27 with the updates relating to the developments that have taken place during the last few days.

1. Persistent elements of the general crisis

The country is experiencing the impact of a severe crisis that is affecting all sectors and areas of life. In addition to being a global, deep and complex crisis, it has recently reached degrees of severity that the country had not known before.

Politically, Tunisia is experiencing a crisis of governance in every sense of the word, despite the relative ease with which President Kais Saied[1] has been able to push through the terms of his plan for the year 2022 since the July 25 coup[2]. It is expected that this crisis will increase in depth and complexity in the coming days, as indicators point to a further escalation in the conflict between the elements of the reactionary regime.

On the economic front, all economic and financial indicators (growth rate, budget deficit rate, debt rate, trade balance deficit, value of the currency, inflation rate, etc.) predict an imminent collapse, which has caused Tunisia to be classified as a country unable to pay

---

[1] Professor of constitutional law, with no political party, no agenda, a proven populist; he was elected President of the Republic on October 23, 2019.

[2] On July 25, 2021, based on an extensive reading of Article 80 of the Constitution, the President of the Republic proceeded to freeze the activities of the Parliament and to dissolve the government in office, of which he himself had appointed the head and most of its members.

its foreign debts and threatened with bankruptcy. The credit institutions, led by the International Monetary Fund, are blocking the possibility of obtaining a loan of $4 billion that the Bouden[3] government needs to mobilize the resources planned for the state budget of the current year, knowing that the debt rate has reached more than 100% of the gross domestic product. Of course, the popular classes and strata are paying the bill for this crisis: unemployment (19% according to official figures), poverty, the collapse of purchasing power, the deterioration of public services and all other signs of misery.

2. More recently, a crisis that is becoming more acute

In the recent period, especially since July 25, the economic situation has become unprecedentedly complicated, and the state would have been unable to pay the salaries of its employees, if it had not resorted more than once to local bond loans and printing money. In the event that the government of Kais Saied fails to convince the International Monetary Fund to obtain a new loan and thus fails to appear on the global financial market (which has become almost certain), Tunisia would logically be forced to officially declare bankruptcy, its inability to pay its debts or to pay its employees' salaries or to provide basic commodities such as fuel and grain. The disappearance on the market of basic necessities such as medicines, semolina, flour and vegetable oil, as well as the appearance of long queues in front of bakeries, are part of the new situation that Tunisian citizens are experiencing against their will; but they also represent serious indicators of the scenario of bankruptcy and famine. Instead of the Saied government taking the necessary measures to mitigate the impact of this crisis, it has designed, on the instructions of the president himself, a campaign to "fight against monopoly and speculation", which the Tunisian people have quickly discovered is spurious and of a misleading nature.

On the basis of these dangerous developments, observers of the internal and external situation unanimously agree that Tunisia is heading for economic collapse and bankruptcy. Some economists consider that the Tunisian state "is in great difficulty, because it has not repaid the debts it owes to private sector suppliers, estimated at

---

[3] Najla Bouden: a career academic with no political experience, appointed by Kais Saied to head the Tunisian government since October 11, 2021, after three months of vacancy of this position.

800 billion, and it has not redeemed the debts of its public institutions, estimated at 6,200 billion"; therefore, by "deferring the claims on its domestic debt, it has already entered into what is called the 'spiral of debt rescheduling', and this paves the way for the rescheduling of its external debt."

This assessment coincides with the verdict of the Fitch Ratings agency, which on March 18 announced that "a downgrading of Tunisia's rating to CCC means that its bonds carry a significant credit risk and that default is a real possibility." The World Economic Forum report (January 2022) predicted "the risks of collapse of the Tunisian state" due to "persistent economic stagnation, unemployment and debt". Some international financial institutions (International Monetary Fund, the U.S. bank Morgan Stanley, etc.) and even some official political circles (the U.S. State Department, the European Union's foreign policy chief, etc.) warn of "a scenario in which the current pace of financial deterioration continues. It is possible that Tunisia will default on its debts." As a result, the International Monetary Fund has postponed negotiations with the Tunisian state and the examination of the loan request ($4 billion) submitted by the Bouden government. For his part, the head of foreign policy of the European Union announced that the Union was studying the possibility of reducing direct aid to the budget of the Tunisian state.

3. International and regional influences

More dangerous than that, the Russian-Ukrainian war is expected to have more serious repercussions and a direct impact on Tunisia in the coming days. In addition to the rapid and senseless rise in fuel prices, where the price of a barrel of oil has reached more than $130 (note that the state budget was based on forecasts of the price of a barrel of oil of $75, that each additional dollar in the price of a barrel of oil would cost the Tunisian budget and the Compensation Fund about 120 million dinars [one dinar is about 33¢, so this is about $40 million – *translator's note*] more). The prices of a wide range of other commodities, including agricultural ones, have seen unprecedented increases, with the food price index rising by 40% in the coming transactions on several U.S. and European stock exchanges. Wheat prices have risen for the third consecutive month since the beginning of the year and in early March they reached their highest level since the summer of 2011.

As a result, the World Food and Agriculture Organization (FAO) and the World Food Program (WFP) have warned that the Russian war in Ukraine could lead to famine in more than 20 countries, due to the expected shortage of food crops, especially wheat. Tunisia (along with Yemen, Libya, Pakistan, etc.) is among the countries that are heavily dependent on wheat supplies from the two warring countries, as has been confirmed by the UN rapporteur on the right to food.

It is known that in Tunisia we produce only one third of our grain needs (1.6 million tons last year out of 3.4 million tons needed), which means that we import annually about two and a half million tons of grain, more than half of which (about 60%) comes from Russia and Ukraine. Given the state of war and its repercussions, the Tunisian state will have to seek sources other than these two countries, which is extremely difficult, in addition to what it will cost the state budget in unforeseen additional costs (1200 million dinars in 2021). On the other hand, it is expected that this year's harvest will be lower than last year (1.6 million tons), which will further complicate the situation. For all these reasons, the fear of famine has increased in the country, especially after the frequent lack of many consumer goods in recent weeks (bread and cereal products, etc.).

4. A catastrophic situation that does not seem to worry the President of the Republic

It does not seem that the path on which the country is advancing (the danger of economic collapse and the specter of famine) is of much concern to Kais Saied; he does not pay much attention to these terrifying threats, which he does not place among his priorities. His main focus is on how to implement his roadmap to take over all state institutions and strengthen his control over them. His main concern was to hold a consultation that failed[4] despite the great means mobilized for its success and to prepare a referendum whose number of participants would not exceed the number of participants in the consultation. Still he would adopt it as a plebiscite to introduce changes in the electoral law and the political system. Kais Saied then proceeded to implement his plan, ignoring the damage inflicted on the

---

[4] This national electronic consultation was supposed to be a kind of plebiscite for President Kais Saied and his policies. But despite the efforts made and the funds mobilized, it ended in failure as the participation rate was below all expectations.

people and the country and the dangers that threaten them. All the data indicates that the political crisis will intensify, which could lead the country to divisions and conflicts that Tunisia has not experienced before, including the possibility of civil war.

The truth is that neither Saied nor the rest of the parties in the power struggle are giving this issue the importance it deserves, as they are only concerned with the struggle for power. The Islamist party Ennahda, ousted from power by the July 25 coup, is now returning in order to inflame the conflict with Saied, having since acted on the saying: "bow until the storm passes." It is clear that it has chosen today to return to the stage and confront Saied openly, after it had been content to do so through its agents in the movement "Citizens against the Coup". Certainly, this return is based on a new analysis of the data of the conflict and the balance of power and leads us to believe that this party may have received the green light from foreign U.S. and European circles, especially after the meetings that Ghannouchi[5] held with the delegations that visited Tunisia recently. It is in this context that we must understand the call for the holding of a parliamentary session[6] whose agenda is the annulment of all exceptional measures taken by Kais Saied since July 25, 2021, as a prelude to a subsequent decision to dismiss him.

As a result, the Ennahda movement pushed Kais Saied to continue his escalation and to make the decision to dissolve Parliament, which was generally welcomed by both the elites and the working class. However, this was with less enthusiasm than the July 25 measures, due to growing disappointment with Kais Saied's inability to respond to the needs of the people. This decision will have other consequences (internal and external) that will accelerate the course of the conflict between the two sides and raise the question of its resolution here and now with greater urgency. Therefore, it is expected

---

[5] Rached Ghannouchi: leader of the Islamist party Ennahda since its foundation in 1981 and current president of the Assembly of People's Representatives, suspended by the President of the Republic since 25 July 2021.

[6] Despite the official suspension of parliament, a parliamentary session was held on March 28 to repeal the exceptional measures taken by the President of the Republic since July 25, following which he announced the dissolution of parliament, a measure that the constitution does not allow.

that the Islamist party will escalate further, taking advantage of the internal economic and social difficulties, Kais Saied's isolation externally, the increase in U.S. and European political pressure on him and the inability to reach an agreement with the International Monetary Fund, and thus the collapse of public finances and the bankruptcy of the state. It is therefore possible that the conflict between the two parties will enter a new phase that may turn violent and mark major setbacks in the area of public and individual freedoms.

5. The positions of the most important political forces

One of the characteristics of the situation in Tunisia since July 25 is the absence of a serious and effective revolutionary opposition movement against the farce that the country is experiencing and the marginalization and denigration of all actors in political life. In addition to the fact that the conflict is limited to the forces of the right, that is, between the Ennahda Party and Kais Saied, the Destourian Liberal Party, the representative of the former regime, has continued to appear as the most prominent political force against both sides of the conflict. It seeks to take advantage of the fall of Ennahda and the beginning of the decline of its influence on the political scene and in society on the one hand, and the failure of Kais Saied to deal with the burning economic and social issues on the other. He is preparing, on the basis of the positive results of the opinion polls, for the next parliamentary and presidential elections, whether they are held early or, according to Kais Saied's schedule, in December 2022. This party has become the center of interest of broad layers of the large and middle bourgeoisie and even some circles of the petty bourgeoisie and some external forces, which point to it as a possible and reliable alternative in the future. This would mean the return of the old regime and the success of the counter-revolution in its most reactionary, most authoritarian version, that of the RCD (Democratic Constitutional Rally, deposed by the Revolution).

6. The Tunisian General Union of Labor and the traditional mission of the union bureaucracy in times of crisis

On the other hand, the Tunisian General Union of Labor (UGTT), after holding its last congress, seeks to return to the scene of political conflict, so the statements of its secretary general are multiplying on various aspects of the current political situation (electronic consultation, negotiations with the International Monetary

Fund, etc.) as well as meetings of its leadership with foreign delegations (European Union delegation and U.S. delegation led by the Undersecretary of State for Human Rights, etc.).

Relations between the union federation, the Palace of Carthage[7] and the government have experienced a significant movement in recent days compared to the period of conflict they had experienced over the past year. And behind this movement there were reasons for both of them. The leadership of the union needed to calm things done with Kais Saied until the holding of its congress, in order to ensure his [referring to Noureddine Taboubi, head of the UGTT – *translator's note*] return at the head of the organization. He feared that some of the cases of financial and administrative corruption that had been raised earlier would be used against him, and he feared the outcome of the complaints filed by the union opposition to invalidate the holding of the congress. For his part, Kais Saied needed the same truce in the hope of persuading the union leadership to commit to the reform program that the Bouden government plans to include in its letter of intent that it plans to send to the IMF to obtain the long-awaited $4 billion loan.

Now that Taboubi[8] is back as Secretary General of the Union, guaranteeing five more years at the helm, its tone has become more

[7] Palace of the Presidency of the Republic

[8] Noureddine Taboubi: General Secretary of the powerful trade union federation, the Tunisian General Union of Labor) for the second consecutive term, while the Statutes of the organization do not allow him to run again. Current leader of the trade union bureaucracy, always at the service of the rulers and the comprador bourgeoisie.

critical of the regime and Kais Said and its threats to resort to sectoral, regional and even general strikes are more frequent. In fact, the role that the UGTT seeks to play in the current political situation is not new. It has become accustomed to this whenever the puppet bourgeois regime is in crisis. Since the 1950s (on the occasion of the decisive Congress of the Destourian Party)[9] until the aftermath of the Revolution of 2010-2011 and the organization of the national dialogue, the union has always been at the service of the comprador state. Let us not forget the 1960s, when it had approved the decision to reduce wages in order to overcome the financial crisis of the Bourguiba State, or the early 1970s, by using the trade union movement and the working class to help the state to get out of its crisis.

Today, the Union is not departing from this tradition and it is using all its weight both domestically as well towards foreign powers (States and institutions) to impose itself as a mediator holding the key to the crisis in Tunisia, by activating the method of national dialogue and forcing Kais Saied to accept it. But the latter reacted very quickly by defining the framework of this dialogue, which will only be the result of the "national consultation" organized by him. It has become clear that this approach of the union leadership is finding positive echoes with the International Monetary Fund and Western governments, which allows us to say that the intention of the union bureaucracy was to pressure Kais Saied to accept its approach for coping with the crisis and saving the dependent capitalist system of our country.

7. The importance of the independent position of the Workers' Party

Our party is almost the only one (besides the Democratic Pole and later the Socialist Party) to have taken a clear position on the July 25 coup, in total and clear contrast with the Islamist Party Ennahda that has led the reaction throughout the post-revolutionary decade. Our party based its position on the class nature of the parties in the

---

[9] This was the 5th Congress of the Destourian Party, held in the town of Sfax in November 1955, on the eve of the signing of the independence agreement which consecrated the control of Habib Bourguiba over the destiny of the country and the irreversible split within the national movement. This congress could not have been held without the help of the UGTT.

power struggle and the nature of the policies and methods that characterize each of them. It courageously defended its assessment of what happened before, during, and after July 25, despite all the criticism and attacks. Over time, many Tunisians, individuals and political and civilian movements and organizations, have become aware of the correctness and relevance of the point of view of the Workers' Party. This represents for us today a source of credibility, months after the July 25 coup and especially after the unmasking of the hypocritical and deceptive nature of the bourgeois and petty bourgeois propaganda under the guise of populism.

Our party, like other political parties, has been affected by the electoral defeat, but losing a battle does not mean losing the war. The class struggle that our society, like other societies in the contemporary world, is experiencing is a prolonged war that can be temporarily won by the reactionary forces of capital, represented by diverse and varied political expressions, which are likely to win other battles given the absence for the working class of the conditions for victory, namely class consciousness and organization.

This is the general context of the struggle of the Workers' Party in Tunisia to achieve a radical and deep change under the leadership of the working class and in its interest and that of all popular classes and strata. It is a context that is generally not favorable to the revolutionary struggle, a context sown with difficulties and obstacles, but at the same time one that provides objective factors of great importance for the development of the revolutionary struggle. These objective factors exist in Tunisia today, and they are expressed in the crisis of the system of government from above and below, its decadence and its exhaustion, the decline of the impact of its political expressions and the worsening of the economic and social situation of this system. The maturation of these objective conditions for launching a revolution in Tunisia represents a favorable circumstance for our party at this very moment, especially if we take into account its strong points: a revolutionary line and the correctness of its tactics on the developments that the country knows. This gives it an important degree of credibility and legitimacy to take an advanced position in the future movement of struggle, provided that it succeeds in strengthening the subjective condition, the necessary element to transform the dream into reality.

8. Our immediate task

Therefore, on the one hand, our task is to make the subjective conditions mature, that is, to widen the circle of revolutionary consciousness, the consciousness of the need to change the situation and eliminate the hegemony of the reactionary forces in our country. We must organize the struggle of the working masses and all other popular strata towards the realization of a powerful historical action to overthrow the reactionary regime and eliminate all manifestations of imperialist domination over our country on the other hand. The accomplishment of this task requires a path that can be long or short depending on many circumstances and factors, including that of the capacity of the conscious element, that is, the party organization, to fulfill its duty in the best possible way. We believe that our party, despite all its shortcomings and obstacles, can take up this mission. Our party has the most important element for this, which is its revolutionary line, its independent position and its revolutionary identity. But this alone is not enough; it is must plan and mobilize the available human energies, however limited they may be.

9. Our plan of action

Our action plan is based on two components: propaganda and activity on the ground. By propaganda, we mean the continuous and diligent work to expose and denounce the policies of the reactionary forces: Kais Saied, the Islamist party Ennahda and the Free Destourian Party, to unmask their tricks and maneuvers, to introduce the alternative policies of our party, to explain their merits in detail, and the solutions that it offers to the working classes.

We will have to make use of all kinds of media, visual, audio and written, each in its own field, at the right time, and with the appropriate methods and means. In addition to this, the struggle on the ground must be linked to the demands of the citizens, their protests and movements. This work will take various forms, those that are known to the general public and that have taken root during the struggle, and those that we must innovate and develop.

Whether it is propaganda, work on the ground, internal organizational work of a formative nature, or seminars on a regional or local scale, etc., the activists of the party and its base structures must leave behind their wait-and-see attitude and not limit themselves only to the campaigns and actions decided by the leading structures of the party. We must rather diversify and intensify our regional, local and sectoral initiatives. Let us start now, with those that the month of Ramadan[10] allows, which offers many opportunities for actions, whether internal (seminars, training, etc.) or external to the general public (distribution campaigns, rallies, political cafes, etc.).

These are the main lines of our plan of struggle in the next stage, in which we will rely mainly on our abilities (although modest) without underestimating any possibility of organizing joint actions with other political and civil forces. We are aware that there are real difficulties in organizing a planned and effective joint action, due to the division of the political scene between the opponents of the coup and its supporters. On this basis, it is difficult to find common ground except with those parties clearly opposed to the coup, which are very few and are currently limited to the Democratic Pole and the Socialist Party. Nevertheless, we must continue to strive to draw up a minimal platform with which some progressive and militant civil forces (National Union of Journalists, League for Human Rights, some trade unions, etc.) could join. The limitation of the number of our comrades and supporters should not become an obstacle; it should rather be an incentive for each of us to mobilize all our physical and mental energy, all our intellectual and technical capacities and our experience. Then the effect of the limitation of numbers will decrease, and this can even become a reason for success.

Likewise, the limited number of central, regional and local leaders should not prevent us from carrying out the plans of struggle that we have set for ourselves and the actions that we have planned. In fact, it is not the weakness of the number of cadres that concerns us, but above all the weakness of the quality of the cadre, who are now required to carry out a process of revolutionizing their status as leaders in the chain of command within the party, from top to bottom and vice versa. Comrades who are members of the Central Committee, members of regional and local committees, and leaders of party organizations are required, each in his or her sectoral or regional field, to share with the party what they have learned in the course of their

---

[10] The month of Ramadan is the month of fasting for the Muslim community. Among its characteristics, human activity, which is very slow during the day, increases in the evening. This has always allowed us as a Party to organize many political or cultural activities in the evenings of Ramadan.

organizational experience of mentoring, sensitizing, refining, guiding, encouraging and promoting in their organizational position. The leading comrades who have learned much in the organization should give much. They must revolutionize their abilities, on their own initiative. Our country is entering a phase of very great danger, and we must stand up and prepare to play our part at this stage. We must define our plan of action under the slogan "maximum exploitation of our energies".

So let us get to work comrades; victory is for the revolutionaries when they conceive and carry out the tasks that they plan.

Tunis, April 2, 2022

Turkey   Party of Labour (EMEP)

The Fallacy of "Green Capitalism"

The environmental movements that emerged in the 1960s with the approach of *"the wind and the sun are enough for us"* with the demand for renewable energy against fossil fuels and nuclear energy, diversified over time and when faced with a bundle of problems, the scope of their demands and *"proposals"* began to evolve.

Within the scope of neoliberal economic policies, the looting of urban assets, the increase of industrial waste and pollution, the emission of carbon and other toxic gases, the depletion of the ozone layer and the increase in the temperature of the planet, etc., all these were factors that attracted the attention of environmentalist-ecologist movements. These developments that led to a crisis that threatened human life and its natural environment not only made the issue interesting and led to the spread of protests, but also forced the monopoly bourgeoisie and state institutions to put the issue on the agenda.

Especially in advanced capitalist countries, no bourgeois government can afford to ignore the ecological crisis. Apart from economic reasons, two factors played an important role in the acceptance of the ecological crisis: first, the symptoms and devastating consequences of the climate crisis have grown with environmental disasters; and secondly, environmental awareness and the movement of the masses who react against the course of development have grown.

At present, almost all advanced capitalist countries, one after another, have announced many *"ecologically"* defined financial packages, legal measures and political decisions in the name of *"protecting nature"* and *"solving the climate crisis"*. At the summits in Tokyo, Paris and most recently Glasgow, "historic resolutions" have been agreed upon. For example, under the Paris Climate Agreement, global carbon emissions must be reduced by 55% by 2030 and down to zero by 2050 in order to limit the rise in the world's temperature to 1.5°.

The *"solution"* developed by the monopoly bourgeoisie and capitalist states against the destruction of the environment came out to be "green capitalism" with production factors of reduced carbon emissions. With an intense propaganda, rosy pictures were painted of *"green capitalism"* (i.e. *"global energy transformation"*, *"green cities"*, *"recycle economy"*, *"green industrial revolution"*, etc.). Even if the objective conditions of capitalism have been dragging the world into destruction and are not suitable for this role, current subjective conditions characterized by the low level of organization and consciousness of the working class, as well as the main ideological environment, allow this "solution" put forward by the monopolies to find a substantial audience, at least for the time being.

*

Although it was generally accepted that the natural and climatic conditions were gradually deteriorating, the views put forward in the name of a solution were mainly in a liberal bourgeois reformist and petty-bourgeois anarchist framework. The so-called *"environmental movement"* included the middle and petty bourgeois sections, as well as a section of rural and urban workers; its main demand in its initial years was the regulation of production in a way that would prevent the destruction of nature and living spaces. In the course of its development, this movement produced splits that formed a barrier against the labour movement with the defence of *"green capitalism"*, as well as those who took a stand against the monopoly capitalist plunder of nature. The "green" movement generally kept the critique of capitalism at a level acceptable to the bourgeoisie and blamed *"humans"*, not capitalists and monopoly capital, for the destruction of nature, suggesting that "individuals bear responsibility" and that the state(s) should follow a *"bioeconomic policy"*.

The increasingly severe consequences of environmental and climate problems led to the suggestion of putting boundaries on capitalism as a solution. This liberal bourgeois approach envisaged certain technical and economic arrangements, such as not exceeding the natural regenerative capacity of resources, avoiding excessive solid and liquid waste, avoiding pollution, maintaining adequate quality of air, water and soil, and protecting biodiversity. This approach blames *"humans"* for the deterioration of nature and climate, and covers up the capitalist commodification of nature, putting the *"disruptive effect"* created by the workers and labourers as human beings by use of heating, lighting, shelter and transportation vehicles, at the same level as the damage done to nature by petrochemical and automotive monopolies.

Liberal bourgeois environmentalism hides the class differences in society and its consequences; it obscures the fact that individuals are in different positions as they belong to different classes in accordance with their relation to the means of production. Though it cannot whitewash capitalism completely, this liberal approach equalizes a monopoly bourgeois with a worker in their relations with nature; it claims that our world has come to a stage where it cannot afford the actions of its population, which will reach ten billion soon, on the environment, and the responsibility for this belongs to all people who consume it nonstop and use technological advances for this purpose! What this *"free market environmentalism"* based on *"sustainable development"* proposes as an alternative is the planned reduction of rapid population growth and the persuasion of international monopolies and bourgeois states to *"alternative projects"*.

There are also those approaches which claim that the *"ecological crisis"* is caused by the rapid change in the relations between humans, society and nature as a result of the capitalist production and industrialization by means of technological advances, that they give *"a Marxist response to the ecological crisis"*. Stating that ecological deterioration has reached a "global and irreparable level" posing a *"threat to all living things"* and drawing attention to the capitalist basis of the problem, the approaches and solutions of ecological socialism (and anarchism) differ when it comes to nuances. Nevertheless, they have common approaches in their conditioning that human emancipation is only possible *"with the end of their domination over nature"*, in their opposition to industry, especially the automotive and chemical industries, and in their defence of limited production and

consumption based on the view that *"environmental resources are limited"*. What they have actually in common is their blindness to capitalism and surplus-value, reaching an extreme point in the views of Murray Bookchin, the defender of eco-anarchism, with the propositions that make capitalism de-capitalist, who argues that the basic contradiction humanity faces is between capitalist continuous growth and the limited resources of *"nature that exists by maintaining a balance"*.

*

It became possible to make propaganda for *"green capitalism"*, which is an overt defence of capitalism, in an ideological atmosphere where the working class and its movement do not have a sufficient level of organization and consciousness, and where bourgeois-liberal and reformist approaches claiming opposition to the existing order had a certain acceptance with their views on environment and nature, especially with regard to relations between nature and human beings that have been detached from their social class content.

For example, a sleight of hand was probably necessary for the capitalists to popularise *"green capitalism"* in society, under the conditions where oil and gas production, with their legendary monopolies, was known to be the driving force of international capitalism for many decades, and a certain connection, even if blurred, was still established between capitalism and the destruction of nature. Liberal-reformist environmentalist approaches prepared the grounds for this, spreading views on the relationship between nature and human beings that was disconnected from their social and class content. What was left to the monopoly bourgeoisie and its ideologues was the naturalization of social relations: they attempted to reflect the current social relation not as that of a particular society at a particular stage in history, but as the most natural and usual relation of humanity. They started out by considering the capitalist mode of production inviolable, not as a specific historical mode of production, but as the natural mode of production of humanity. There was no other way; only with purely natural capitalism progress could and would be possible!

With this approach, the ecological crisis has been brought into a form that is compatible with its universal character as a phenomenon. Ecological disaster was a universal problem of all humanity and therefore all people, all societies and countries should take responsibility! Thus, the undeniable causal relationship between the capitalist mode of production and ecological catastrophe has been transformed into an ordinary manifestation of the relationship of *"human nature"* with nature by naturalizing capitalist relations. In this way, the problem of ecological disaster, a problem that interests all humanity and living things as a whole, appeared before us as an inevitable consequence and problem of *"human nature"*, i.e. of production and consumption! The conclusion that can come out of this is simply that "We humans are responsible for the ecological crisis with our production and consumption"! Thus, the problem was isolated from the systemic dimension of the mode of production and reduced to a style of life and consumption or a technology problem. Capitalism has been shrewdly whitewashed and a point that is acceptable to monopolies has been reached: it is not capitalism that is responsible for the ecological crisis, but this or that sector, company party, or politician!

So, in order to act on a solid ground in the struggle to overcome the ecological crisis, the fundamental link that needs to be highlighted is the fact that the capitalist mode of production is neither the most natural nor the only mode of production without alternatives. It is capitalism that must be eliminated in order to survive ecological destruction.

*

There are many characteristics that distinguish the capitalist mode of production from previous social formations, but the aspect we need to emphasize in terms of our subject is that in the production of surplus-value it realizes the production of relative surplus-value in a large-scale, scientific and systematic way in addition to absolute surplus-value. The production of relative surplus-value is primarily based on the increase of labour productivity over a given period of time. There are many dimensions and necessities of this increase in labour productivity, but its result is clear: capitalism gets the opportunity to organize a much more widespread, rapid and large-scale production than the previous modes of production. By putting science and technology at the disposal of capital, increasing productivity and therefore production capacity on an enormous scale means that all the underground and aboveground natural resources are plundered at a scale not seen in any pre-capitalist social formation, turning them into a means of obtaining surplus-value.

Thus, the reckless destruction of nature and ecological balance becomes a natural necessity for capitalism. Moreover, because of competition between capital and especially monopolies, the faster and greater the plunder of nature, the more successful the people responsible for this destruction are considered. In short, the reckless plundering and destruction of nature is inherent in the capitalist mode of production, whose sole purpose is the production of surplus-value, which is an indispensable aspect of it.

Ecological crisis means that the level of sharpening of the contradiction between the limitless drive for capital accumulation and the natural conditions of living things has reached a point where it cannot operate as before in the form that has hitherto been able to hold together the mutually excluding aspects of the two. And when this trend cannot be stopped, it means that a threshold will be crossed where irreversible destruction will occur in the natural conditions of living things.

Capital's approach to nature takes place on the basis of a measure that does not exist in nature itself, that is the production of value and surplus-value. As the increased productivity of labour and the brigand plunder of nature go hand in hand, nature, like everything else, is subordinated to the law of value and capitalist commodity production.

However, while this is the character of the relationship between capitalism and nature, the market and its laws are the basic criteria of all the measures taken under the name of the fight against the ecological crisis at the ecology summits where capitalist states and their representatives come together. This is the pinnacle of hypocrisy.

It is not only that mines, waters, minerals, soils etc. have been commodified, but nature itself has also been transformed into a huge sea of commodities with the new possibilities offered by science and technology. Today, bio and gene technology is applied to agricultural commodity production; genetic information contained in some seeds and certain endemic plants is patented; and the sun and wind is converted into energy and sold. Interestingly, we are witnessing the fact that, under the name of combating the climate crisis, carbon dioxide emission, which is considered to be the main cause of the climate crisis, is itself turned into a commodity that can be bought and sold!

As a matter of fact, the Emissions Trading System is a striking example of this, and it reveals how and with what kind of logic the climate crisis is being fought under capitalism.

As is known, in line with the *"climate change prevention target"*, the Kyoto Protocol introduced a regulation regarding the amount of worldwide carbon dioxide emissions: emissions trading. This takes place according to the *"cap-and-trade-principle"*. A cap was set on the amount of worldwide carbon dioxide emissions, and this amount was shared between states in the form of a carbon emission right (certificate). Every country that has signed the Kyoto Protocol (191 at present) obtains the right to emit carbon in the amount determined in the protocol. It goes without saying that the right to carbon emissions is the right to pollute the atmosphere. When some countries reduce their carbon emissions, they accumulate their unused polluting rights in the form of emission certificates, which are then put up for sale on the international market and bought by states that have released more carbon than they are allowed. And just like governments, companies can buy and sell their carbon emission rights (emission certificates).

The truth is that the amount of carbon released into the atmosphere is left to the laws of the market. The market, on the other hand, operates according to the law of value, not the laws of nature!

Two news articles from Bloomberg reveal another fact: The first one, titled *"Raw material price pressure on the green transition"*, states the following:

"Large price increases are on the horizon for key raw materials such as cobalt, copper, lithium and nickel. According to a study published by the German Economic Research Institute, the demand for these raw materials will increase rapidly in the coming years.

"Of course, this could become one of the hurdles that will complicate the transition to green energy, because these raw materials are currently indispensable for the production of electric cars, solar panels and wind turbines. Large amounts of copper are needed to build wind and solar power plants; and cobalt, lithium and nickel are needed for electric car batteries. According to the International Energy Agency (IEA), copper consumption is expected to double, nickel consumption is expected to triple, and cobalt consumption is expected to increase six-fold in the next 20 years.

"The largest increase in demand is expected for lithium. It is predicted that the demand for lithium in 2040 will be exactly 20 times higher than today. It seems difficult for supply to keep up with this level of demand, because large investments are needed for the extraction of these metals. According to the scenario announced by the German Economic Research Institute, copper prices may be 70 percent

higher and lithium prices 180 percent higher in 2030 compared to 2020." [1]

The second piece is about the calculation of Bloomberg New Energy Finance. By that reckoning, the "global energy transition" characterized by the shift from oil and gas to wind and solar energy *"will require investments worth $173 trillion in energy supply and infrastructure over the next 30 years."*

It is undeniable that the data in the two reports show the reasons behind the "green passion" of finance capital: profit and new investments for it.

While the trend towards *"green capitalism"* is causing the monopolies that have invested in oil and natural gas, which has long been at the top of the *"largest companies"* lists, to lose power together with their discredited sectors, it is clear that the increase in raw material prices will be in favour of the capitalists who invested in these raw materials and against the capitalists who use them in production. And it seems inevitable that this situation will intensify the competition between capitalists and spark new investments by including sectoral innovations as well as innovations in the technology used. Considering that oil and gas resources will be depleted in a few decades, *"global energy transformation"* as a fundamental aspect of *"green capitalism"* was actually necessary, and it seems inevitable that the monopolies that have invested heavily in this sector cannot avoid their *"destiny"* unless they diversify their investments and take precautions. However, the price increase in certain raw materials shows that sectoral fluctuations are also normal and that the uneven development of capitalism is evident in all areas, and all this will intensify competition, especially among monopolies.

*

"Green capitalism" is the propaganda that the ecological crisis can be overcome within the current capitalist mode of production. Accordingly, the fight against the ecological crisis must be done in accordance with the laws of the capitalist economy and the market. Then, if capitalism will not cease to be capitalism with *"green capitalism"*, which no one claims, the following question needs to be answered: Are the laws of the capitalist economy and the market

---

[1] https://www.bloomberght.com/yesil-gecise-hammadde-fiyati-baskisi-2297569

compatible with the steps required to overcome the ecological crisis? Leaving aside all other questions, examples of carbon emissions trading, possible increases in raw material prices and the enormous investments required by the energy transition all indicate that they are not compatible. Just as it is not surprising that the capitalist pursues profit, there is no reason to be surprised at this! A capitalist is a capitalist because his sole aim is profit, and the capitalist economy and the market have their own laws which differ from the laws of nature.

The main reason why capital is turning to the *"green transformation"* today and not 20 years ago, for example, certainly has nothing to do with the increase in global warming, but with the changing rates of profit.

The proof is simple, given the transformation highlighted in the energy sector: The technology used today in renewable energy is not new and has been around for decades. However, until recently, factors such as the cost of production using this technology, labour productivity, market volume, preventing or delaying the devaluation of the capital invested in fossil fuel, has kept the monopolies away from investing in this field, because it was not profitable enough. However, the ecological crisis has not been a problem of just a few years and it made the use of these technologies necessary many years ago. However, because it was not profitable, these technologies, which are now being promoted at a high pitch, were not invested in then. Today the situation has changed. In addition to the limited oil and gas reserves, for example, the *"hydrogen market"* alone has now reached $150 billion. By 2050, it is expected to reach at least $600 billion. Investing in this field is now worth competing for it! And now capitalist states with their "ecological funds" have begun to meet the cost and competitiveness challenges for their classes of capitalists.

Marxists have never found it strange that capital pursues profit. On the contrary, Marxists have exposed capital and capitalism, which are not and cannot be based on human beings, their health or nature in general, since profit is their sole reason and purpose of existence. What is interesting is that those who describe Marxists who advocate overcoming the capitalist order as *"dreamers"* expect capital not to behave like capital using *"green capitalism"*!

A question may come to mind: Is it not better to turn to *"renewable energy"*, *"green transformation"*, *"clean industry"* now, even if it is for the purpose of capital accumulation? Is it not true that every lessening of the destruction of nature counts as a gain?

No doubt. However, the point where the destruction of the ecological balance has been reached has already made the best-of-evil approaches meaningless. The current magnitude of the ecological crisis and the dynamic in its development trend imply that possible *"gains"* will not actually be gains, and every lost day, that is, leaving the historical task of overcoming this crisis to the selfish and frivolous interests and impulses of capital, means that we are getting closer to the turning point where the *"irreparable rift"* (Marx)[2] that capitalism is causing in nature can no longer be reversed.

*

On the other hand, the emergence of "green capitalism" on the agenda as a result of the *"ecological crisis"* also implies that the capitalist mode of production itself is open to discussion on the basis of a criterion that capital is unable to control directly. This is the criterion of the question of existence or non-existence of nature which creates the conditions for humanity and all living things. This debate takes two forms today. 1) The common and dominant approach is as follows: If nature is in question, this is a universal and supra-class problem which concerns all humanity equally and everybody should take responsibility. 2) This is a problem that is universal and therefore has a dimension that interests the entire planet and humanity but is specific to a certain mode of production (capitalism) in which a certain class (capital) is dominant in terms of responsibility.

Obviously, it is the subjective dimension of the problem that makes the first approach dominate. The main reason for the

---

[2] Reading Jesus von Liebig's book "Agricultural Chemistry", Marx was interested in the causes of soil depletion and approached the problems of the social material exchange with nature from an ecological perspective, considering them as a contradiction of the capitalist mode of production. The plundering of nature was a problem of modern capitalist social production, and according to Marx, the plunder of nature would continue: "in this way it produces conditions that provoke an irreparable rift in the interdependent process of social metabolism, a metabolism prescribed by the natural laws of life itself. The result of this is a squandering of the vitality of the soil, and trade carries this devastation far beyond the bounds of a single country." (Karl Marx's Economic Manuscript of 1864-1865, translated by Ben Fowkes, p. 798)

dominance of the bourgeois approach is that the *"ecological crisis"* has emerged at a stage where the multi-faceted devastation of the historical defeat of the working class has not yet been overcome and where the working class cannot leave its mark on political struggles with its independent movement. As a matter of fact, it is today's reality that those who believe that the end of the world may come due to carbon emissions, climate change and rapid temperature rise, do not believe that there is an alternative to capitalism, and unfortunately this approach keeps the majority under its influence.

However, the historical reality is that we are faced with an objectively overripe capitalism in that it is overdue to be replaced by a social order that is its opposite. This is capitalism that is objectively outdated, not only in terms of the severe economic, social and cultural contradictions in the social life of the peoples of the world, but also in terms of putting the natural living conditions of the human species at risk on this planet.

The ecological crisis we are in manifests itself in the erosion of the form in which the contradiction between the conditions of existence of capitalism and the natural conditions of living things has undertaken up until now. Where we are now requires the termination of capitalism's exploitative and plundering relationship with nature, at least in terms of nature's reaction. However, the current situation of the subjective factor determined by the consciousness and organizational level of the working class, which is the main force that will end the domination of capital, is not ready to take this urgent step, at least in terms of guaranteeing the survival of the life at risk.

The so-called *"green capitalism"* is an attempt to reshape the contradiction that has reached its peak in capitalism's relationship with nature in favour of capital but against ecology, and thus to continue the destruction of nature by plundering it. This initiative will have an ecological, economic and social bill which the workers and laborers of the world, especially the youth and the oppressed peoples, will be expected to pay.

March 2022

United States of America	American Party of Labor

We Reject Biden's and Putin's War

"It is the duty of the socialists of every country to wage an un-relenting struggle against the chauvinism and patriotism of their own country (and not only of the enemy)."
Vladimir Lenin

Immediately following the final dissolution of the Soviet Union, US imperialism and its pundits went into a frenzied victory dance, loudly announcing a New World Order that signaled the "end of history" and the emergence of a unipolar world headed by the United States and its allies. However, the celebration was short lived as, following a period of instability in the 1990s, a new imperialist power emerged as a regional contender against the United States, Putinite Russia.

Let there be no mistake: US imperialism is the foremost enemy of the peoples of the world. However, this must not blind us to the aggressive intent and actions of Putin's aspiring imperial regime. Putin's Russia is not part of an "axis of resistance" to US imperialism, as some have termed it. It is a capitalist/imperialist state that fully intends to stake out its claim as a world power, whether in opposition to US imperialism or in partial partnership with it, as evidenced during the years of the Trump administration.

The rivalry between US and Russian imperialism has escalated to the point of possible armed conflict between the two, as each is championing their chosen proxies in Eastern Europe, with the United States supporting the Ukrainian government and Russia throwing its weight behind the breakaway regions of Donetsk and Lugansk.

The years of saber-rattling, posturing, and covert actions on the part of both imperialist states has now reached the breaking point. Both powers are at the brink of war.

The American Party of Labor firmly and emphatically rejects the war moves of both Biden and Putin. We are not deceived by Biden's hypocrisy and sanctimony. Neither are we taken in by Putin's chauvinistic claims that Ukraine is "historically Russian land."

We call on the peoples of Ukraine, Russia, and the United States to resist the warmongers with every sinew of their strength. We demand the immediate withdrawal of all troops from the region, an end to threats and sanctions, and a political solution to the Ukraine crisis on the basis of the Leninist principle of self-determination for all peoples; a self-determination free of all imperialist pressure, blackmail, extortion, and subterfuge.

The imperialists in Washington and Moscow care nothing for the Ukrainian people; they care only for their own power and profits — power and profits which they seek to gain with the blood of the peoples of the region and the world.

We Say "No!"
No to Biden's and Putin's War Moves!
For a Revolutionary Solution to the Crisis of Capitalism!

April 2022

Uruguay	Marxist-Leninist Communist Party of Uruguay – PCMLU

Breaking with the Two-Party System, a Task of Historical Perspectives

From the moment that the electoral reform of 1996 established the runoff (second round) for the election of the President in the Uruguayan electoral system, the two-party system developed significantly, expressing itself with great force at the electoral level.

The bankruptcy suffered by the Colorado Party in 2004, a historical party of the industrial bourgeoisie and of an important sector of the agrarian bourgeoisie, after the presidency of Jorge Batlle [President of Uruguay from 2000 to 2005 from the Colorado Party – *translator's note*] came to deepen an electoral model in which two large coalitions contest both the presidency as well as the government and parliament. In fact, these remain the two large blocs throughout the parliamentary period.

These blocs, which were initially composed of the Broad Front and smaller parties on the one hand, and the Colorado and National Parties on the other, have remained without great variation in these last 25 years. They vary only in the relation of forces and adding some other support, such as the incorporation of Cabildo Abierto, a heterogeneous party with a strong presence of sectors with careers in the Armed Forces. This was the last large incorporation into this system, forming part of the second bloc mentioned above.

There is no doubt that the existence of two large blocs led by different sectors of the native bourgeoisie and the petty bourgeoisie favor the support of the current system. A false antagonism is created between two models of managing a political system that is only responsible for adjusting some aspects of the backward and dependent capitalist mode of production that has not been questioned by the successive governments of different parties. They have only been concerned with complying with the mandates of the multilateral credit organizations and maintaining a good investment grade in order to attract capital. All this has happened without any fundamental discrepancies when it comes to accepting every command of imperialism.

Meanwhile, those political organizations that have tried to stay out of these blocs have gone without shame or glory to being absorbed, or, at best, remaining inconsequential while waiting patiently for their assimilation, given their inability to overcome the schemes imposed by the political agenda of the two large coalitions.

A brief review of the formation of these blocs

Since the emergence of Uruguay as an independent republic, the two-party system made itself felt with the existence of two major bourgeois parties, the Colorado Party and the National Party, parties that did not hesitate to bring their disputes to the military level on more than one occasion.

Despite this, the economic deformations of backward and dependent Uruguayan capitalism have created various complications when it comes to understanding the class representation of each of the factions of these parties. This has made the political analysis superficial, putting aside the material aspect of the contradictions between them, putting aside the concrete interests of the social classes and their sections in their different positions in the course of history.

As an example, we can mention the many contradictions between the pro-Rivera sector and Batllismo within the Colorado Party, which far from being contradictions of "power" were the reflection of the contradictions between the native bourgeoisie linked to the incipient industrial sector with another bourgeois sector more closely associated with finance capital and agro-export production. This explains in part the flirtations of a large part of the National Party – a party led by agrarian sectors – with the pro-Rivera section heir to much of the oligarchic structure that followed the independence of the Uruguayan State.

Undoubtedly, the explanation of these contradictions and their concrete expression in the country's history deserve a much broader explanation that can be given in this article, but this mention helps us to briefly understand the evolution of these blocs and how what ends up predominating are class interests and not party colors.

Moving forward a few decades in history, the second Batlle failed in the attempts to promote a developmentalist model. The subsequent agreements of the Uruguayan government with the multilateral credit organizations dominated by US imperialism entering the 1960s, would put an end to any form of an independent capitalist project in order to deepen Uruguay's subjection to the international organization of labor. This strengthened its role as an exporter of raw materials and an importer of capital in this area, to the detriment of industrial development and an independent economy.

This qualitative leap in the economic development of Uruguay would separate the sections, clarifying much further the political expression of the different sections of the native bourgeoisie and the petty bourgeoisie. This was after the mass abandonment of several contingents of both the National Party and the Colorado Party that were the most consistent representatives of the interests of the petty bourgeoisie interested in an independent capitalist development. These would group themselves around the old Parties of the left and the MLN-Tupamaros in a process of unity of the left that would materialize with the formation of the Trade Union Unity through the CNT [National Convention of Workers] and later with the appearance of the Broad Front in the national elections of 1971.

It is worth noting that, despite the official narrative, the proletariat was absent as a politically independent class due to the absence of a Communist Party guided by Marxism-Leninism, a product of the ideological decomposition of the PCU [Communist Party of Uruguay] and the elimination of different revolutionary organizations at the dawn of the coup d'état. This makes the working class, throughout this process and at present, a class without effective political leadership, forced to choose between one or the other sector of the bourgeoisie.

The development of this whole process, including that of dependence on imperialism, has helped to further crystallize the interests of the different sections of the native bourgeoisie, so that today there are only minor differences summarized by questions of management of resources and the state apparatus. As a class, the bourgeoisie is not capable of carrying out a political project different from the one it began almost two centuries ago. It cannot establish its own independent productive model, since the degree of dependence on imperialism is such that, without destroying the relations of capitalist production, without leaving the framework of the capitalist world market, it is impossible to break with dependence and therefore develop a different program that would lead to their disappearance as a social class and their corresponding privileges.

The rupture of Uruguay's economic dependence not only requires good intentions on the part of the political bureaucracy, as some sectors of the left claim, but it also requires a new economic organization that allows effective planning of the national economy and its subsequent reorganization, a significant increase in the productivity of labor by concentrating production, and definitively putting an end to those unproductive or barely productive sectors of the economy. With this would come a radical reform of the state that completely destroys the current legal system and the entire state bureaucracy.

All this, obviously, has as an absolute condition the expropriation of foreign companies, of local capitalists and also of large sectors of the petty bourgeoisie dedicated to being parasitic intermediaries and to speculation that unnecessarily inflate prices and hinder the system of distribution. With a stroke of a pen, this would erase almost an entire social class – the bourgeoisie including a considerable part of the petty bourgeoisie – and a wide range of well-to-do officials in the commercial and financial sector and also in the State.

In short, the bourgeoisie can only contest the administration of the state and keep the economy as it is or make itself disappear; the latter, of course, is impossible except in science fiction.

This was proven in Uruguay during the 15 years in which the left ruled, unable from any point of view to change absolutely anything in terms of the economic destiny of the country. In the most developed of cases in the region, the left has only been able to change masters; if it ceased to depend on the United States, it is because it became dependent on China, the USSR (Cuba) or shared its dependence among several powers.

It must be borne in mind that the left, from its beginnings, never considered overcoming the capitalist mode of production; on the contrary, its program was aimed at strengthening it, at the development of a "serious," "good" capitalism, which would allow a greater creation and distribution of wealth starting from the development of national industry – always in the hands of the bourgeoisie or the bourgeois state, which is the same thing. The historical subject of their transformations was always the "national" business owner and the State, also without eliminating foreign investment. For some reason, they thought that they would be willing to invest from abroad in the development of the country, only because the Uruguayan State was willing and had good ideas for doing so.

The impossibility of putting this program into practice, the impossibility of confronting imperialism on which it depends, makes the program of the left impossible, making them govern like their predecessors. This is not the product of the "betrayal" of such or such a leader, as sectors that analyze the facts in a romantic way say, but a product of the objective conditions. It is due to the framework in which Uruguay is incorporated into the world market, since we insist: no imperialist power, no foreign investor has an interest in investing in Uruguay so that it develops itself while, on the other hand, the native bourgeoisie lacks the capital to do so.

This leads all those sectors of the left that are outside of the Broad Front to claim the historical project of the left, especially industrial development that is led by the native bourgeoisie or "national liberation" as a way to break with imperialism and to develop an independent economic model, are only a romantic caricature. Both have the same project with the difference that some have already beaten their heads against the wall when trying to start it and others want to stumble on the same stone. This also explains why the "critical" left throughout the region, once progressivism went into opposition, has not hesitated to ally itself with its former enemies and tail it: its program is the same, its methods are the same, the class interests they defend are also the same.

As a result, as was pointed out at the beginning of the article, we have two large blocs: the left as a fundamental expression of the petty bourgeoisie, the most affluent sectors among the ranks of the workers (state, banking, technical, white-collar workers in industry), professionals and intellectuals. On the other hand, the Multicolor Coalition [a coalition of center and right parties – *translator's note*] most clearly represents the interests of the comprador bourgeoisie (the intermediaries), the agro-exporters, the industrial petty bourgeoisie and the hierarchy of trade and services.

Although it seems redundant and we run the risk of falling into repetition, it is worth insisting that none of these sectors have great contradictions with the current model. On the contrary, they are sectors that are mostly well-off and manage to function with relative ease; although it is true that some of them run the risk of joining the ranks of the working class in the face of each crisis, the relative economic bonanza experienced in recent years has taken away all forms of combativity. Today, when some of its privileges were questioned by the pandemic, they did not hesitate to launch the struggle opportunistically and in a business-like way, the state being the best example of that.

The working class, unorganized and politically demoralized, despite being the majority of the population, today lacks leadership. It has lost its independence and unconsciously vacillates between the left and the right; it remains outside the trade union movement that on more than one occasion had to admit its inability to organize it.

Indeed, to be able to reach the working class, to offer it a program, a tactic and the forms of organization that it needs in order to face the successive attacks on its living conditions, to achieve the demands it needs to cement the foundations for a broader struggle for socialism, is the great historical task that our Party must face in order to break with the current two-party system, to gain the sympathy of the majority class of society and to add to its ranks its best elements; that is the reason for our existence.

The experience of the left outside the Broad Front and a great example of what not to do

With the coming into office of Luís Lacalle Pou with the consequent change of the role of the Broad Front, which was forced to go into opposition, the parties of the left outside the Broad Front – except for some honorable and minuscule exceptions – did not take long to join the agenda of the Broad Front. They made the Front's struggles their own and even, in many cases, showing a total lack of shame, also endorsed its slogans as the continuation of a long process that leads to the definitive absorption of these organizations.

As we said, the unity of the entire left, led by the Broad Front, is a process that has been cooking "over low heat" as a result of the inability of those sectors to transform themselves into a real alternative and in their immobility in some cases; in their inability to effectively break with the tradition of the Broad Front with which they had broken verbally temporarily, always at a time when the apparent rupture could not lead to great contradictions for the Government of the Broad Front or a new re-election.

The truth is that outside and inside the Broad Front a very wide range of organizations and parties have been built that, throughout their history, have been unable to seriously contest for the leadership of the labor movement and, on the contrary, they continuously vacillate in a stagnant way through the social movement without being able to grow beyond a small handful of militants despite already being the oldest such group with more than 50 years of existence.

The eternal lack of development of these organizations could not have occurred if it were not for their lack of effort in the understanding of reality and starting from this the development of a program that responds to this, together with a concrete tactic that has the objective of promoting it and making it known to the masses.

These sectors of the left throughout their existence have ignored the responsibility of achieving a serious theoretical development or they have reduced it to a very select group of their membership, limiting their practice to the repetition of magical formulas coming from dystopian realities copied mechanically: artiguism [the ideas of José Gervasio Artigas – translator's note], the tactics of the Comintern, Trotskyism, the theory of focos [armed struggle by small groups – translator's note], Maoism are ideas that, although they could have had value (which in itself is already debatable) and importance at some point, for more than 60 years they have not been successfully applied anywhere, because our current society and the development of capitalism are not the same.

People have tried to apply and are still applying these formulas as a shortcut to avoid the headache of the scientific elaboration of a program and a tactic, a task that involves meticulous work over several years or decades and that in Uruguay, as an alternative to the political project of the bourgeoisie, only a very small group of organizations has tried to do it in an incomplete manner that were the product of the social explosion of the 1960s and the subsequent coup d'état.

On the contrary, the theorists of the left outside the Broad Front are in the best of cases cadres borrowed from the University, or they have dedicated themselves for decades to reproduce stories of what they had experienced when they were young. This is why today the left does not have strategic debates but rather sporadic talks when the time comes to remember a date.

The lack of a serious analysis of reality, of a program and an effective tactic makes all this a chronic problem that is also expressed in its practice. The consequence of this has been the inability to have promoted any struggle, let alone to win them. This, as much as it sounds like pedantry, is the sad reality. These sectors have been characterized by "accompanying" the struggles, "being with the workers who are fighting", participating "in a minority" in what drives the union bureaucracy, but there is not a single example where these sectors promote a concrete demand without the impulse or approval of the bureaucracy; on the contrary, its history is the decades-long repetition of a very primitive spontaneity.

Yes, it is true, we will not deny it, that the left outside the Broad Front has been able to promote mobilizations, which are a much more transparent reflection of what we mentioned. These are always mobilizations on the defensive and within the frameworks of bourgeois legality, such as rejecting a bill or in response to some concrete and partial event. This highlights the lack of a program and the impossibility of having a policy that anticipates the future or organizes the masses for a different future, which makes the eternal anarchist slogan of "resist" the only formula of its political practice.

Clearly, it is impossible to create a lasting movement, to consolidate a project organizationally and politically that broadly includes the working class without proposing a clear and concrete program, without calling on the masses to win it by organizing them during the process.

Bearing in mind that the Broad Front as the majority sector and leader of the left has given itself over hand and foot to imperialism, that it has been unable to express in practical terms a program different from the historical program of subjection to the native bourgeoisie, and that the sectors of the left that are "critical" of progressivism directly lack program and initiative, we can say that the left, and above all the left outside of the Broad Front, are the clearest expression of the cult of spontaneity, which makes our work of consolidating and developing our Party among the working class as a tool that surpasses the left ideologically, organizationally and politically/practically.

In order to break with the two-party system, no effort must be spared in the fusion of Socialism and the workers' movement.

For quite some time, our Party has insisted on the difficult subjective situation in which the working class finds itself, politically and ideologically unarmed, absent from the trade union movement – co-opted by well-to-do sectors – and without a clear program or even systematic propaganda that moralizes it when facing the misery to which it is subjected.

In recent years their living conditions have been severely affected, losing rights of all kinds, experiencing periods of extreme uncertainty and working for subsistence wages without resistance, which clearly reflects their state of demoralization and their lack of effective organization of which we have spoken.

As we have already pointed out, the left outside the Broad Front has been unable to take advantage of this situation politically and the very brief and few spontaneous outbreaks that have occurred in recent history have run like sand through its hands without being able to take advantage of the situation.

Being aware of this, our Party, despite being still young, is facing a challenge of great importance in historical terms by considering the correct task of elaborating a program, which is based on the objective reality in which capitalist society in general and Uruguayan society in particular finds itself. It can respond to the endless sorrows that the working class experiences; to develop a tactic on this basis that can involve the greatest number of workers, which requires, as a result of the political-ideological disarmament that we mentioned, a hard work of previous organization.

Undoubtedly, the correct development of these two tasks – the drawing up of a program and the work of the Party among the masses – is the Chinese wall that separates us broadly from fulfilling our historical mission and drowning in the ocean of acronyms that exist today and that are condemned to perish in the future.

We believe that the Second Congress of our Party has given us a strong impetus in terms of the need to break definitively with the left by establishing general directives on how to continue advancing in this sense. These, if applied correctly, will achieve a qualitative leap that allows us to develop more efficiently among the masses.

We need to develop an active practice to put on the table the fundamental problems facing the working class, patiently and without voluntarism: to improve working conditions, to lower the prices of popular consumer products, to improve housing conditions, to improve access to quality education for working students or children of workers, among others; these are some of the points to be addressed. But we would be lying if we said that we have the tools to carry through an effective struggle; this requires considerable programmatic and tactical development without absolving ourselves of the responsibility of raising awareness of these problems.

The need to advance in building a program, without neglecting, of course, the development of our concrete practical work, raises the objective of strengthening party work in a precise and forceful way in those places where we do have development and doubly where we have programmatic development and presence.

This means establishing the principles and the line of the Party in a clear and transparent way, with the necessary flexibility for each location, but above all developing practical work that serves to organize the masses in each location and thus fight for their demands against the practice of resolving immediate and excessively specific problems of the location that creates tasks that only serve electoral politics. The first is the communist style of work, the second is the opportunist style of work of the left that we want to eliminate from the mass organizations.

Therefore, far from what some distracted people may think or what some opportunists may blame us for, the tactics of our Party, far from being based on immobility, have the double challenge of radically transforming the style of work among the masses, on the one hand, and of advancing in a broad study and knowledge of objective reality, using the materialist-dialectical method and inspired by the experience that the classics of Marxism-Leninism have left us. This is a hard and complex task that mortally wounded our adversaries in their attempt.

The rupture with the bourgeois two-party system, establishing a proletarian political alternative that politically raises the working class to being a class for itself, is a task of historical perspectives on which our Party will not vacillate and in which it already places stone upon stone after 70 years of havoc perpetrated by opportunism.

Is a third force needed at the national level?

We live in a deindustrialized country, based on services and the export of raw materials. Every successive government, whether of the right or left, plunges Uruguay deeper and deeper into dependence and economic backwardness. We cannot aspire to have a standard of living similar to that of industrialized countries with an economy based on tourism, on the export of raw materials or on services. Only on the basis of a developed economy can the life of the working class be raised to the levels that modern society makes possible.

The capitalist class in Uruguay is tied to imperialism; this society is sealing the destiny of our country by imposing what is produced and how. As long as the capitalist class runs the country, as long as it controls the economy in conjunction with the monopolies, as long as they have the state at their service, the future will be one of worsening, precariousness and impoverishment for the majority of society.

The Uruguayan bourgeoisie has shown its inability to develop the national economy. The current model of production promoted by all the governments, and which respond to the economic and political interests of the bourgeoisie of our country, does not need skilled labor, nor high levels of training, nor that many active workers. For this reason, the economic restructuring that is being promoted has as a result the disappearance of skilled jobs and workplaces. As in the whole region, this result is aimed at imposing social assistance programs and underemployment administered by NGOs that serve as a retaining wall against possible social demands and outbreaks.

Both political blocs that are contesting for the national government do not intend and cannot break with the current model. Only by breaking with the relations of production is it possible to change the course of the country, only by concentrating the productive forces to develop and enhance them is it possible to achieve industrialization and national development. But the driving force of this operation does not belong to either the current state or the native bourgeoisie. Only the Uruguayan working class uniting its forces with the working class of the region can create the bases to get out of backwardness and dependence, to achieve the standard of living that modern society allows us.

Neither the left nor the right bloc in general nor the political bureaucracy that responds to one or the other bloc are interested in breaking with the current economic relations. The sectors that these blocs represent have their existence assured, at least for the moment. That is why the answer is in the affirmative: yes, a third force is necessary at the national level, which breaks with the two-party system and represents the vast majority of the working class, but above all, that puts forward a possible and alternative program.

The program of a third force that seeks to represent the working class, both in its immediate demands and in its historical interests, has to be based on three premises:

1. It must break with the entire political bureaucracy, of the left or right, which lives by defrauding the working class, both by the State and by the official unions and associations.

2. Only by the concentration of the productive forces under Workers' Power for the development of industry, particularly of the means of production, will the social base be created that allows for raising the standard of living of the entire population.

3. This is not possible without destroying the economic and political power of the bourgeoisie, without destroying the current social relations that limit our possibilities for development.

The bourgeoisie in our country is not going to do today what it did not do in the last hundred years; the working class has to take over the destiny of our country and the first step is to form itself as an independent social force. Thus the immediate task today is to take the first steps in the formation of a third force that leads us out of the swamp of the two-party system and proposes a socialist program.

March 2022

Venezuela	Marxist-Leninist Communist Party of Venezuela – PCMLV

A Time of Wars and Revolutions

To analyze the reality of today's world, we must take into account the sharpening of the fundamental contradictions of the time, which are seen on three levels:

1. The struggle between two imperialist blocs, a traditional one, experiencing economic stagnation, led by the US and the EU. Another, an emerging one led by China and Russia, with a process of economic growth that has allowed it to assert itself and drag other countries into its policies; this is seen as a threat by the traditional bloc, which is creating permanent struggles.

2. The contradiction between the imperialist powers and the dependent countries that want to carve out a path of their own is rising.

3. The struggle between the bourgeoisie and the proletariat is emerging and is seen in mobilizations, strikes, conflicts, demands of the working class to defend its rights that are being suppressed or eliminated by the capitalists in order to increase the surplus value stolen from the wage earners and to increase the concentration and centralization of capital, while the workers are living under worse conditions every day.

These contradictions have been escalating to the point of leading to open war. The confrontations that still persist in Palestine, Iraq, Libya, Syria, Afghanistan and Yemen are only stages that have pushed the confrontation towards Europe itself. They are wars with economic causes that confront the two imperialist blocs in the struggle for a new distribution of markets, sources of raw materials, cheap labor, strategic points for the big monopolies and the ruling bourgeoisie. This is expressed as a confrontation between Russia and Ukraine for nationalist reasons, confusing the unwary; but it is really another step in the clash between both imperialist blocs, since the emerging bloc needs a new division of the world to expand its share of the pie, while the traditional imperialist bloc tries to oppose this by various methods, without achieving its goal so far.

China, Russia and their partners are seeking greater space for their capital and commodities, while the U.S. and the EU want to block their way and maintain their hegemonic control of the past.

War is the answer for the imperialists because it is the suitable instrument to resolve the control of wealth and to overcome the economic crises since war allows them to stimulate their industrial apparatus, produce weapons, vehicles, logistics, declare a state of emergency, limit the rights of the workers and increase their exploitation. With it the surplus value and profits of the great imperialist monopolies increase while they take advantage of the resources of the State to finance their projects at the expense of of the hunger of the peoples.

For the working class, the peasants and the exploited majorities, imperialist war means only destruction, death, wounded and social dramas, while for the big monopolies it is the way to revive their economies.

The proletariat also seeks an answer to its situation; it is clear that the highest stage of capitalism is a time of wars and revolutions. The oppressed of the world must not become cannon fodder in an imperialist war for a new division of the world; that is why we must reject imperialist wars and prepare the conditions, in the midst of them, to advance towards revolution.

In the war between NATO and Russia, historical references and fascist practices become evident, this is clear. For revolutionaries this is something very serious that expresses at a higher level the process of fascistization that capital utilizes and that we have been denouncing. It is no longer just a group of skinheads threatening people on the streets. In Ukraine they are armed and trained groups that openly call themselves Nazis and that have managed to control a country, the

government and the state, leading fascist actions towards ethnic cleansing and the structuring of a completely Nazi program with shock groups and slogans of segregation.

The ICMLPO and each of its member parties have the responsibility to adjust our methods of work and accelerate the processes of coordination in order to respond efficiently to current and future challenges.

Hard struggles are coming as a result of the sharpening of the fundamental contradictions; confrontation will be the order of the day. Today the main forms of struggle can already be seen and it is to be hoped that they will continue to develop towards higher levels in which the proletariat, and the oppressed of the world in general, will be directly involved. Regarding this we must ask ourselves: How will our organizations take up the challenges of the future? Our party has asked itself this question and considers that it is urgent to raise our organizational levels, our ability to respond, our propaganda and mobilization in order to guide the popular masses in the coming struggles.

The guiding principles are the analyses and policies elaborated by the Communist International in its time, and although it is true that in their particularities the conditions are different, we are still in the imperialist stage of capitalism, with the control by the monopolies, finance capital and the struggles for a new division of the world.

As in the past, capitalists resort to extreme methods, to the elimination of rights, imposition of governments, persecution of revolutionaries, destruction of productive forces, concentration and centralization of capital by violent methods, attempts to apply colonial forms, imperialist invasions and wars, placing the weight of crises on the shoulders of the working class and peasants, while the big capitalists obscenely increase their wealth.

Confrontation is inevitable, we are very clear about this. Fascism is a weapon of capitalism to advance in retaliation against the working class and peoples, especially against the vanguard. Against the Marxist-Leninist communists it is especially vicious because historically we have been able to organize the peoples and lead them to the struggle until the defeat of the bloody monster.

The tactics implemented by the Marxist-Leninist Parties have had success and have put our comrades at the head of the struggles and sacrifice; the Antifascist Popular Front has been a line of action to bring the proletarians to the fight together with the different democratic and popular strata under the red flag with the hammer and sickle, which under the leadership of great Stalin managed to mobilize the healthiest forces of humanity until it was placed on the rubble of the fascist Nazi empire.

The fascist danger did not disappear, and today, with the sponsorship of big capital, it is trying to rise again and therefore the ideological, political and military struggle takes center stage and forces us to take firm steps to confront such a dangerous monster.

Socialism Is Only Built with the Worker-Peasant Alliance in Power and the People in Arms.

BP of the PCMLV.
Caracas, March 2022.

www.ingramcontent.com/pod-product-compliance
Lightning Source LLC
Chambersburg PA
CBHW070417290526
45791CB00005B/1732

* 9 7 8 1 3 8 7 9 4 1 3 0 8 *